American Zion

American Zion

The Old Testament as a Political Text from the Revolution to the Civil War

Eran Shalev

Yale UNIVERSITY PRESS

New Haven and London

Published with assistance from the foundation established
in memory of Amasa Stone Mather of the Class of 1907, Yale College.

Copyright © 2013 by Yale University.
All rights reserved.
This book may not be reproduced, in whole or in part, including illustrations,
in any form (beyond that copying permitted by Sections 107 and 108 of the
U.S. Copyright Law and except by reviewers for the public press),
without written permission from the publishers.

Yale University Press books may be purchased in quantity for educational, business, or promotional use. For information, please e-mail sales.press@yale.edu (U.S. office) or sales@yaleup.co.uk (U.K. office).

Set in Granjon and Garamond types by
Newgen North America.
Printed in the United States of America.

Library of Congress Cataloging-in-Publication Data

Shalev, Eran, 1970–. American Zion : the Old Testament as a political text from the Revolution to the Civil War / Eran Shalev.
pages cm
Includes bibliographical references and index.
ISBN 978-0-300-18692-5 (cloth : alkaline paper) 1. United States—Politics and government—1775–1783. 2. United States—Politics and government—1783–1865. 3. United States—Religion. 4. Bible. O.T.—Political aspects. 5. Bible. O.T.—Criticism, interpretation, etc. 6. Bible and politics—United States—History. 7. United States—Relations—Israel. 8. Israel—Relations—United States. 9. Nationalism—United States—History. 10. Political culture—United States—History. I. Title.
E302.1.S525 2013
322'.10973—dc23

2012026939

A catalogue record for this book is available from the British Library.

This paper meets the requirements of ANSI/NISO Z39.48-1992 (Permanence of Paper).

10 9 8 7 6 5 4 3 2 1

publication of this book is enabled by a grant from
Jewish Federation of Greater Hartford

To Gabi and Uzi, with love

Contents

Acknowledgments ix
Introduction 1

Chapter 1. "The Jewish Cincinnatus":
Biblical Republicanism in the Age of the American Revolution 15

Chapter 2. "The United Tribes, or States of Israel":
The Hebrew Republic as a Political Model before the Civil War 50

Chapter 3. "A Truly American Spirit of Writing":
Pseudobiblicism, the Early Republic, and the Cultural Origins of the
Book of Mormon 84

Chapter 4. Tribes Lost and Found:
Israelites in Nineteenth-Century America 118

Chapter 5. Evangelicalism, Slavery, and the Decline of an
Old Testament Nation 151

Conclusion. Beyond Old Testamentism:
The New Israel after the Civil War 185

Notes 193
Index 231

Acknowledgments

American Zion has profited enormously from a supportive cadre of friends and colleagues. Many helped and encouraged me as ideas matured into chapters, which in turn developed into a complete manuscript. I am particularly grateful to friends who read the manuscript generously and provided me with indispensable criticisms and suggestions. Although I carry the sole responsibility for the book's content and form, the unsurpassed advice and support of David Bell, Jack Greene, Laura Kalman, Ken Moss, David Nirenberg, Peter Onuf, Carl Richard, and Avihu Zakai helped and inspired me to an extent and in ways that they would find hard to imagine.

I had the good fortune of working with a thoughtful and supportive editor in Jennifer Banks, and to profit from the astute and most helpful comments of the manuscripts' reviewers, James Byrd, Shalom Goldman, and Mark Noll. I would also like to deeply thank Ory Amitay, Ayelet Ben Yishai, Menachem Blondheim, François Furstenberg, Dan Heaton, Richard John, Nitzan Lebovic, Phil Morgan, Fania Oz-Salzberger, Nathan Perl-Rosenthal, Murray Rosovsky, Dorothy Ross, Jonathan Sarna, Zur Shalev, Milette Shamir, Hannah Spahn, Yael Sternhell, Molly Warsh, Amit Yahav, and Michael Zakim.

The Israel Science Foundation provided me with a generous grant to write this book, for which I am very thankful. I presented chapters at Notre Dame's history department, New York University's Atlantic History Seminar, the Kennedy Institute of Berlin's Free University, and the American Studies Forum at Tel Aviv University. I thank Patrick Griffin, Karen Kooperman, Hannah Spahn, and Millete Shamir and Michael Zakim, who invited me to those thought provoking venues. An early version of chapter 1 appeared as "'A Perfect Republic': The Mosaic Constitution in Revolutionary New England, 1775–1788," *New England Quarterly* 82:2 (June 2009), 235–263. Parts of chapter 3 appeared as "'Written in the Style of Antiquity': Pseudo-Biblicism and the Early American Republic, 1770–1830," *Church History* 79:4 (2010), 800–826. Discussions on Mordecai Noah in chapters 2 and 4 are based on "'Revive, Renew, and Reestablish': Mordecai Noah's Ararat and the Limits of Biblical Imagination in the Early American Republic," *Journal of American Jewish Archives* 62:1 (2010), 1–20. I thank the MIT Press, Cambridge University Press, and The Jacob Rader Marcus Center of the American Jewish Archives for permitting me to make use of those articles.

Finally, I thank my family, Michal, Yonatan, Yuli, and Ben, for all they gave me while I was writing this book. In return I can only offer my love.

American Zion

Introduction

> Our American Israel is a term frequently used.
> —ABIEL ABBOT, 1798

> The whole of America is Zion itself from north to south.
> —JOSEPH SMITH, 1844

Between two American wars, one to replace British imperial rule and found a republic, the other, fourscore years later, to secure the Union created by the first, a biblical world of Hebraic political imagination burgeoned and then withered. The idea of America as a new Israel, founded on a Calvinist ethos that was not narrowly denominational but inclined toward the Old Testament, originated in an insular seventeenth-century outlook that singled out New England as a "chosen nation." It reverberated and expanded with the onset of the Revolution throughout the colonies-turned-states as Americans repeatedly heard that they were "at present the People of Israel," or were establishing "our Israel." This image of an American people chosen for a special destiny was to remain a mainstay of American self-fashioning and the negotiation of nationhood for years. We still live with the legacy of that centuries-old identification.[1]

So prevalent was the Old Testament in the early culture of the United States that for decades after the start of the nineteenth century it was, in the words of Perry Miller, as "omnipresent ... as ... the air that people breathed." But despite a rich historiography of the religious quality of politics in the early United States, we have still to recognize some of the central components and characteristics of the identification of the United States as Israel, hence to come to terms with its meaning and significance. In *American Zion* I explore the role that the Old Testament played in the politics of the early republic and in Americans' negotiation of nationhood. By analyzing for the first time some of the most widespread interpretations of the Hebrew Bible as a political text, or a text about national politics, I intend to reveal the extent of that biblicism in American culture and uncover its distinct character. One of my central aims is, in short, to expand vastly our sense of the role of the Hebrew Bible, and particularly the role of biblical Israel, in the formation of an American national and political culture from the Revolution to the Civil War.[2]

In *American Zion* I explore a robust discourse which mobilized the Old Testament, or specific sections of the Hebrew Bible that recounted the political history of the Israelites; in so doing, I seek to bring about a better understanding of the debate about the early national life of the United States. Taking these political readings of the Bible as a springboard, I describe key tropes and images through which contemporaries identified with—and as—the Israelite political community. This identification provided politically conscious Americans with a powerful rhetorical mode ("the American Israel") for expressing a boastful patriotism and a budding national sentiment. Yet that biblicism also reveals a political cosmology ridden with terrific anxieties relating to the sustainability of the Union and its future. The idea of American chosenness and its corollary that the United States was a new Israel manifests a deep ambivalence toward a secular vision of modernity and Enlightened politics based solely on human reason and will. Politically conscious Americans, who in many ways broke with orthodox Christianity, operated for years after the creation of the republic in a civic universe impregnated with a Calvinist-tainted biblicism. While Americans, in Thomas Paine's words, might have had it in their power to start the world over again, they chose to create it in the shadow of ancient worlds long departed. Such impulses reveal a persistent American national need to dress up the new in the old and familiar, and a deep ambivalence toward modernity that complicates straightforward understandings of a "nation born modern."[3]

This Old Testament biblicism, the identification of the United States as a God-chosen Israel, provided a language to conciliate a modern republican experiment with the desire for biblical sanction; it could thus help alleviate anxieties related to the limits of human authority and legitimize the unprecedented American federal and republican endeavor. Tense and contradictory, republican and biblical, the early United States was forward looking and, as Theodore Bozeman would have put it, "primitivist," or deeply attracted to the narratives, language, and ordinances of biblical times.[4]

From its earliest days Christianity has had a complex relationship with the Hebrew Bible, starting with the conflict between Peter and Matthew, on the one hand, and Paul on the other, regarding the place of Hebrew law in the Christian order. As a political text, the importance of the Hebrew Bible has had its great explorers for millennia, beginning perhaps in the Christian world with Eusebius, Constantine's ecclesiastical counselor. Although that history cannot be retold here it is worth noting that early modern thinkers frequently dwelt on the political aspects of the Hebrew Bible, although many of them rejected an ecclesiastical framework for political life: Spinoza, Hobbes, Bayle, Voltaire, and Rousseau all recognized and grappled with the meaning of such biblical Hebraic themes as the Mosaic constitution as crucial to the history of political thought, even as they differed sharply on the meaning and desirability of the biblical example. Once reformed Christianity, particularly its Calvinist form, reinstated the Old Testament to a central place within Christianity, it reopened the issues of national chosenness and election. The revolutionary stakes in this clash are most dramatically evident in the case of seventeenth-century England, which has the most developed historiography in this area. But the United States is where that the political legacy of the Old Testament blossomed latest and has endured most strongly.[5]

Calvinism, whose Reformed Protestantism was particularly attuned to the Old Testament, outnumbered other denominations from early in the history of the North American British settlements. With their distinct modes of public rhetoric and action, Calvinist colonists frequently characterized themselves as the modern equivalents of the chosen people, as a New Israel. The Puritans, the first and dominant group of British North American Reformed Protestants, saw themselves as Israelites fleeing a new Egyptian captivity, crossing a sea to reach freedom and taking possession of a promised land; it was they who introduced the "chosen people" doctrine into the New World and viewed themselves as the successors of the Children of Israel and the bearers of a renewed covenant with God.[6]

We have recently learned about the wider context of seventeenth-century European Christian Hebraism through Hebraic political studies, a discipline whose interest is the Hebraic tradition in political thought. We can now better appreciate that many European and Atlantic communities similarly felt themselves to be new Israels in the seventeenth century. By the late eighteenth century the moment of Hebraic introspection was long over in Europe. Yet as historians have recognized, "although Puritanism had collapsed as a total way of life by the eighteenth century, it continued to exert a powerful influence on the public life of the new United States." One of its lasting intellectual legacies was the central role that the Old Testament played in American public life. An obsession with these scriptures permeated "the writing of the elite and the speech of the humble" in the early United States, to the extent that it became "the common coinage of the realm." And it was *after* the Bible's primacy began to corrode in Europe that Americans performed a last great act of political Hebraism, as the citizens of the young American republic witnessed a remarkable effort to construct their newly established polity as an Old Testament nation, an American Zion. Americans of the early United States may have already been far removed from Calvinism strictly understood; yet they elaborated a discourse whose origins can be traced to Calvin's Geneva and which prospered, thrived, and gained a life of its own in the early republic.⁷

We now know much about the Anglo-American millenarianism engendered in the wake of the eighteenth-century imperial military conflicts in the New World, especially the French and Indian War (1754–1763), which ended in a sweeping British victory in North America. That chiliasm, which fed into the old notions that America was favored by God, flourished in the ensuing Revolution and became adapted to the needs of the new nation. Public speakers subsequently intensified the rhetoric of the young republic's millenarian role as the "Redeemer Nation."⁸ The American political theology that stands at the center of this book coexisted with that national or civic millenarianism and occasionally intertwined with it, but was more concerned with worldly affairs. Its adherents were less troubled with (although often aware of) America's role at the End of Days and more attuned to the history of the Israelites and its bearing on the United States' national politics and the politics of nation. In the most basic sense this stance reflects Americans' quarrel with the meaning of becoming and being a nation by providing a historical example of the God-favored Israelites against which to measure and construct their own American nation.

The Bible in the early United States was, in the words of a cogent historian, "the most imported, most printed, most distributed, and most read written text in North America up through the nineteenth century." Its narratives and language dominated the intellectual and spiritual lives of untold millions of Americans, a preeminence that may have coincided with the American Bible Society's great drive of 1829–1831 to distribute a Bible to every household in the nation. But as universal and critical as the Bible was as a whole, it was its opening Hebrew Testament that was for decades after the creation of the United States the source for a massive outpouring of speeches, polemical newspaper articles, and sermons on issues from independence to war, constitutionalism to federations; the Old Testament's themes may indeed have "suffused the minds" of the citizens of the young United States.⁹

If, as Sacvan Bercovitch has demonstrated, New England clergy extended the promise of a covenant from New England to cover "America," Americans from other regions and denominations embraced such notions as well. For example, Thomas Jefferson, who is not suspect as either a Calvinist or a New Englander, envisioned as early as 1776 a Great Seal for the young United States that represented on one of its sides the people of Israel led by the pillar of fire in the desert. Decades later, as the president of the United States, Jefferson still harbored such sensibilities, referring in his first inaugural address to the United States as a "chosen country," and appealing four years later, in his second, to "the favor of that Being in whose hands we are, who led our fathers, as Israel of old, from their native land and planted them in a country flowing with all the necessaries and comforts of life." That such language was so powerfully entrenched in the most deist of minds demonstrates how common understandings of America as a Second Israel became in public discourse of the early United States, and how a language permeated with Calvinism provided a constructive mode of political expression for an emerging American national culture long after rigid orthodox Calvinism itself had begun to fade. That Old Testamentism would further expand in the age of the Second Great Awakening through the powerful "Christian-Republican synthesis," the unique and characteristic American amalgamation of evangelical Protestantism, republican ideology, and commonsense moral reasoning.¹⁰ As I demonstrate in this book's final chapter, the unprecedented religious expansion and intensification of that Great Awakening was to become, however, a two-edged sword that eventually did more to diminish than increase the role of the Old Testament in public politics.

The participants in the discourse of this Old Testament biblicism were almost exclusively Christians, and were likely to be educated and politically conscious. They often treated "the American Israel" in terms that were not metaphorical but rather demonstrative of their conviction of a God still operative in history. Nevertheless, that political discussion was commonly conducted in terms that were rather neutral to the question whether the Bible carried revealed theological truths. A contemporary reconstitution in the Bible's authority, which the historian Jonathan Sheehan described illuminatingly in the European context, dictated that while American Old Testamentism would never be "secular," it frequently mobilized the Bible in a detheologized fashion that might be better understood through cultural than in religious terms.¹¹

In many accounts the Exodus functioned as a towering narrative and trope, fundamental in shaping the form and content of early American biblicism. The story of the enslaved Israelites who flee Egyptian tyranny, are elected by God as his chosen people during their long sojourn in the desert, and take possession of the Promised Land exerted tremendous influence over various segments of American society. Throughout the pre–Civil War years Exodus remained a fundamental source for talking about politics and for exploring the meaning of nationhood. On the verge of civil war Americans such as the University of the City of New York law professor William B. Wedgwood still provided full-fledged accounts of the United States' history as a repetition of the Exodus. Retelling the biblical story, Wedgwood pointed out that the Israelites "were in bondage in Egypt for four hundred and thirty years. Then God brought them out of Egypt, leading them by a pillar of cloud . . . he opened the gates of the sea for their passage . . . he gave them his covenant amid the thunders of Sinai. . . . For forty years he led them through the wilderness. . . . He then . . . planted his chosen people, in thirteen [Canaanite] States. . . . Prosperity and happiness followed them, and their names and their fame went out to the ends of the earth."¹²

Wedgwood, like numerous Americans before him, saw a direct link between biblical Israel and the new, American Israel. Now, "in after days," Wedgwood asserted, God "selected another people . . . led them through the Red Sea of the Revolution," and finally "planted them . . . in thirteen States." The creation of the two nations—of Israel and the United States—was sealed by the act of political compact, the Federal Constitution being "another covenant, [delivered] by the hand of another Moses," George Washington. Wedgwood's was a typical rendition of the United States as a New Israel, which made use of typological-like exegesis to tie biblical and modern events. Remarkably, such interpretations not only biblicized the United States by representing it in terms of a New Israel but also Americanized biblical Israel: describing ancient Israel as a confederacy of tribes—as a "Union" in the manner of the United States—as Wedgwood has done was common; so was dubbing the Israelite tribes "states" and (mis)counting them as thirteen, conforming to the sacred number of American patriotism, instead of the conventional twelve.¹³

Exodus, then, has been a key trope in the construction of the United States as a New Israel and has consequently received much attention from scholars who study its shifting permutations through centuries of American history, from the Puritans to the civil rights movement and beyond. Yet the Exodus's enduring influence in America, long after other biblical tropes were forgotten, may have obscured other equally important Old Testament structures and narratives. It is thus imperative to unveil the breadth of that American Old Testamentism, and in *American Zion* I explore central Hebraic narratives and tropes, particularly those pertaining to Israel's "republican" phase, which were as relevant as the Exodus for coming to terms with the challenges and obstacles that the young United States confronted in its early decades.

While I recognize the attraction contemporaries felt to the republican period of Israel's history, that phase in the annals of the Israelites (and the Exodus) was not the only one that captured their attention. For example, the notorious Hebrew kings Rehoboam and Ahab assumed an important role in ongoing deliberations in the United States on political authority and its limits. Rehoboam, whose tyranny and folly split Israel into rival kingdoms, emerged in the public discourse with the recurrent anxieties about the viability of the American Union: from the Revolution, when George III was seen as America's Rehoboam, through the periodic threats of secession leading up to the Civil War, American public speakers revisited that king's disastrous reign, which ended with the dissolution of the union of Israel's tribes. Characteristic was a powerful speech in which John C. Calhoun fiercely objected to the "tariff of abomination" by referring to the people of Israel's demanding from Rehoboam, in the speaker's telling choice of words, "a repeal of the tariff." With the biblical example and the prospect of secession on the former vice president's mind, he asked whether it was possible "even for a careless reader to peruse the history of that event without being forcibly struck with the analogy in the causes which led to their separation, and those which now threaten us with a similar calamity." The South Carolinian senator was only one of many antebellum Americans, southerners and northerners, "struck with the analogy" of Rehoboam's Israel and the United States.[14]

Ahab, the king who conspired to murder his subject Naboth in order to inherit his coveted vineyard, exemplified an even more malicious misappropriation of political power. Throughout the late eighteenth century and well into the nineteenth, Americans of many sorts and creeds repeatedly depicted their land as "vineyards" craved by "Ahabs," first imperial Englishmen, then whites appropriating Indian lands and northerners attempting to force the South into their sphere of economic and political domination. As with Rehoboam, contemporaries saw "striking parallels" to Ahab's conduct in various alleged usurpations; perhaps the best known of these appeared in the context of midcentury American expansionism, which David Lee Child helped identify as an act of coveting Naboth's vineyard in his celebrated tract *The Taking of Naboth's Vineyard; or, History of the Texas Conspiracy* (1845). Herman Melville's Ahab, the tyrannical and monomaniacal captain of the *Pequod*, testifies to the power of that image in mid-nineteenth-century America.[15]

A few paragraphs cannot cover discourses as rich and long-standing as those involving Rehoboam or Ahab in pre–Civil War America. Note, however, how these kingly tropes—whose full chronological extent and full impact are yet to be recognized—functioned for decades in dramatically shifting historical contexts. The two figurative models emerged simultaneously and for decades were mainstays of American political discussion, providing the young nation with versatile political idioms, hence a much-needed discursive stability to come to terms with the republic's predicaments. Rehoboam and Ahab further suggest the impressive life span of an American Old Testamentism, as both kings emerged as political tropes in the mid-1770s and all but disappeared after the Civil War (during which southerners and their sympathizers likened Abraham Lincoln to both), never to regain their antebellum prominence.[16]

Their chronological trajectory—from the Revolution to the Civil War—is not the only characteristic of the larger Old Testamentism manifested by these tropes. The use of Rehoboam and Ahab in the political discourse demonstrates the extent to which the Hebrew Bible's narratives were embedded in the political grammar of the young nation, providing observers with vocabularies through which to express their political attitudes and misgivings. The importance of these errant Israelite kings lies not in any of their particular materializations in a specific historical context but in demonstrating at significant moments in the life of the republic how the biblical language was available for communicating and articulating shared assumptions on the nature, uses, and abuses of political power. Most important, while Rehoboam and Ahab may differ from the larger biblical discourse in significant ways— for example, both derive from Israel's monarchic (and thus postrepublican) era, they still participated in and reflected the intellectual construction of the United States as a second Israel.

Rehoboam and Ahab were more than ciphers for political disunion and encroachment; through these Israelite kings generations of politically conscious Americans struggled to come to terms with the pitfalls that awaited their American Israel—that is, with their unease and fears of becoming *un-*

chosen or *de*selected. Election was not an unqualified blessing; its contractual nature implied, as both biblical Israelites and Americans came to realize, a national life beset with high, almost unobtainable standards and ridden with a dread regarding Providence's continuing approval and affection. While being chosen may have abetted concerns regarding the secular nature of the American republican endeavor, it stirred a new array of anxieties related to the fragility of the favored situation that it promised.

One of the most remarkable aspects of the biblicism that I intend particularly to underscore in *American Zion* is its facilitation of attempts to transcend traditional figurative exegesis, expressing a striving for "biblical authenticity," a radical typological sensibility that disposed contemporaries to present their nation as concretely or historically related to Old Testament history. They demonstrated such dispositions time and again, as they were not content with rendering America a metaphorical Israel. Understandings of national election and the notion of an American Israel were more than rhetorical and allegorical flourishes; they presented America's identity as a latter-day Israel in various ways but most often as something deeply meaningful, tangible, and factual. This extreme biblicism, the attempt to construct concreteness into the bond with biblical Israel, was not concerted or planned but was evident through a variety of otherwise unrelated phenomena that shared an underlying motivation to craft an American nation that in significant aspects was understood as Israelite. The construction of a sacred American geography by applying a biblical nomenclature to numerous towns and places is a well-known (and comparatively mild) manifestation of an intense and steadfast outlook originating in the colonial era; the Book of Mormon is another familiar manifestation of entwining Hebraic elements and America.[17] In the following chapters I elaborate other measures and efforts to similarly shape the United States as a biblical nation. These remarkable attempts reflect, as we shall come to see, the Janus-faced qualities of pre–Civil War American political culture that I shall stress, one that was simultaneously boastful and in constant need of reassurance, self-assured and perpetually anxious regarding its abilities and ultimate destiny.

This polarity was evident already in the revolutionary years. Ezra Stiles's renowned sermon *The United States Elevated to Honor and Glory* (1783) has extraordinary buoyancy, shining through a sermon of tens of thousands of words. Stiles's optimism represents a recognizable facet of the identifications of the United States and biblical Israel: for him being "God's American Israel" meant the promise of future prosperity and national splendor. Stiles, the president of Yale University, was confident—as soon as the Revolutionary War was over—that the states recently united "may prosper and flourish into a great American republic; and ascend into high and distinguished honor among the nations of the earth." This sanguine outlook was based on a biblical history that demonstrated time and again that "the secular welfare of God's ancient people" depended on their own conduct. Self-reliance promised Americans that as long as they continued to make the right choices America's future "prosperity and splendour" would be secure; a paramount example of a correct choice was placing at the head of the Continental Army a leader such as George Washington, "the only man on whom the eyes of all [America's] Israel were placed . . . this American Joshua."[18]

American biblicism also entailed less upbeat sentiments. During the dark days of the Revolutionary War, Nicholas Street, pastor of East Haven Church, did not celebrate but lamented the American Israel's predicament: in Street's remarkable Jeremiad Americans in their national capacity were "acting over the part of the children of Israel in the wilderness"; when times got hard they, like the Israelites of old, began "to murmur against Moses and Aaron." Street chastised his compatriots: "We are prone to act over the same stupid vile part that the children of Israel did in the wilderness." Such anxieties, which manifested the early modern quarrel with virtue-based politics, did not end with the American victory in the war. Triumph on the battlefield, to extend Street's elaborate metaphor, did not secure the United States' "entrance into Canaan's rest." Hence the symbiotic relationship between biblical and recent history, between the ancient and modern chosen nations, did not entail only the uplifting narrative of Israel's nation and state building. Such concerns were still expressed three generations after the Revolution, when the aforementioned William Wedgwood, who witnessed the disintegration of the American federacy after the election of Abraham Lincoln as president, warned his compatriots: "In the midst of their [Israel's] prosperity there was a dissolution of their Union."[19] In ominous moments in the life of the republic it seemed too obvious that America's Union could falter, just like Israel's in the past.

While Ezra Stiles and his numerous optimistic followers persistently reflected on a bright future of "prosperity and splendor" for the American Israel, others continued to identify their condition as a "wilderness, i.e. in a state of trouble and difficulty, Egyptians pursuing us, to overtake us and reduce us." Chosenness meant that some Americans would always dread the

"Red Sea before us."[20] As long as this was the case, Canaan's rest, like a mirage in the desert, would remain ever elusive.

As I have shown elsewhere, contemporaries also appealed to historical models other than biblical Israel, particularly to republican Rome, which was a central element of late eighteenth-century American historical and political imagination. Some of the differences between Israel and Rome are obvious: Rome's paganism contrasts sharply, for example, with the Hebrews' status as God's chosen. The two models also peaked in American culture at different times: Rome's intellectual presence was most powerful during the constitutional era, and that aristocratic republic became less relevant as a political model with the swift democratization of American society after the turn of the nineteenth century. Biblical Israel, however, not only adapted to the dynamism of the early nineteenth century but peaked during the Second Great Awakening (conventionally dated 1800–1840), especially between 1820 and 1830. By the era of the Civil War it was not uncommon to hear that "the popular idea taught our youth," namely that "civil liberty was born and cradled in the ancient States of Greece and Rome," was false, but that the principle rather was "first taught by God himself to the ancient Hebrews."[21] Differences aside, in chapters 1 and 2 I elaborate on deep connections and interrelations between the examples of republican Rome and biblical Israel in the American political imagination.

The political scientist Donald Lutz was able to back up quantitatively Perry Miller's intuition regarding the prevalence of the Bible in the early United States. Lutz observed that during the founding era (which Lutz defines as 1760–1805), the source most frequently cited in political expositions was the Book of Deuteronomy. Perhaps even more surprising and significant is that even discounting the 75 percent of biblical references that appeared in reprinted sermons—a huge cottage industry that accounted for 10 percent of all contemporary pamphlets—Lutz found that the "nonsermon source of biblical citations [was] roughly as important as the Classical or Common Law categories."[22] The prominence of the Bible would only increase during the second and third decades of the nineteenth century.

Studying the rich political culture of the Revolution, the early republic, and antebellum America by scrutinizing political pamphlets, histories, public orations, private correspondence, sermons, poetry, newspaper essays, and other polemical and partisan writings is how we latecomers may come to terms with the roles of the biblical history of the ancient Hebrews in the early United States. Such a broad reading provides a sense of the depth of American political culture's Old Testamentism. It also demonstrates how American authors, public speakers, and commentators developed sophisticated modes of probing through the Old Testament the new nation's key problems, dynamics, and relationships, which enabled them and their contemporaries to better visualize their nascent national project. The fostering of a national consciousness was not, of course, an inevitable or foreordained result of the American Revolution, as a recent historian of the making of an American public reminds us.[23] The Old Testament, specifically the history of biblical Israel, provided a productive intersection between politics and religion, a political theology which legitimized political novelties but could also help unite a growing number of dynamic political entities—the American states—around well-known and revered scriptural narratives, structures, and models.

Throughout the pre–Civil War era the Bible provided American revolutionaries with a critical perspective on Britain's management of the colonies and later on antebellum American politics; a medium for political discourse in the process of constitution making and then state building; a common fund of linguistic structures, legitimizing images, and organizing assumptions; and a usable political and sacred past.[24] But as this book is focused more on the political imagination—the intellectual construction of social interaction—than on "politics" as the negotiation and implementation of policy, its chapters are not organized as a linear narrative. Instead, *American Zion* consists of a series of investigations into overlooked and central aspects and themes of American political biblicism. The book takes "Hebraic" moments and distinct vocabularies as vantage points from which to gain fresh insights into the processes that were shaped by, and in turn helped to drive, the momentous transformations of the young American republic from the Revolution to the era of the Civil War. This chronology is not an arbitrary periodization but points to the time frame in which this political biblicism first rose during the 1770s, peaked sometime around the year 1830 as the Second Great Awakening raged, and withered (but did not vanish) as the Civil War approached; by the end of the war this American Old Testamentism had lost its vigor and morphed into a less-committed abstract language. By the late nineteenth century biblicism can no longer be considered a major component of national political discussions.

The voices articulating the notion of the United States as a New Israel were overwhelmingly male, in step with much of the pre–Civil War political discourse. Nevertheless, there were extraordinary contributions by women who shared and further expressed the prevailing interest in the Old Testament. Such were, for example, Hannah More's doctrinaire biblical dramas, focused on Old Testament figures and intended to promote "the love of piety and virtue in young persons." Decades later Hannah Adams's expansive *History of the Jews* (1812) provided another example of feminine participation in the contemporary in Hebraic discussion. Tellingly, female figures such as the prophetess Deborah and Jeptah's daughter were useful in the contemporary biblical republicanism. Nevertheless, these examples underscore the rule, namely that the theonational idea of America as the New Israel was a discourse articulated and dominated by the hegemonic group of white educated males.[25]

American Zion's chapters demonstrate that revolutionary Americans and subsequent generations read the Old Testament, particularly the history of the Israelite nation, as a civic humanist text to explore and propagate their republicanism (chapter 1); that for decades politicians and commentators, clergymen and laymen, continued to appeal to the "Mosaic constitution" as a template for organizing their community and justifying their distinct republican federalism (chapter 2); and that they relied on the Old Testament's distinct language, narrative forms, and history to formulate a biblical past for America and to sanctify their present (chapters 3 and 4). The book, in short, illustrates a powerful biblical consciousness that lifted the notion of the Second Israel to new heights and spanned decades, peaking in the first third of the nineteenth century. Without grasping that biblicism, we cannot fully appreciate how, and to what effect, contemporaries conceived their sprawling republican federation. In *American Zion* we see unveiled a lost world of biblical political imagination, or the negotiation of nationhood, which deepens our understanding of some of the most profound aspects and enduring issues of the American experience. Hence this potent biblicism helped invigorate, for example, the construction of such ideologies as Manifest Destiny and the self-righteousness that justified, and thus facilitated, the carnage of the Civil War.

Comprehending such crucial yet hitherto unnoticed dimensions of the distinct Old Testament biblicism that emerged during the Revolution and played out in the first half of the nineteenth century transforms our understanding of early American political culture. In fact, we cannot properly understand the political culture of early America unless we appreciate how and to what effect contemporaries drew on their sense of ancient Israel's political history and the ways in which that history helped construct their views of their nation. The identification of the United States as the Israel of its time made contemporaries aware of the possibility that their nation might eventually fall from grace. Yet before the Civil War, with the Union periodically seeming deficient and fragile (and in hindsight rightly so), that identification enabled contemporaries to cope with the hardships that plagued the commonwealths of the past, which republicans traditionally attributed to *fortuna,* the amoral goddess of secular chance.[26] When the Children of Israel did wrong in the sight of the Lord, they may have been punished, but even then they were not left alone to face fortune's whims.

The history of biblical Israel enabled contemporaries to express and shape understandings of history and politics, even as their experiences reshaped their attitudes to the Bible (chapter 5). Since the Hebrew Bible began receding in the political discourse after the first third of the nineteenth century—to an extent and for reasons that were not sufficiently clear until now—we have yet to fully appreciate the degree to which American national culture was carved out in a deeply Hebraic setting. While the Bible may not have provided contemporaries with new ideas about the conduct of modern polities—that is, it did not constitute a new political philosophy—their Old Testament biblicism operated in a cosmology that was arguably more important than straightforward declarative propositions. This biblicism furnished a powerful justification, a rationale and motivation for ideas and modes of action which otherwise may have been unacceptable or even inconceivable.[27] This book reveals a political culture of an American people who, like the patriarch Moses, forged a nation and were within the reach of the promised land of modernity; like Moses they grappled with questions of human legitimacy, authority, and agency and fought to set the better angels of their nature free; like Moses they had to wait for future generations to make the final step and fulfill their nation's promise.

I

"The Jewish Cincinnatus"
Biblical Republicanism in the Age of the American Revolution

An early-nineteenth-century essay in *Jenk's Portland Gazette* described the Israelite judge Gideon in a fashion reserved for virtuous yeomen-generals, from the Roman Cincinnatus to the revolutionary American "Washington, Greene, Lincoln, Putnam and others." The biblical Israelites under Gideon's lead were threatened by their Canaanite adversaries, and like Cincinnatus's Rome and Washington's America, their condition "was extremely distressing." Similar to the way in which the revered Roman and American republicans were mythologized, Gideon too, according to the anonymous American author, left his farm at once when he "was called to lead the army of Israel, while he was threshing wheat." Like wartime Rome and the young United States, Israel was consequently headed by a virtuous leader who provided a model of self-effacing republicanism, so different "from those spurious patriots, who trumpet their own praises, scramble for promotion; and impudently thrust themselves into offices." Yet Gideon, like other great republican leaders, performed the greatest service to his nation *after* returning victorious from battle: upon winning he "refused the offer of an hereditary throne," starkly reproving the Israelites: "I will not rule over you, nor will my son rule over you. The LORD will rule over you" (Judges 8:22–23). Like George Washington, who refused to become king after leaving the field to save his country, the Israelite Gideon was transformed in America into a classical republican in the Cincinnatian tradition.[1]

In recent years we have gained a deeper appreciation of politically conscious Americans' attraction to the history of classical Greece and Rome from the early days of the Revolution and throughout the early national period. We now know better how, why, in what contexts, and for whom, those ancient polities provided laudable and heroic examples of public virtue; we also know of negative models of villainous and corrupt intrigues. Consequently, we are better informed about the roles that classical antiquity played in the construction of the American federal republic, hence are able to assess more accurately the modern political doctrine of classical republicanism in the early United States.[2]

Less noticed, however, is that revolutionary-era Americans frequently discussed, adapted, and absorbed the fundamentals of classical republicanism through Old Testament narratives and figures. Indeed, by the early nineteenth century representations of biblical Israelite history through civic humanist language, such as the foregoing portrayal of the Israelite judge Gideon, were common, joining a tradition established in the early days of the Revolution.[3] This biblical republicanism enabled revolutionaries and successive generations of Americans to conciliate two distinct cosmologies and harness them, indeed amalgamate them, to advance their political goals. This largely unnoticed biblical republicanism significantly expands our understanding of the ways in which contemporaries constructed their political worldviews, and sheds new light on how they made that revolutionary ideology meaningful for their lives. Identifying and charting this biblical republicanism will thus provide a fuller picture of the form and content of contemporaries' political cosmology, and consequently a better understanding of the parameters and forces shaping the political and intellectual history of the early United States.

In this chapter, then, I demonstrate how classical republicanism's ability to occupy an important role in the political discourse was supplemented by a hitherto unacknowledged branch of the republican language, one that cast biblical narratives and tropes in a civic humanistic mold. As we shall see, adding the Old Testament to our understanding of contemporary modes of political thought, or rather to the ways in which late-eighteenth- and early-nineteenth-century Americans thought about politics, may answer questions about classical republicanism's rise, prevalence, and impact in the early United States. Further, biblical republicanism underscores the importance of the Bible as a political text in that nation's formative years. It also offers a glimpse at the lost intellectual world that politically conscious Americans inhabited, hence a better understanding of their idiosyncratic ideological synthesis.

It would be an understatement to point out that republicanism has been a major analytical concept in the past few decades for understanding the ideological and intellectual universe of early America. It would also be a platitude: on few topics in American history has so much ink been spilled. After the paradigm shift that occurred in the late 1960s and early 1970s, when the ideas of the school of Consensus History lost ground to those of the "republican synthesis," historiographic wars have raged between "liberals" and "classical republicans," each camp asserting its intellectual idols as better equipped to explain American (particularly early American) history. The contours of that debate are well known and need not be repeated here; suffice it to state that while "liberals" take rights, liberties, and their pursuit as the drivers behind the dynamism of American history, "classical republicans" underscore the primacy of liberty, virtue, and public duty.[4] Nonetheless, the vigorous debate between individualist and communitarian interpretations of American history began to wane during the 1990s, as historians largely sidestepped a controversy that has rightly come to be seen as arid.

However, although classical republicanism was obviously a salient component of early American political language, questions about its role and its ultimate contribution to early American political consciousness remain unresolved. For example, while classical republicanism clearly pervades the political discourse after the mid-1760s, it is unclear how an ideology based on classical education, from which only a fraction of eighteenth-century Americans benefited, could have enjoyed widespread appeal. An arguably even more important question is how people as permissive as revolutionary Americans (who by the nineteenth century would become citizens of the swiftly democratizing—hence decidedly "liberal"—United States) could maintain for decades a stern, collectivist, and demanding ideology such as civic humanism as, in the words of the political scientist Alan Gibson, a "distinguishable political language."[5] Indeed, it is fair to say that the burden of explaining this puzzle—the apparent mismatch between the social and political antiauthoritarian and centripetal character of American culture and the restrictive and communitarian nature of classical republicanism—seems to lie on those who would suggest that civic humanism had a significant impact in the early United States. At the very least, one would have to explain how contemporaries could overcome their cultural inclinations, bring themselves to internalize civic humanism, and make that creed meaningful to their experiences and compatible with their cognitive paradigms.

Biblical republicanism may help alleviate such tensions as it sheds light on the adjustments and calibrations to civic humanism to make it more easily co-opted and absorbed through the Bible's mediation. Biblical republicanism enabled potentially every literate American—not merely the formally educated elites—to come to terms with civic humanism through the use of well-known Old Testament structures, narratives, forms, and metaphors, which functioned throughout the era as, in the words of Mark Noll, "the common coinage of the realm." In the Protestant universe that emerged in colonial British North America and the early United States, the Bible was, according to Paul Gutjahr, the "most printed, most distributed, and most read written text in North America up through the nineteenth century." This biblical supremacy led to the Good Book's dominance of the world of American print, creating countless shared "idioms, metaphors, narratives [and] themes." The Bible was the chief source for school-age children from which to learn reading and writing; together with a few other heavily doctrinal texts, such as catechisms and the New England Primer, it yielded the form and content of education in early America. In such an intellectual environment, biblical references and motifs permeated the rhetoric of revolutionary and early-national politicians and commentators.[6]

The prevalence of the Bible in the American Protestant world was of course no accident, but the consequence of a theology that emphasized a direct relationship with the Word as an essential component of spiritual life and necessary for salvation. From early in the history of Protestantism, in stark contradiction to centuries of Catholic dogma and practice, Protestant vernacular Bibles proclaimed themselves, in the words of the Great Bible (1539), the first authorized translation of the Bible into English, as intended for all "manner of persons, men, women, young, old, learned, unlearned, rich, poor, priests, laymen, lords, ladies, officers, tenants, and mean men, virgins, wives, widows, lawyers, merchants, artificers, husbandmen, and all manner of persons of what estate or condition soever they be, may in this book learn all things that they ought to believe, what they ought to do, and what they should not do." The Protestant doctrine of *sola scriptura*—by Scripture alone—eventually raised the readership rates of the Bible in America to unprecedented if not quite universal levels.[7]

Sandra Gustafson reminds us of the inherent tension between republican deliberation on the one hand and inherited systems of belief on the other. Nevertheless, for quite some time now historians have recognized that religion had a unique role in the formation of American republicanism. In the words of the historian Dorothy Ross, while the "republican rhetoric of corruption formed an alliance with the jeremiad," fervent Protestants "identified the American republic with the advent of the millennial period." Historians from Edmund Morgan to Nathan Hatch, Ruth Bloch, and Mark Noll, among others, have indeed recognized the interrelatedness of religion and classical republicanism and have consequently offered religion-oriented explanations pertaining to revolutionary Americans' political consciousness.[8] Nevertheless, the significant merging of civic humanism and millennialism that they have revealed does not cover the whole spectrum of late-eighteenth-century intersections between classical republicanism and Protestantism in America. The role of Scripture, particularly the Old Testament, in the formation and evolution of an American republican worldview has gone unnoticed as yet.

The best-known example of an American republican reading of a biblical narrative is the Exodus, a liberation story that echoes throughout American history. Students of American history have long recognized the central role of the Exodus, as generations of historians explored the influences of the story of the Israelites, rising from the house of Egyptian bondage, led by a charismatic and god-inspired Moses to escape Pharaoh and his host. They roamed the wilderness for forty years, eventually conquering Canaan and settling in the land of milk and honey. By the time of the Revolution, Exodus already had a long typological history in the British North American colonies, especially in New England, where the Puritan immigrants and succeeding generations interpreted the Great Migration of the 1630s as a crossing of the Red Sea and an escape from the British Egypt.[9] That trope was little employed after the decline of the Puritan orthodoxy and throughout the first half of the eighteenth century. Once the imperial conflict between Britain and its American colonies erupted in 1765, however, Exodus once more became central to contemporaries' typological imagination and historical understanding of their conflict.

The Exodus was certainly the story of "the miraculous deliverance of the children of Israel from the Egyptian Bondage." Nevertheless, revolutionary preachers also portrayed the Exodus, perhaps more significantly, as "a very signal instance of God's appearing in favour of liberty, and frowning on tyrants." The late-eighteenth-century God of Israel was a republican god, who "shews how much he regards the rights of his people, and in how exemplary a manner, hard hearted tyrants, and merciless oppressors, sometimes feel his vengeance." Some, such as Nicholas Street in his remarkable but characteristic sermon *The American States Acting Over the Part of the Children of Israel in the Wilderness, and thereby Impeding Their Entrance into Canaan's Rest* (1777), referred to the Exodus to elaborate the precarious American situation. Street's impressive typological reading, coming at a time of dire straits for the young American confederacy, lengthily juxtaposed "the history of the children of Israel in Egypt, their sufferings and oppression under the tyrant Pharaoh, their remarkable deliverance by the hands of Moses out of the state of bondage and oppression, and their trials and murmurings in the wilderness." In Street's wartime Jeremiad, Americans "act[ed] over ... the children of Israel in the wilderness, under the conduct of Moses and Aaron, who was leading them out of a state of bondage into a land of liberty and plenty in Canaan."[10]

As the Revolution continued, it became clear that the Exodus was not a model that applied merely to New England, and that not only New Englanders would use it. Historians have noted the process through which, in the words of Harry Stout, "speakers engrafted New England onto the sacred history of Israel, and then extended that history to America." This graft included the typological relevance of the Exodus to the young United States. Americans outside New England, particularly in the middle colonies–turned–states, were becoming accustomed to think that although they, like the Israelites in Egypt, were enslaved in foreign bondage, with "a wilderness still before us," they should expect soon to "have crossed the Red Sea of our difficulties."[11] Although "crossing the Rubicon" would arguably better describe the stakes before declaring American independence than crossing the Red Sea, the biblical metaphor seems to have been at least as popular during the early months of 1776. Even the most deist of revolutionaries such as Thomas Jefferson and Benjamin Franklin imagined the revolution as an Exodus-like deliverance from slavery, as evident in their proposals for the American Great Seal in 1776. Numerous references to the tyrannical English "Pharaoh" and his Israelite-American subjects-turned-enemies during the Revolution attested to that popularity. In 1785 it was manifested in Timothy Dwight's epic and metaphoric poem *The Conquest of Canaan,* which he dedicated to the American Moses (and now victorious Joshua), George Washington.

The centrality and importance of the trope of the Exodus to the Revolution's political imagination is undeniable. Nevertheless, historians' focus on that particular discursive strand, which may have intensified still more due to its future importance for diverse American groups, from enslaved and free African-Americans and Mormons in the nineteenth century to the civil rights movement in the twentieth, may have obscured the presence and significance of other key contemporary biblical narratives and tropes for the revolutionary cosmology. The Exodus has overshadowed a larger world of

Hebraic revolutionary political imagination. Other biblical idioms reveal how deeply invested American revolutionaries were in representing their political situation in biblical terms. Further, the "other" biblical tropes we shall now examine differed significantly from the Exodus: while that was a story of deliverance from slavery to freedom which could be convincingly presented as antimonarchical, it was not necessarily a civic humanist plot.[12] Once we appreciate the full spectrum of revolutionary biblical language, the familiar classical republican picture appears: of corruption versus stern virtue, of self-aggrandizement versus sacrifice and self-effacement. To that biblical civic humanist language we now turn.

Corruption is a crucial yet elusive concept in the civic humanistic creed. While early modern republicans wished to preserve the health of their polity through active and disinterested citizenship, they knew that from the time of the classical polities, humans were too weak to preserve indefinitely free republics, which depended on the virtue of their citizens and magistrates. The civic humanist worldview, which idealized self-sacrifice and disinterestedness, and dreaded the advancement of personal or sectional interests at the expense of the public good, saw "corruption" as a vicious and potent force; men could hardly be expected to withstand the egotistic temptations of self-betterment. Corruption was thus believed incessantly to undermine virtue, hence to ruin the innately frail republic.[13]

Present-day understandings of corruption tend to be concerned with moral perversions related to monetary and sexual excesses. Although such debaucheries were in no way unrelated to the early modern civic humanist worldview, they seemed to contemporaries more the consequences than the causes of corruption. Early modern corruption was fundamentally a political concept, concerned with the human ability and will to control the temptations of power: on the one hand a citizen should preserve at all costs his—and a man's world it was—independence (hence the classical and neoclassical belief that only economically self-sufficient and armed yeomen were truly independent and politically autonomous) and on the other hand control the temptation to dominate others by usurping power not his own. Historians have long noted that this outlook, which originated in the classical world of Greece and Rome and was revived and transformed in Renaissance Italy and the seventeenth- and eighteenth-century Anglophone world, shared assumptions with reformed Protestantism, especially its Calvinist branches. The aggressiveness of sin and corruption, and the frailty of piety and virtue ery similar republican and reformed Protestant worldviews. ᴣd on corruptible human beings and could thus share their po‌nptions. Neither the reformed Protestant nor the civic humanist ₌an was expected to withstand temptation, whether religious or politiᴄ‌, humanity was corrupt, or at least corruptible in a most fundamental sense. Those who beat the odds and prevailed were deemed "saints," or in a less theologically committed fashion, "virtuous." While certainly not all late-eighteenth-century Americans held a full-blown pessimistic Calvinist belief regarding humanity's irrevocable corruption, the historian John Murrin points out that the belief "that humankind [was] highly corruptible and that a surrender to corruption had destroyed nearly every republic before their day" was widespread. Murrin concluded that the classical dread of corruption had "a genuine affinity" to orthodox Christian values.[14]

As compatible as Christian and classical republican views about human corruptibility were, early modern political thinkers who tried to understand why republics had failed in the past and how they could—if indeed they could—be constructed to endure, drew far more directly from civic humanist sources than from Christian theology. Educated contemporaries learned from the histories of past republics and the teaching of the ancient historians about the ways in which corruption had advanced and spread. Corruption was part of a large scheme of the historical process, ensuring an unending flux in human events that perpetuated recurrent rises and declines in the lives of political entities. Free republics were prey to the destructive forces of corruption and were often horrifically quick to succumb because of their citizens who preferred to indulge their desires and yield to their vices. (Ironically, this was often facilitated by riches pouring in from foreign conquests, which were made possible through virtuous conduct in the first place.) Preoccupied with self-indulgence, corrupt citizens rapidly forfeited their autonomy to ambitious men who hastened to encroach on their freedom. Yet this process operated not just on the personal level but also on larger social scales, as historical communities depended on their citizens' virtue, that is, lack of corruption. The advancement of individual corruption thus signaled the immanent decay of virtuous government. Tyranny, or anarchy, was soon to follow.

The inimical forces of corruption and decline that have worked throughout history display time and again the painful sight of the decline and consequent fall of virtuous republics. One grand example of this process towered over all others in historical imagination for millennia. The Roman republic's devastating tale of virtue turning into power and its eventual loss conveyed the whole gamut of civic humanistic beliefs regarding corruption, rise, and fall, on a major scale. Many historians, including the Roman Tacitus, the Greek Polybius and more recently the English Gibbon, have described the transformation of the Roman polity from republic into a perverse and eventually faltering empire.[15]

It thus comes as little surprise that many revolutionaries, notably elite southern planters, found the Roman decline useful for understanding the dangers before their revolution and young nation.[16] Many others, however, biblically rather than classically literate, were more psychologically invested in the Bible and thus potentially better instructed in political concepts and processes through the biblical world. Consequently, the years of the War of Independence (1775–1783) were characterized by remarkable representations of the biblical Israelite polity as a corruptible, and eventually corrupt, body politic.

"Bodies politic" was indeed a conventional way in which early moderns understood polities and through which they interpreted their corruption and decline. In the body politic the monarch typically functioned as the head, while the other organs stood for discrete governmental branches and social classes. Eighteenth-century British commonwealthmen adopted this idiom to their needs, representing the commonweal as a living organism that experienced youth, maturity, and eventually the declension of old age. Revolutionary Americans, such as Joseph Huntington (1735–1794), soon adapted this useful metaphor to their needs. Huntington offered his Coventry, Connecticut, church a biblically steeped revolutionary sermon, which he aptly titled *On the Health and Happiness, or Misery and Ruin, of the Body Politic, in Similitude to that of the Natural Body*. In the sermon Huntington presented an elaborate rendition of polity-as-body, asserting that like the well-functioning body politic, a salubrious human body was "perfect in every part, and enjoy[ed] perfect health," while needing "no man, no angle, no creature" to mend it. One historical body politic answered in particular to that qualification of perfection: the "ancient plan of civil policy, delineated for the chosen tribes of Israel" boasted a "divine constitution" that rendered "the most perfect form of civil government."[17]

The "united states or tribes of Israel"—a common understanding of the constitutional arrangement of biblical Israel that we shall examine further in a later chapter—referred to an Israelite "republicanism" which Huntington and his contemporaries fruitfully imagined and articulated. They envisioned, for example, Hebrew officers, like their counterpart American magistrates, "elected by the people at large," as well as a Hebrew "general congress" appointed "with a president at their head." Regardless of its perfection, the Hebrew polity was a body, and as such was bound to decay like every living organism. Its successful constitutional arrangement prevailed only until "the days of Samuel, when the constitution was subverted" by the Hebrews requesting, and getting, a king. The Hebrew republic perished, and was consequently ruled by a dynasty of unelected, often inapt and sinful, officers.[18]

Huntington's identification of the nexus of the Hebrew republic and civic humanist decline was characteristic, as other commentators similarly postulated an original virtuous era of political perfection in Israelite history, one that would eventually succumb to corruption and decay; the Israelite republic would consequently be replaced by a monarchy. Patriots such as David Jones believed in the Hebrew polity's virtuous beginnings: "Israel, when first planted in the land of Canaan, were a brave, heroic and virtuous people, being firmly attached to the true worship of God." Like other past virtuous polities, "they were both formidable and invincible: when their armies went forth to battle, thousands and tens of thousands fell before them." The Israelites in their prime, according to Jones, were thus uniquely "cloathed with the majesty of virtue and true religion." Similarly, the Congregationalist Samuel Langdon (1723–1797), in a sermon that fixated on corruption and was revealingly titled *Government Corrupted by Vice* (1775), portrayed a prelapsarian moment of political virtue that made sense of the Jewish republic's subsequent dissolution. In the early Hebrew republic, according to Langdon, "the public good engage[d] the attention of the whole; the strictest regard [was] paid to the qualifications of those who held the offices of the state; virtue prevail[ed]; every thing [was] managed with justice, prudence, and frugality; the laws [were] founded on principles of equity rather than mere policy; and all the people [were] happy." Langdon went so far as to pronounce the Hebrew polity a "perfect republic," endowed with a godly constitution.[19]

Yet even in a perfect republic, such as the Israelites' may have been, this happy virtuous state could not last. Explanations for such a dramatic reversal of fortunes could take the guise of the standard accounts of republican decline, portraying the advance of vice in Israel with the "riches and glory of an empire," which in turn corrupted the constitution, and "in time [brought] on it dissolution." Like the history of other past republics, the Israelite commonwealth's annals proved that "if the people in general are not engaged to promote the strength and honor, wealth and happiness of a nation

. . . all must fall to the ground." Corruption could be discerned not only during the life span of the Israelite republic (from Moses to Samuel) but also in other periods of Hebrew history. As in every monarchy, corruption—in the republican imagination—raised its head in the Hebrew monarchy after the halcyon yet fleeting reigns of David and his son Solomon. Corruption advanced in Israel under the House of David due to the "the bad policy that prevailed under the reign of [King Solomon's] successor. Solomon's funeral is scarcely finished, before fatal dissensions arise: the Jewish tribes separate, through the imprudence and tyranny of Rehoboam, and the empire is suddenly divided into two independent states." It appears that corruption and decline were regularly interpreted in relation to imprudent policy, or bad personal choices made characteristically by egotistical tyrants.[20] Although corruption was deemed inherent to the historical process, it was often seen as initiated by the personal choices of powerful individuals.

The pristine beginnings would thus be overshadowed by corruption even before war was to drag on and bring with it anguish and pessimism. As early as 1775 David Jones warned that when "pride and luxury predominate, we cannot expect such a nation to be long happy." So "when vice and immorality became prevalent; when [the Israelites] forsook and rebelled against their God, they lost their martial spirit, and were soon enslaved." Another episode in Israel's history in which corruption seemed to have operated was the Maccabean Revolt (167–160 B.C.). The revolt began after the Selucid tyrant Antiochus Epiphanes forbade the practice of the Jewish religion and made use of "chicanery and flattery," the well-known methods of political corrupting, in an attempt to "bring people to favor and assist him in his wicked practices." Antiochus was at least partly successful, as he was able—Jones here drew a direct parallel to George III ("his Antitype in England")—to build a "corrupt party" of "minions and vassals." It was clear then, as John Murray concurred, that "whence prosperity frequently becomes a poison in disguise—the sweeter in taste, the more fatal in effect: nations, as well as individuals, are generally intoxicated by it." Even the Bible confirmed this view, as Murray suggested, citing Deuteronomy 32:15: Jeshurun, a poetic name for Israel indicating a now bygone uprightness, had "waxed fat and kicked at the hand by which they were nourished."[21]

As we have just seen, contemporaries used their civic humanist imagination to understand the decline of the Hebrew republic. It is worth citing at length the following revolutionary American text, which describes the fall of the Hebrew republic, as it demonstrates the striking rendition of Israel as a corrupt classical polity. Indeed, it reads as if it were written by Sallust about first-century B.C. Rome and its transformation from republic to principate:

> The whole body of the [Israelite] nation, from head to foot, was full of moral and political disorders without any remaining soundness. Their religion was a mere ceremony and hypocrisy, and even the laws of common justice and humanity were disregarded in their public courts. They had Counsellors and Judges, but very different from those at the beginning of the common wealth. Their Princes were rebellious against God, and the constitution of their country, and companions of thieves, giving countenance to every artifice for seizing property of the subjects into their own hands, and robbing the public treasury. Every one loved gifts and followed after rewards; they regarded the perquisites more than the duties of their office; the general aim was at profitable places and pensions; they were influenced in everything by bribery; and their avarice and luxury were never satisfied, but hurried them on to all kinds of oppression and violence.

The grim description of the Rome-like Israel concluded with the weary observation that "the whole body being so corrupted, there could be no rational prospect of any great reformation in the state, but rather its ruin."[22]

The question contemporaries understandably asked themselves was how such a shocking subversion took place, since "so long as [the Israelites] abode firm in this reasonable and divine [Mosaic] constitution, supported it, and made the best of the happy privileges contained in it" they were "by far the happiest nation under heaven."[23] If contemporaries could make sense of the Roman republic's decline in terms of corruption, as Europeans had been doing for centuries, the Israelite case necessitated an additional effort. How could a "perfect republic" of a chosen people decline? Were common portrayals of civic humanist corruption enough to explain the severance of the godly covenant? Apparently they were not, as American commentators appealed to a "godly republicanism," in which virtue was not restricted to its civic terms but expanded to encompass religiosity. Revolutionary clergymen thus wedded constitutions and piety, virtue and religion, and blamed the derailment of a godly constitution on ungodly conduct.

Joseph Huntington asserted, for example, that as long as "true religion and good moral principles prevail and rule, that nation is in health"; once "religion dies away," however, "morality decays, infidelity, vice and iniquity prevails among the people in general." Such theological causality had evidently little bearing on the pagan classical republics (to the contrary, Christians had to deal with the opposite accusation, made just before by Edward

Gibbon, that Rome fell *because* of Christianity); but it did strike a chord in the anxious hearts of American Protestants, especially Calvinists conditioned by a tradition of Jeremiads. The new element in this civic humanist historical explanation, which Huntington was by no means alone in adopting, was the fundamental role of religiosity in maintaining a virtuous republic.[24] With religion waning, commentators asserted, a Christian (or Hebraic) republic could not stand.

Traditional historical explanations relied on the destructive work of such worldly forces as *fortuna*, the Roman goddess of fortune which traditionally stood for the whimsical nature of secular occurrences. Yet in order to explain the ever-changing fortunes of republics, revolutionary commentators believed that the transformation of the Jewish republic occurred "not only as the natural effect of vice," as in the case of the classical republics, "but as righteous judgment of heaven, especially upon a nation which has been favor'd with the blessing of religion and liberty, and is guilty of undervaluing them, and eagerly going into the gratification of every lust." Religiosity (or lack of it) and political independence closely corresponded, as did piety and corruption. If Roman decline was conventionally told as a story of secular rise and decline, it was God, however, in "righteous judgment," that left the biblical Hebrews "to run into all this excess of vice to their own destruction, because they had forsaken him, and were guilty of willful inattention to the most essential parts of that religion which had been given them by a well attested Revelation from heaven." With their religion in shambles classical-style corruption would become inevitable and terminal, and in vain would the Jewish nation hope "for a change of men and measures and better times."[25] Israel, a chosen nation that established a perfect republic which lasted for hundreds of years, from Moses to Samuel, succumbed to Rome-like corruption. The causes of that corruption may have been different, secular in the Roman case and religious in the Hebrews', but its results were painfully similar.

Ancient Israel was not the only biblical polity that revolutionary Americans interpreted as experiencing and demonstrating civic humanist corruption. A striking example for such an interpretation was the Persian kingdom ("empire") under its king Ahasuerus (Xerxes), the memorable setting of the Old Testament Book of Esther. That eastern kingdom was characteristically seen during the years leading to independence through a republican prism, as a monarchy not unlike Britain, which was at the "zenith of its greatness" and "had gained the summit of its glory, extent and wealth." This, as every student who dabbled in history knew, was an ominous moment when polities were most vulnerable to the alluring seductions of corruption. Just as in first-century B.C. Rome, and presumably in contemporary England, "luxury and riot began to rage" within Ahasuerus's Persia. A once glorious kingdom "now became prolific in the production of cockatrices and vipers, that began to prey upon the bowles of the empire." Once more, the descriptions of Persia were interchangeable with traditional depictions of the collapsing Roman republic: Ahasuerus's Persia became festered with "minions, and court parasites, those blood-suckers of the constitution" who successfully "establish[ed] unrightousness by law." No less portentously, American commentators argued, "legislative authority [was] prostituted, to the iniquitous." The mortal blow to a state, "of which wound it will certainly perish," occurred when the "low purpose of aggrandizing individuals" came before and "instead of the good of the whole."[26]

Fierce opposition to the threatening and new imperial British policy gathered almost instantly after rumors of a Stamp Act reached the North American colonies in 1765. Americans immediately began to describe Britannia's empire as corrupt in civic humanist language. Learning from the examples of Rome, and now of Persia, both of which signaled and demonstrated Britain's looming fate, patriots imagined how corruption brought about the death of once glorious states: "One set of hampers will flow in after another, till the juices of the political body are consumed—and death is the consequence. . . . Convulsions shake the state, it totters, and then falls."[27] Consequently, Britain was could be understood as the declining empire in the Roman style, and, as we have seen, through the examples set by the perverted Israelite republic. The biblical Persian empire provided yet another useful biblical model of debasement and corruption, as well as virtue.

As historians have long acknowledged, it took colonists more than a decade to direct their anger openly at King George III. During the decadelong contest over Parliament's repeated attempts to tax the colonies following 1765, even militant patriots at least superficially kept their loyalty to their monarch; that would change only during the last months before independence. If patriots elevated the king above the political fray and beyond disparagement, they had to find other culprits toward whom to channel their harsh criticism. This structural (and psychological) need to find perpetrators responsible for what seemed a sudden change in British policy found an outlet through a political tradition that blamed the monarch's corrupt and machinating ministers and counselors for mistaken policies, as well as for the colonies' woes.[28]

Such archetypal explanations customarily portrayed rulers as encircled by scheming and nefarious advisers who purposely separated the monarch from his people, alienating him from the people's wishes and good. Such an interpretation was useful in deflecting criticism from the monarch's person, maintaining the king's immaculate image, which was crucial in old-regime political cultures that cultivated the cult of the king. Denigration and censure trickled down to a group of allegedly wicked and subversive henchmen, "ministers." Such explanations enabled monarchs to act as they thought necessary without allowing considerations of the crown's popularity to outweigh all others, while still maintaining the king's image as a ruler who would not willingly hurt his people. Nevertheless, upholding the king's benevolent image by blaming scheming counselors did carry a price: such interpretations presented the king either as detached and thus as caring insufficiently for his subjects' suffering, or, worse, as a fool maneuvered and manipulated by his aides to act in ways against the good of his kingdom and dangerous to the well-being of his subjects. American patriots found biblical kings, and particularly a certain biblical king, Ahasuerus, who perfectly suited this image.

Colonials considered a distant Hanoverian ruler such as George III, who never even contemplated setting foot on American soil, hard to blame for America's suffering because he was not expected to be aware of the grave infringement of his American subjects' rights. In "royal America," a British North America that the historian Brendan McConville has described as innately royalist and cultivating a cult of the king, such understandings were apparent in patriots' interpretation of the king's role, or rather its nonexistence, in the unfolding imperial crisis.[29] During the decade preceding independence and the creation of an American republic, patriots were quite successful in keeping the king detached from their harsh criticism of the management of successive imperial crises, a pattern that changed dramatically only in the early months of 1776—after the publication of Thomas Paine's *Common Sense* and George III's proclamation of the colonies as rebellious and outside his protection.

American colonials were not especially naïve in absolving the king and putting the blame solely on mischievous ministers. This interpretation of imperial politics demonstrates their reversion to traditional modes of political analysis and expression. That the Continental Congress made repeated appeals and petitions to the king, never losing hope that on learning in person of the colonists' sufferings the benevolent George III would immediately return to the policy of salutary neglect, demonstrates the persistence of this mindset.

So after the repeal of the Stamp Act in 1766 Americans wished to assure the "royal Mind" that the man ("whoever he be, and whatever is his Station") who had been "the instrument of conveying to his Majesty such Sentiments of his faithful [American] and loving Subjects ... is a vile Slanderer and Accuser of the People, and a Traitor to his Prince." In short, such a man was "as great an Enemy ... as was wicked Haman to the Jews."[30] As this last quotation hints, the repeated appeals to the story told in the biblical Book of Esther, with its Persian king's villainous counselor, became a popular way of demonstrating this mode of interpretation of imperial politics, which while protecting the king severely criticized his policies. It also underscores the attraction and benefits that patriots found in the years and months preceding independence in using the Bible as a guide and manual on oppositional politics in a still monarchical political culture.

The story of the Persian king's pious Jewish wife, Esther, and her virtuous uncle Mordecai, who together foiled Haman's planned genocidal massacre of the realm's Jews, provided British North American colonials with important tropes that would assist them in interpreting court and imperial policy. British North American colonials who, according to Bernard Bailyn, were "generally acquainted" with that biblical story, enlisted it frequently from 1765 until the separation from the British monarchy in 1776, after which it became irrelevant once the United States was no longer ruled by a king or influenced by court politics.[31]

The contemporary tendency to interpret history as a stage on which great men determined singlehandedly the fate of nations helped in ascribing political ruin to a single powerful and malevolent enemy of the common good. While a ruthless general such as Julius Caesar was understood to have destroyed the Roman republic for his own selfish purposes, American republicans observed that Persia boasted its own villain: the king's bloodthirsty prime minister. The focus on the character and role of Haman is deeply instructive for understanding the ways in which authors, commentators, and preachers—hence presumably their large audiences—made sense of civic corruption through biblical narratives. The still monarchical but embryonic republican context in which this discourse was so unmistakably useful is evident as American commentators told their audiences, which were not restricted now to New England, that Haman's friends accused the Jews of being "inclined to republican principles" (which would have been a dangerous accusation in monarchical Persia but a badge of honor in opposition circles in America).[32] This interpretation of court politics and British policy along biblical lines may have eroded the legitimacy of the British monarchy in the long run; more immediately, it helped in articulating commonwealthean modes of thought which were strongly related to notions of civic corruption.

Revolutionary-era Americans seemed to agree that among "the many wicked men, whose characters are handed down to us in the scripture-history," Haman was "one of the most remarkable." If earlier generations would probably have interpreted his character in theological terms, revolutionaries represented the scheming minister time and again in civic humanist language. The story was particularly useful, as we have already noted, for colonial Americans still working within a political tradition that exempted monarchs from misdeeds: like George III, the Persian king Ahasuerus "reigned over many distant provinces" and was, "by his prime minister, induced to oppress, and take measures to destroy many of his subjects." The New York author's use of the passive voice is particularly instructive: he underscores that the king was "*induced*" by his active "prime minister"—who "*led* his sovereign to view many of his innocent subjects as rebels"—to destroy lawful and law-abiding subjects. While ultimately eroding the legitimacy of the king, this language identified the modern Hamans as King George's familiars such as Lord Bute and later Lord North, or even military commanders, such as John Burgoyne, sent to pacify America. Those British Hamans were deemed the main perpetrators in a conspiracy against American liberties, a conspiracy as much against their king as it was against his colonial subjects. It was surely against the king's and the kingdom's best interest to outlaw the Persian Jews, or to rob Americans of their British rights, and then, Americans claimed frantically, to "appoint the time of their destruction." But Haman's evil genius, and apparently the English counselors' as well, enabled them to persuade their respective kings to act against their best interest, and their countries'.[33]

Yet another characteristic made Haman so useful for American patriots, more useful than the notorious enemies of the Roman republic Catiline and Jugurtha: Haman, unlike the Romans, did not attempt to attack the polity from the outside with military power. Instead he manipulated and duped a monarch to subvert an empire from within. So at least until the beginning of open warfare with the British in April 1775, Haman the king's courtier was much more relevant for Americans than the enemies of the Roman republic. Nevertheless, Haman's character as portrayed in contemporary polemical literature bore the distinct marks of classical corruption: through his relentless scheming and lying, his ruinous pride and ambition, his political power and consuming hatred for the Jews, the king's adviser was a menace to society, even to a monarchical one that was supposedly less vulnerable than a republic to the harms of corruption. Americans had to speculate on how Haman secured his position in Ahasuerus's court in the first place, as the biblical text gives little evidence on this; they determined that it was not through any distinct merit or ability, but only by being "an adroit courtier, expert in flattery, and by falling in with the king's humours, and ministering to his pleasures, [he] artfully wrought himself into favor."[34]

This view of Haman in light of the imperial scuffing was not confined to New England; South Carolinian clergymen such as Thomas Reese also found it convenient to preach the political corruption of Britain's leadership as a story of biblical decadence. Reese, a southern Presbyterian minister, remarked in a sermon titled *The Character of Haman* that ambition "sticks at nothing to compass its designs. It wades to empire through seas of blood. No principles of religion, virtue or humanity can restrain the wretch, whose ruling passion is the lust for power." A conniving courtier such as Haman would sacrifice all to achieve "his beloved object," the destruction of his innocent enemies. He will "stop at no act of cruelty, however horrid, which he thinks may forward his designs. Treachery, poison, daggers, and all the instruments of death are employed without remorse. He cares not how much blood he spills, nor how much misery he causes, if he can only gain his point." Haman, just like other dangerous ambitious men from Julius Caesar to Lord North, "would risk an empire rather than lose this gratification."[35]

The ordeal of the Jews, as told in the Book of Esther, began when Mordecai, depicted by contemporaries as "that great patriot," would pay "no compliments to the ambitious Haman," refusing to bow to the minister and satisfy his limitless pride. Haman, "the second man in the empire, and highly in favour both with the king and the queen," could have been satisfied with his elevated position within the empire, as the king and queen "had every favour shewn [on] him that he could expect." In a language that was still tolerant of monarchy, American colonials depicted the king's aides as British embodiments of Haman, who in republican language was an evil creature whom nothing would please "unless poor Mordecai was brought to his feet." All Haman's honors and riches "were nothing as long as Mordecai the Jew did not cringe to him.... His whole heart was set upon this one object, and all his glory could not ease his melancholy while this rub was in his way." So despicable and antisocial was Haman's behavior that he was "ready to tell over all

Shusan [biblical Persia's capital city], that this Mordecai was one of the King's enemies, because he did not bow to the nod of his prime minister."[36]

Thus started Haman's egotistical and ferocious campaign against the Jews that would end in his own destruction; the slight to the minister's pride, the fact that Mordecai would not pay him the respect he thought he deserved, initiated the chain of events that ended with the Haman falling "into those very pits" that he had dug for his righteous enemies, and "hang'd on the very gallows . . . [he had] erected for others." This gallows, "the tree, which proud Haman for Mordecai rear'd," was a symbol and sign that "virtue endanger'd is spar'd," and that ambitious men "whom no bonds and no laws can restrain" might be "stript of their honors, and humbled" once more.[37] Americans sounded a stark warning to the British Hamans.

Yet Haman's pride was not the most dangerous of the minister's traits. His more fundamental flaw was one well known in the republican idiom, his "insatiate lust for power . . . and influence." Bernard Bailyn showed long ago that power, the aggressive strife for dominion over other men and its war on liberty, stood at the center of classical republicanism. Patriots repeated this notion time and again when referring to Haman: "The lust of power is a strong passion! It is a sweet thing to ambitious men to see all the world cringing as their humble servants." Had Haman, "whose ruling passion is the lust of power," succeeded in his "bloody purpose . . . do you think he would have been satisfied?" Obviously he would not; such consuming narcissistic ambition, the opposite of virtuous republican disinterestedness, would have continued to propel the "empire through seas of blood." Haman's perceived lust for power was thus repeatedly interpreted in a civic humanist light, as combining "the worst passions of the human heart, and the worst projects of the human mind, in league against the liberties of mankind." While Ahasuerus and George III might have been "naturally of a compassionate and benevolent heart," behind them "court-locusts . . . designing men, this kind of patriots, always lay their plan with a view, to sculk behind the king's authority." However, if Haman, the "haughty prime-minister—and his junto of court parasites," was able to influence the king and obtain from him "that horrid decree to slaughter the Jews in all the provinces," what did this speak of the king? As the contest between Britain and the colonies grew more bitter, the patriots became less forgiving toward the king. As time passed Americans could see George as "brought into a state of magnificent servitude" by his Haman-like ministers. The Book of Esther told of the danger that "over-grown ministers and courtiers" posed both to kings and states. But now the king too came under censure, as being "too ready to believe evil of his subjects, and to comply with the oppressive measures of his prime minister." Even if still not a perpetrator of acts against Americans himself, George III was still seen through the prism of Ahasuerus, "taken up with his Queen and the luxuries of the court, and committ[ing] the management of his political affairs to a very bad man."[38] Once the split between Britain and its colonies became final, and the British king openly declared his former subjects to be enemies, the Book of Esther became irrelevant. Nevertheless, during the decade of American resistance to British attempts to impose taxes on the colonies, the story of the Book of Esther, with its monarchical context, offered Americans an invaluable outlet through which to interpret and contextualize their grievances. Ultimately, it may also have helped them in the process of desecrating and disposing of a king who was now seen as a dupe led by a corrupt and murderous minister.

Demonstrating the classical mindset through which Americans interpreted Haman's character and actions, commentators described him as among history's "greatest conquerors, or absolute monarchs," who were never "satisfied with their power." If such juxtapositions were not bold enough, there were those who compared Haman's genocidal ferocity to the psychopathic Roman emperor "who wished that all the Romans had one neck, that he might have the pleasure of cutting them all off at one blow." This conflation of biblical and classical corruption enabled revolutionary Americans to identify a history of repeated attacks of power-hungry men of the likes of Haman, sinking once virtuous nations and empires, from Persia to Britain, "into the very jaws of slavery, vassalage, and ruin."[39]

American patriots identified corruption not only in external Haman-like threats but also in homegrown Tories, perceived as working against the good of their own community. Here, too, a biblical trope played an important role in assessing, articulating, and contextualizing the danger posed by Americans who would not rally to the patriot's cause. The Curse of Meroz, a well-known trope among American ministers, appears in the Song of Deborah (Judges 5), sung by the Hebrew prophetess after the military victory of the judge Barak over Israel's Canaanite enemy. In the twenty-third verse of her song, the prophetess curses the Israelite town of Meroz for not joining its brethren in their battle against the Canaanite army commanded by Sisera:

"Curse ye Meroz, said the angel of the LORD, curse ye bitterly the inhabitants thereof; because they came not to the help of the LORD, to the help of the LORD against the mighty."

English Calvinists had already invoked the Curse of Meroz during the Puritan Revolution in the seventeenth century, and in America, the historian Alan Heimert has pointed out, colonists had done likewise from the early days of settlement. Ever since, the Curse had functioned as one of the most "honored [and] . . . continuing themes of colonial American literature." Already during the seventeenth century such colonists as Roger Williams had called up Meroz against those perceived as the "glozing neuters" of the day.[40] A century later the Curse of Meroz became significant during the First Great Awakening for societies divided between "old lights" and "new lights," which could not tolerate "neuters" on theological issues.

The "Merozites" of the Great Awakening were religious transgressors who violated a godly command. As Jonathan Parsons put it, "In vain do Men hope to shun the Censure of being against Christ, who are not active in his Cause. . . . [Those who] make any Thing serve for an excuse to lag behind, is mean Cowardize, and a dark sign that men don't care to engage in a critical Day and a difficult service, when their help is most expected." Parsons was only one among a group of leading revivalists who mobilized the Curse to "arouse the slothful people of God in whatever operation the Calvinist ministry happened to be engaged," as well as to separate Christ's friends from his enemies. Other revivalists such as Jonathan Edwards threatened not only those who actively opposed the Awakening but also the "many that are silent and inactive" that "the Lord . . . will bring that Curse of the Angel of the Lord upon themselves, Judg. 5. 23." Other leaders of the Awakening from Gilbert Tennent ("Was not Meroz cursed, because he did not come up to the Help of the Lord against the Mighty?") to George Whitfield ("Think of that awful Saying of the Angel of the Lord, Curse ye Meroz"), among others, repeatedly invoked the cursed biblical city of neutrals who defied the divine decree to assist their brethren.[41]

The Great Awakening–era invocations of the Curse were reconfigured by the time of the French and Indian War, as public speakers mobilized the accursed Meroz for patriotic and military, not religious, reasons. Samuel Davies, in a sermon revealingly titled *Religion and Patriotism the Constituents of a Good Soldier* (1755), reminded Captain Overton's Independent Company of Volunteers, raised in Hanover County, Virginia, that he was "concerned that there are so few to join you." He referred to "the people of Meroz [who] lay at home in Ease, while their Brethren were in the Field, delivering their Country from Slavery." Similarly Isaac Stiles and Samuel Finley (as well as Davies himself again in 1758) warned through the example of "the dastardly Inhabitants of Meroz, who refused to take up Arms for the Defence of their Country." In a sermon aptly titled *The Curse of Meroz,* Finley concluded, "British subjects, who refuse to assist their labouring Country, in the present War, are obnoxious to the Curse of Meroz."[42]

Only a few years after the French and Indian War ended, the Curse of Meroz became, according to Alan Heimert, "probably the favorite text of the Calvinist ministry in the years of the Revolution," as the biblical imprecation was mobilized to focus the animus of the people against American Tories. So widespread would such invocations be that preachers would remind American armies preparing for battle "of the curse which the Lord had placed on Meroz for not coming to the aid of the mighty." Yet the use of the Curse of Meroz underwent a significant and hitherto unfamiliar transformation during the years of the Revolution: revolutionaries applied once more the logic of civic humanism to represent the inhabitants of the accursed Meroz as corrupt, antirepublican citizens. This is particularly remarkable since not only is the city of Meroz mentioned just once in the Bible, but beyond the single verse in Deborah's Song there are no details whatsoever regarding that accursed city; all the Bible says is that the Merozites did not come to the help of their brethren and were consequently cursed.[43] Hence the representation of Meroz's betrayal and the subsequent revilement it received in civic humanist colors reveals a republican exegetical mode through which Americans read and applied the republican Bible to their revolutionary needs.

As early as 1770, five full years before the military conflict began, a long piece in the *New York Gazette* retold the story of the Israelites' battle with the Canaanites under the rule of Jabin and his commander Sisera (that Israelite victory, told in Judges 4 and 5, was the subject of the song of the Hebrew prophetess). The language of the article was steeped in the classical republican idiom, emphasizing military ardor and sacrifice for the common good. The author portrayed, for example, the Israelites as "behav[ing] themselves valiantly, by opposing so violent an Oppression" as the Canaanites, while the tribes Zebulun and Naphtali were applauded for being "willing to attempt the throwing off the Yoke of Slavery by risquing their all in the Service of the Country"; other commentators concurred, concluding that "the little army—raised from two tribes only out of twelve—of Deborah and Barak march out and wage war against their oppressor, for the recovery of their freedom." Republican-like sacrifice for the cause of liberty was not the only lesson that that biblical struggle conveyed; while "some other of the Tribes came down and assisted in the Pursuit," there were always, as "in all Nations and in all Communities," Merozites, "dead to the delicate Feelings of Liberty," who found it "their Interest to court the Oppressors Rod." There were traitors other than Meroz who would betray the Israelite's cause: the tribe of Dan, who "pretended he could not leave his Ships," recalled Americans who broke the colonial commercial boycott and "would no longer be faithful to their Country, than it comported with their personal Lucre!" However, there was only one community singled out for severe punishment. Only "Meroz is condemned with a Curse." The Inhabitants of Meroz, the pastor Nathaniel Whitaker pointed out late in the war, "did not commit any acts of violence, insult, barbarity or murder; they did not burn, or assist in burning the towns and dwellings of their brethren." Indeed, the sin of the inhabitants of Meroz seemed less than the transgressions of contemporary Loyalists, since "they did not, that we know, go over to assist, counsel, or comfort the enemy, as our tories have done." No, the only sin of the Merozites was to "neglect . . . their duty; they did not come to their [brethren's] help, when their enemies oppressed them, nor assist in casting off the galling yoke."[44] This language of service and duty, of liberty and the common cause, was clearly a manifestation of the ideology modern historians came to call classical republicanism. That doctrine deemed the neglect of civic responsibility as corruption. Under *biblical* republicanism, corruption led to a divine curse.

And cursed Meroz was. The city's fate raised considerable interest in revolutionary America but also posed difficult questions that the Bible left unanswered. Under the intense political and social strains of the Revolution, those questions became urgent: why of all sinning communities was Meroz singled out for being cursed, and why did not Scripture mention it ever again (or before)? A contemporary commentator conjectured that it "was undoubtedly a considerable City, Since something great seems to have been expected from it." After sinning it might have just "dwindled away" becoming "utterly detested," and thus never being mentioned again.[45]

More revealing, however, than such speculation and overreading of the biblical text was the particular language in which revolutionary commentators chose to describe the inhabitants of Meroz: "Philo-Patria" observed in the *New York Gazette* that "Meroz altogether refused to assist in the one Common Cause." Such behavior meant, in the prevailing revolutionary sensibilities, that the inhabitants of Meroz were seen not as mere sinners but as corrupt republicans, a representation which obviously had no textual basis. The language of revolutionary republicanism emphasized active citizenship and a personal sense of duty and sacrifice, which was evident in wartime pronouncements such as George Washington's: "It is not sufficient for a Man to be a passive friend & well wisher to the Cause. . . . Every person should be active in some department or other, without paying too much attention to private Interest."[46] Passivity and neutrality, not to mention loyalty to the crown, were deemed then in the world of revolutionary American classical republicanism a civic sin. Meroz thus provided many revolutionaries with an alarming example of such deviance, one that was biblical but understood through the civic humanist cosmology.

It comes as no surprise then that revolutionaries described Barak and Deborah, who won the battle that the Merozites dodged, in language preserved for virtuous republicans: the Israelite leaders were "Worthies who had so nobly denied themselves to save their distressed Country." The inhabitants of Meroz presented a negative image of such republican disinterestedness: in their corrupt, antisocial, and antirepublican conduct, they preferred "their petty Interests to the general Good" and their "secular Interest to the public Emolument." Another commentator, calling himself "Hampden" to invoke the English commonwealthman John Hampden, wrote that the inhabitants of Meroz, "instead of defending their country," were the "advocates for tyranny and oppression." Referring to the Curse of Meroz, the American Hampden declared in the language of civic humanism (with a biblical twist) "that a person or people, that neglect to defend their country, their religion and liberty, deserve to be cursed, or at least to be treated with neglect and contempt."[47]

Patriotic Americans thus found it convenient, if totally unfounded, to describe the view of the inhabitants of Meroz as "dastardly, low-spirited, court sycophants" who "trembled at the power of Jabin [the Canaanite king], and thought him invincible." Meroz became an instructive parable of a corrupt community "so lost to all noble and generous feeling, that would not choose to die in the field of martial glory, rather than accept such insulting terms of peace or rather of misery." Corruption led to slavery, and indeed by staying "neuter," the people of Meroz chose to remain "subjugated to the arbitrary will and disposal of a merciless tyranny." The Curse of Meroz thus taught Americans a republican lesson, namely that "God himself abhors the sluggish Spirit, who tamely submits to the galling Yoke, and from a slavish Love of Life, or a more iniquitous, Love of gold, prefers his own private Interest to the more permanent good of Posterity." Hence the story of the accursed and lost city demonstrated that "factious and party Spirits in a State or Community, who are seeking their own private Emolument, to the public Loss, however powerful they may seem to be, will in the End be justly exposed, and receive the due Reward of their Iniquities." In short, Meroz was a glaring example not only of civic corruption, but—just as in the case of Haman—also of godly retribution for a civic, republican sin. American Tories, who "opposed, or even neglected to assist us in our endeavors to secure our liberty," were "guilty of the sin of *Meroz*."[48]

Americans would thus perceive the biblical people of Meroz through a vocabulary traditionally preserved to describe decadent Romans: the Merozites were "dastardly, sordid, and selfish," characterized by "their *Effeminacy*, Luxury, false Notions, Confinement to little Party-Interests, and absolute Want of public Spirit."[49] Their corruption seemed even far worse than the decadence that inflicted classical societies, since beyond their civic sins they defied a godly call. Once more, the treatment of Tories-Merozites as civically corrupt manifested the ways in which the revolutionary imagination transformed the Bible into a republican text.

Revolutionaries could find examples of "biblical Tories" more active than the people of Meroz, who were after all mere "neuters," harmful to the common cause through lethargy and indolence. The Book of Maccabees, a scripture of ambivalent pedigree (actually an eclectic corpus which may have consisted of two to eight books), provided them with such an example. As an apocryphal text it was not part of the Protestant (or Jewish) canon, hence potentially less appealing, and less known to the predominantly Protestant population of American colonials. Nevertheless, Americans could have been acquainted with the history of the Maccabees through the popular writings of the Jewish-Roman historian Josephus Flavius, which were available in late-eighteenth-century America through multiple printed editions.[50] Maccabees chronicles second-century B.C. events, which are much later than the rest of the Old Testament corpus. The book tells the story of the Maccabees, the leaders of a Jewish rebellion against the Seleucid Empire, a Hellenistic kingdom carved out of the divided empire of Alexander the Great. The Maccabees were the founders of the Jewish Hasmonean dynasty, which would rule an independent Israel from the successful rebellion in 140 B.C. until 37 B.C., when Rome installed a non-Hasmonean king, effectively turning Judea into a province. In their long and costly uprising for national independence, the Maccabees, who were commonly seen as saviors who resisted Hellenistic encroachments and revived the Jewish state, faced formidable dangers from external threats but also from within; not all of their coreligionists believed in the Maccabees' risky and bold revolt.

Once again, American patriots framed this biblical struggle in the conceptual world of early modern republicanism, describing the leaders of the rebellion as striving "with a gallantry" to "the cause of freedom," and as able to "frustrate many attempts made by the Syrian [Seleucid] monarchy to destroy their liberties and reduce them to absolute vassalage." Not surprisingly, they respectively perceived the Jews who refused to go along with the Maccabean leadership during the rebellion as epitomes of classical corruption, juxtaposing them with their own Tories. Like "Judea [that] suffered from her apostate sons, America's calamities are chiefly owing to degenerate Americans." Those who refused to take up the struggle against Antiochus Epiphanes, the ruler of the Seleucid Empire at the time of the rebellion, were "Jewish Transgressors." Those "insidious Israelites" betrayed their brethren in that they applied "to Antiochus, addressed his fears, rendered him jealous of his regal prerogatives, misrepresented the sentiments of their countrymen, [whom they] insinuated . . . intended to throw of all subordination to his government, that they wished to live independent of his authority." The analogy "between the state of Judea . . . and the present situation of America" seemed remarkable: just as those "sycophants formerly entertained their sovereign with tales of a contemplated revolt," so did "a Hutchinson, Oliver, &c."—Massachusetts natives and high-ranking royal officials "in these modern times by letters fraught with fallacies and replete with malice." "These corrupted Emissaries of the Tyrant," Epiphanes, American Patriots now clearly saw, "were among the Jews, what the Tories are in this Country in the present Day."[51]

Peter Powers (1728–1800), a New England pastor, preached in 1780 on the same "apostates and vile mercenaries among the Jews, called the Transgressors," who after the Maccabean rebellion erupted, gave the Seleucid leader "intelligence of every design of the Jews, and who were in opposition against him, what their situation, power and strength; nothing could pass in Judas Maccabeus's camp or Councils" without his foes' knowledge.[52] The lesson for Americans was that Israelites and Americans alike had "more to apprehend from the treachery of residents among them, that they can possibly dread from the most dangerous foreign invasion." However, to answer what motivated the ancient Jewish Tories, and accordingly their American counterparts, to betray their own people, American political commentators had to interpret the Maccabean revolt through the ideological world of classical republicanism.

Seen through a civic humanist lens, the Jews who sided with the Seleucid Empire were "corrupt and abandoned Men," who were "lost to the feelings of shame, so dead to the sensations of honour." Epiphanes won them over easily by "brib[ing] and flatter[ing] out of all their Liberties, and their Religion." In a civic humanist view, these "traitors" were represented as acting against their own people "for the Sake of filthy Lucre: The Love of money was to them the Root of all Evil." In language similar to that in which Jugurtha, the great corruptor of the Roman republic, described the late republican Rome—"Yonder is a city put up for sale, and its days are numbered if it finds a buyer"—Peter Powers described the Jewish Tories who were "ready to do any Thing for Money and are nosed about by Flatteries to commit Murders, and every vile Thing." Interestingly, even southern observers could disregard altogether the appeal to the problematic religiosity of the Hellenized Jews who did not wish to rebel against the Seleucids; they chose to condemn the Jewish Tories for civic misdeeds, for proving "regardless of their country's welfare." Their offenses were thus not deemed religious transgressions for being swayed by Hellenic paganism, but were antirepublican in nature: they did not "hesitate at any steps tending to promote or gratify their resentment, avarice or pride," which led them to "league with tyrants [and] aid and abet the ravages of their natal climes." Avarice, pride, egotism, and lust were, as should by now be clear, the distinct characteristics of classical republican corruption.[53]

We have seen how easily American commentators could read classical corruption into Old Testament narratives and figures, enabling audiences to become familiar with and make sense of an ideology that was a significant force in shaping their revolution. This was possible, however, only if a more general Whig interpretive mode prevailed, namely one that could read the Old Testament as a narrative of resistance to tyranny. Such understandings were indeed prevalent. The New York author "Philalethes" was characteristic in concluding days before the commencement of hostilities in Lexington and Concord, that "passive obedience and non resistance" was "contrary to the word of God," a stance he proved by citing a string of biblical anecdotes; the Bible persuaded Philalethes that "oppression, tyranny, and unrighteous acts of government, are odious to the supreme Being." The Patriots' God emerged as a republican deity. "From the beginning," they commonly believed, God "had a regard for liberty, and that tyrants, and oppressors, have been the objects of his abhorrence." This truth manifested itself in sacred history, as "oppression and tyranny began to work in early ages . . . and spread abroad its baneful influence, and pernicious effects among men." Although "injustice, tyranny, and oppression" often prevailed, the history of the Israelites indisputably demonstrated God's "favour of liberty, and frowning on tyrants; and it shews how much he regards the rights of his people, and in how exemplary a manner, hard hearted tyrants, and merciless oppressors, sometimes feel his vengeance." The Old Testament thus provided many other revolutionary readers and listeners a store of justified rebellions against despotic domination and political repression (while simultaneously providing Loyalists with a justification of monarchy and obedience). A "Moderate Whig" pointed out in a tract dedicated to George Washington that "the lawfulness of taking up arms to oppose all tyranny, oppression, and those who abase and misuse their authority" is obvious when examining the history of numerous biblical despotic rulers, from Rehoboam to Sennacherib, and the resistance to them by liberty-seeking people.[54]

The common Whig view of liberty as a positive but fragile and ever-threatened political element, together with a traditional and common cyclical understanding of history, facilitated readings of the Bible that underscored the repetitive sequences of the Israelites' oppression by their enemies, followed by successful, if temporary, resistance to tyranny and the regaining of political autonomy and liberty. The same biblical narratives examined earlier in this chapter that could demonstrate classical corruption, such as Haman's character and the people of Meroz, also furnished biblical exempla of republican public virtue, the polar opposite of civic decadence. For every corrupt Haman there was a virtuous Mordecai, "that great patriot," who "refused to do homage to a hangman, Haman," and an Esther, both of whom "bestir[red] themselves, and even risk[ed] their lives" in their people's cause. For every prosecuting Antiochus Epiphanes, "a tyrant, and he one of the greatest and worst that ever existed," who "used chicanery and flattery, corrupting and bribing people to favor and assist him in his wicked practices," there was a virtuous Judas Maccabeus.[55]

The Maccabean case demonstrates a larger pattern in the contemporary readings of biblical narratives: the Bible, as Christian exegetes have known for two millennia, did not merely provide lessons in politics and morality but was a stage for elaborate typological analysis. The tyrant Antiochus was "exactly answered in his Antitype in England [George III], who for these five or six years has been laying many of our populous towns in ashes, and pouring out the blood of hundreds and thousands of peaceable inhabitants by the force of the sword." Judas Maccabeus, on the other hand, the leader of the rebellion against the Seleucids, who "vigorously prosecuted . . . the quarrel of religion and liberty, against the mighty tyrant," would provide an antetype for Washington for decades to come.[56]

Similarly, countering the Tory-like people of Meroz were virtuous redeemers in the guise of the judge Barak and the prophetess-judge Deborah, who "behave[d] themselves valiantly, by opposing so violent an Oppression" as the Canaanite king Jabin's in order to recover their liberty. In taking arms against Jabin and his general Sisera, the prophetess and the military leader Barak "acted agreeably to the law of nature . . . [aiming only] to recover and secure the liberties and rights which had been wrested from them." Political readers of the Bible characteristically and typologically understood the "struggle with Great Britain [as] very similar to that of Israel and Jabin," and reached the republican conclusion that since it was the Israelites' "duty to fight for the recovery of their freedom, it must likewise be ours." The duty to fight tyranny to regain lost liberty was of course fundamental in the republican creed since the early days of the foundation of the Roman republic. Framing their contemporaneity in light of a republican reading of the Bible, Americans could call out in exasperation before armed resistance mustered to fight the "English Jabin," "Is there not a Barak in the land? Are there no Deborahs to be found amongst us?"[57]

Yet Barak and Deborah were only two among a host of Israelite judges that revolutionaries mobilized for their republican cause. The Jewish judgeship, as will be further discussed in a later chapter, was a noninherited military and judicial magistracy, which elicited civic humanistic readings throughout the Revolution. Ehud Ben-Gera, the first judge of Israel after Joshua's death, who restored the Israelites' liberty from the oppression of the Moabite king Eglon, characteristically stimulated republican interpretations. His bold regicide of Eglon was perceived as the ultimate antimonarchical deed: "If the Lord's people, serving a haughty tyrant, may shake off the yoke of the subjection, then it is duty to defend themselves and resist."[58] Yet while patriots lauded many judges for their republican virtue during the Revolution, the most intense and remarkable discussion was preserved for one judge in particular.

Gideon, whom the Bible also identifies as Jerubbaal, was the fifth judge of the Israelites, who saved his people from their enemies the Midianites and the Amalekites. Victorious on the battlefield, Gideon was renowned for his military leadership, which would suffice for revolutionary Americans to discuss a biblical figure in republican terms. However, Gideon's character was multifaceted and more elaborate than, say, that of his predecessors Barak and Ehud, providing American republicans reasons to admire him greatly. Gideon's humble origins and modesty, his military prowess, and especially his refusal to become king over Israel all made him a perfect republican model.

Only during what would become the final attack on the institution of monarchy could a starkly negative discourse regarding kingship emerge; the man perhaps most responsible for antimonarchical sentiment in America was he who injected Gideon's antimonarchism into the American discourse. The significance of Thomas Paine's *Common Sense* for understanding the shift to antimonarchical sentiment in early 1776 is undisputed among historians, and lately we have learned about the importance of republican Hebraism in Paine's antimonarchism.[59] It may thus come as a surprise that some elements of that most renowned, examined, and important of revolutionary tracts have still not been sufficiently contextualized. In particular, the Israelite judge Gideon's role in this pamphlet, as well as his more general place in the revolutionary republican imagination, has gone hitherto unnoticed.

Algernon Sidney, the seventeenth-century English republican martyr best remembered for his magisterial and rambling *Discourses Concerning Government* (1698), of which Americans, in the words of the historian Caroline Robbins, made a "textbook of revolution," may have been Thomas Paine's inspiration with regard to Gideon. As Sidney briefly acknowledged, "Gideon was indeed much pressed by the Israelites to be their king . . . [but they] desisted when [the] offer [was] refused." A century later Paine further developed this theme in *Common Sense,* imparting a civic humanist flavor to the biblical story of Gideon's rejection of dynastic monarchy: the Israelites, *Common Sense* pointed out, so elated with their rescue by Gideon's small army, "proposed making him a king, saying, Rule thou over us, thou and thy son and thy son's son." Paine pointed here at the basest and most dangerous of sentiments in the republican lexicon at work, the corrupting lust for political power, "temptation in its fullest extent." Gideon, however, "in the piety of his soul replied": "I will not rule over you, neither shall my son rule over you, THE LORD SHALL RULE OVER YOU." "Words," Paine concluded, "need not be more explicit."[60]

As other American revolutionary exegetes soon discovered, Gideon enacted what could be construed as the ultimate republican deed of disinterested rejection of political power. Polemicist writers interpreted his actions as equivalent to the most praiseworthy of the Roman republic's heroes, Lucius Quinctius Cincinnatus (519–438 B.C.), the retired senator who returned to the Senate his dictatorial powers shortly after winning a victory and saving Rome. No one elaborated more on this notion than John Murray in a prolonged revolutionary pamphlet, *Jerubbaal* (1784), which took as its subject the relevance of Gideon (Jerubbaal) to revolutionary America. Murray's civic humanistic interpretation of Gideon's conduct demonstrates, however, not only the relevance of the Israelite judge to the American situation but also the utility of collapsing the worlds of the Old Testament, Rome, and America into an amalgam fused through civic humanism.

Murray emphasized Gideon's aversion to power and his negative response regarding "the ambition which would prompt some men to court so high an honor—or to grasp the nomination to office." When first approached by God's angel, "the judge-elect modestly declines the appointment—remonstrates the smallness of his tribe—the obscurity of his family—and his own inferiority in it—represents himself as the last person, of the last family, of the last tribe, from which a commander in Israel should be expected—and persists in his doubts." To the ears of a republican audience young Gideon's behavior was no demonstration of timidity (which could after all be a plausible interpretation of the biblical text). For American revolutionaries a much more likely explanation was that Gideon was acting the virtuous role of republican self-effacement, of avoiding the slightest appearance of the pursuit of power for one's own sake, of personal gratification and ambition. Classical republicans, Murray's Gideon included, would accept political power only for the sake of the common, namely the polity's, good. In this context, especially in light of Murray representation of the biblical Gideon, the similarity between the Israelite Judge's refraining from power and George Washington's statement to the Continental Congress upon his appointment as commander of the Continental Army is striking: "Tho' I am truly sensible of the high Honour done me, in this Appointment, yet I feel great distress, from a consciousness that my abilities and military experience may not be equal to the extensive and important Trust."[61] Good republicans, from Gideon son of Joash to George Washington, were supposed to erase the slightest impression that they were power hungry, to act humbly to the point of self-deprecation. Little wonder that, as we shall now see, Americans would construct George Washington, the master of classical politics of virtue, as a latter-day Gideon.

As contemporaries well knew, throughout history it was at the dangerous moment of victory that military leaders capitalized on their battlefield success to solidify and perpetuate their power. Such a crucial moment arrived when Gideon, who had valiantly won a war and saved his people, was consequently "crowned with the blessings of his rescued country—and loaded with laurels" (laurels themselves of course being classical and pagan, not biblical). At that dramatic moment the children of Israel invited Gideon "to ascend a throne." Not only were the Israelites "ready to receive him as Monarch in Israel," they also invited Gideon "to settle the crown upon his issue-male, as their hereditary property in lineal succession." Like the Romans who presented Julius Caesar, their republic's destroyer, a dictatorship for life, the Israelites "consent[ed] tamely to surrender to their General, those precious liberties with which heaven had made them free." Murray presents here Gideon not as a judge but as a general holding a dangerous military chieftainship, a figure that was traditionally suspected of seeking to usurp the republic for personal gratification, Caesar-style. However, unlike Caesar, who was remembered for disingenuously rejecting—thrice!—the diadem offered him by the Roman people, only to become a monarch de facto of the republic he ruined, Gideon's "patriotic greatness of soul" obliged him to "positively refuse the unadvised present" of a king's throne. Gideon declined perpetual sovereignty and refused "rewards which none ever did better deserve." Not only did the Israelite Judge "accept no pay for his laborious services," he did not even accept "any pension to himself or family."[62]

Once more the American author may have been alluding here to George Washington, who famously set a magnificent republican example upon becoming the Continental Army's commander: "As to pay, Sir, I beg leave to assure the Congress, that, as no pecuniary consideration could have tempted me to have accepted this arduous employment, at the expence of my domestic ease and happiness, I do not wish to make any proffit from it." When Murray finally described Gideon as "greatly retir[ing] to his farm ... while he withdraws from the command," the archetypal model he was referring to was obvious. Gideon was "the Jewish Cincinnatus."[63]

This conflation of the Roman dictator Cincinnatus—who rose from the field to assume absolute power in order to save Rome from its enemies, only to retire victorious days later and return to his oxen and plow—with an Israelite judge is remarkable. The merging of two characters from the remote worlds of the Bible and classical antiquity was not fleeting but a theme Murray thoroughly explored. Even the language of classical republicanism was applied to describe Gideon, who was repeatedly referred to as "Israel's Dictator," a term associated in classical republicanism (and in Roman history) not with tyranny but with absolute powers limited in time and granted to confront grave emergencies.[64] Gideon's self-effacement, modesty, and disinterestedness all fed into the Israelite's Cincinnatian image. However, Murray's careful representation of Gideon as a Cincinnatus was more than an exercise in historical comparison; it was meant to link the most famous of American Cincinnati, the now retired general George Washington, with the biblical—and republican—Jerubbaal.

"We," Murray exclaimed, "were blessed with a Gideon too." "Like Gideon," George Washington was "singularly qualified" for his mission. Further, "the American Gideon, with scarce that number of men, equally destitute of every military advantage," was able to defeat a superior enemy; and "Like Israel's Dictator, the American Gideon rose—like him he conquered—and like him too, he retires." The image of George Washington, already widely renowned among his compatriots as a retired Cincinnatus who after winning the war returned his commission to Congress to retire to his Mount Vernon farm, was now constructed from a trio of leaders: a classical Roman, a biblical Israelite, and a self-effacing, power-rejecting American. The three seemed inseparable: "As Jerubbaal, when his work is done, returned to his native city," Murray asked his fellow citizens to "behold the AMERICAN CINCINNATUS greatly retiring to his beloved privacy!" After winning the war speculation indeed ran high whether Washington could or would indeed become king. While this of course did not happen, Murray assured his audience that even had Americans "copied the weakness of Israel," and one may add the weakness of the Romans, "and rashly invited him to a throne," Washington's "past conduct affords unequivocal proof, that the offer would have met the deserved repulse." Murray fantasized Washington's answer to such a vile offer in Cincinnatian fashion and in Gideon-like language: "*I will not rule over you;—neither shall my son rule over you:—the Lord alone shall be king in* AMERICA."[65]

Political commentators continued to portray Gideon after the Revolution and into the nineteenth century in the most Cincinnatian of representations, as a modest, self-effacing "perfect able young farmer, [who] was called to lead the army of Israel, while he was threshing wheat." Americans, north and south, thus kept thanking their Gideons, that although they "might have bound a yoke of iron" upon "tame and submissive necks" if they had only wished, both the biblical and American Cincinnatian Gideons refused the offers of a hereditary throne. Rather, they respectively said to the people of the Old and the New Israel, "I will not rule over you, neither shall my son rule over you."[66] The ties binding the Bible and America, the Old and the New Israel, were intensified through civic humanism, an ideology forged in the tyranny-hating, duty-bound Roman republic.

Throughout the early national period, the Old Testament continued to provide Americans with invaluable venues for expressing and contemplating the tenets of republicanism, namely the moral language of liberty. Political readings of the Bible would not cease after the conclusion of the War of Independence, as the Old Testament affirmed its position as an integral part of the United States' moral and political economy for decades to come. Americans continued to address and interpret the Old Testament as a republican text well into the nineteenth century, as even a glance at antebellum public rhetoric reveals. As I shall demonstrate in the rest of this book, this "republican Bible" was a dynamic and flexible text, which Americans were able to preserve and mold according to changing needs and in response to shifting circumstances and evolving sensibilities. A brief look at the story of the Israelite judge Jephthah hints at the ongoing and evolving significance of this language.

Jephthah, who vowed before God that upon winning in battle he would sacrifice the first person who came out to congratulate him when he returned to his home, kept his vow when his only daughter emerged to applaud his triumph over the Ammonites. On the face of it, this story most resembles that of Lucius Junius Brutus, the founder of the Roman republic, whose vow never to reinstate monarchy in Rome came back to haunt him as he stoically watched the execution of his two conspiratorial sons. Nevertheless, when Americans invoked the tragic story of Jephthah in the nineteenth century, it was not in relation to the stern civic humanist sensibilities that characterized the earlier, founding-era biblical (and classical) discourse. Rather, it manifested the evolving Victorian sensibilities of republican womanhood. Hence Americans chose to praise not the homicidal father but his stoic nameless daughter for her "dignified . . . composure [and] heroism." Jephthah's daughter symbolized the "sweet simplicity" of a newly feminized notion of virtue, as she "prepare[d] herself for a death more glorious than that of the most celebrated heroes of ancient or of modern ages." If late-eighteenth-century

Americans celebrated Cincinnatus (or Gideon) for his manly republican disinterestedness, Jephthah's daughter provided them with an example of "devotion more sublime than that of Codrus and Curtius," exemplars of civic humanist patriotism and self-sacrifice. The republican landscape was shaking as feminine virtue could successfully compete with the symbols of manly antiquity. If it was the business of a soldier and a king to die in the field of battle, "what could a poor rural girl feel of martial enthusiasm or expect of future fame?"[67] The Old Testament with its store of narratives and tropes would accommodate these changes, and cater to the new sensibilities as long as it served as the nation's primary political text.

2

"The United Tribes, or States of Israel"

The Hebrew Republic as a Political Model before the Civil War

Enoch Wines (1806–1879), a Congregationalist minister from New Jersey, mused in 1853 that he had "sometime imagined all the legislators of America gathered into one vast assemblage, and the Jewish lawgiver [Moses] appearing suddenly in their midst. 'Gentlemen,' he might say to them, 'at length my word is fulfilled. What you boast of doing now, I accomplished, as far as in me lay, in a distant age.'" Moses went on, in Wines's imagination, to recount to the American legislators how he had led Israel out of the house of Egyptian bondage through the wilderness. But the ancient Hebrew also detailed to his American listeners his perceived political accomplishments, such as proclaiming "the principle of universal equality among men," and first and foremost, founding an Israelite republic. Cling to republican principles, Moses entreated the "legislators of a world that had no being when I founded my republic, Give them a broader development, a higher activity; and the civilization, the prosperity, the happiness flowing from them, shall outstrip your fondest hopes."[1] American republicanism seemed inherently connected to an ancient, biblical experience.

Wines's conjuration of the Hebrew lawgiver appeared in his remarkable tome, the 640-page *Commentaries on the Laws of the Ancient Hebrews* (1855). This volume joined an interpretive tradition that understood, in the author's words, "the Hebrew constitution, in its substance and forms, in its letter and its spirit," as "eminently republican." A further premise of that tradition, which in America could be traced to the early years of the Revolution (some eighty years before Wines published his book), was even more dramatic: the so-called "Hebrew constitution" of the Israelite nation not only was republican but had "important and striking analogies with our own constitution." Wines, and his revolutionary-era predecessors, saw that the American and Hebrew constitutions' "fundamental principles are identical; and many of the details of organization are the same or similar." While there may have been variants in the analysis of the Hebrew republic and in the specifics of the comparisons between the Mosaic and American constitutions, all participants in that prolonged discussion would have agreed with Wines that "the Hebrew polity was essentially a system of self-government. It was the government of individual independence, municipal independence, and state independence,—subject only to so much of central control, as was necessary to constitute a true nationality." The Mosaic constitution was deemed, in short, a federal constitution, and thus, according to numerous American commentators, "remarkably resemble[d] our own, and as remarkably differ[ed] from other ancient polities."[2]

By the 1850s Wines was among the last that would provide a full-fledged exposition of a political tradition that originated in early modern Europe and was Americanized during the Revolution. In recent decades scholars have begun to appreciate the European richness of this tradition, and the extent to which early modernity, for a century and a half after the Protestant Reformation "between Bodin and Locke, with Machiavelli as a significant Predecessor," experienced the efflorescence of political Hebraism, namely the analysis of the Hebrew republic in the political context.[3] In this chapter I aim to demonstrate, however, that a full century *after* Locke, and following the decline in European political interest in the Hebrew Bible, revolutionary New England in particular spawned a similar and prolonged Mosaic moment, one that was to evolve into a distinct dialect of national scope in the political culture of the antebellum United States.

The Old Testament was a significant intellectual sphere through which pre–Civil War Americans articulated and constructed their political and national consciousness. In this chapter I address this larger trajectory by examining an intriguing dimension through which Scripture interacted with contemporaries' reflection on their young polity: taking the initial lead of revolutionary New England clergymen, antebellum politically conscious Americans, from northern Congregationalist ministers such as the aforementioned Enoch Wines to evangelical statesmen such as Elias Boudiont and southern politicians like John C. Calhoun, attempted to make sense of, justify, and reconcile the experimental constitutional arrangements of the young United States and the hallowed political models introduced through the history of what they often called the "Jewish republic."

American patriots, commentators, and politicians appropriated throughout the early national period, a time when they confronted novel political contexts and dilemmas pertaining to legitimacy and authority, a biblical constitutional paradigm of their historical circumstances. The Mosaic constitution, "the oldest complete constitution in our possession" according to one of its modern students, provided early Americans with a divinely sanctioned historical archetype. They found in the political history of the ancient Israelites a model for republicanism, but not less important for the *federal* republicanism that was developing during those years. The discourse of the Hebrew republic and its Mosaic constitution emerged from robust reformed Protestant sensibilities, forged through years of absorbing religious sermons, "the only regular voice of authority" in colonial northern communities. This biblical constitutionalism, which first appeared in revolutionary-era sermons in New England and later diffused into national debates, was not a conventional theological discourse (it mostly consisted of a *political* analysis of the structure of ancient Israel), nor was this constitutional mode of analysis an American innovation, as it had already been known in Europe for centuries.[4] However, focusing on this overlooked biblical strand of constitutional and republican exegesis brings to the fore a significant contemporary mode of thinking about, and structuring Americans' understanding of their young federal republic; it also situates American political analysis in its broad and deep Atlantic genealogy. This discussion of the Mosaic origins of the American republic was particularly meaningful for a nation that was actively forging its identity as a "second Israel" as it was alleviating the apprehensions regarding its experimentation with republican politics.

Historians of America, and particularly of the early United States, are still to take full advantage of a relatively new scholarly discipline that defines itself as "Hebraic political studies." The aim of this new field is to analyze readings of the Old Testament "in a political context, whether or not the authors read those texts in the original Hebrew." Its students insist that such readings, rising dramatically after the Renaissance, were intimately concerned with the political questions of the time, and manifested a remarkably wide spectrum of predominantly Christian readings of the Hebrew Bible. Rather than a particular ideologically coherent reading of Scripture, they insist, political Hebraism should be "seen as a common mode of discourse [rather] than as a defense of a specific political position," and should thus "take its place of honor among other [contemporary] languages or paradigms." As Guy Stroumsa has recently pointed out, that Hebraism was "essentially . . . a modern phenomenon, directly linked to the radical change that occurred in the early modern period in the scholarly approach to ancient texts."[5]

The potential benefits of pursuing such a line of inquiry should be evident to early American history in particular, which is conceived nowadays as Atlantic due to its ongoing intellectual exchange with the Old World, but is also markedly defined through the common, if not universal, self-conceptions of that historical society as a chosen nation on a God-sanctioned mission. But students of the political uses of the Bible habitually conceive their historical field as flourishing in both geographic and temporal remoteness from the American Revolution and the early United States.[6] This field of erudition not only is self-consciously Eurocentric (at least in its early modern interest), but its adherents also understand its zenith as having occurred at least a full century before the commencement of the Age of Democratic Revolutions.

The fact is that regardless of the centrality of religion in America, as well as the vigor and extent of religious American studies, political Hebraism has to date been insufficiently employed by early American historians. Only recently we have benefited from studies that appreciate, if not focus on, the Atlantic dimensions of political Hebraism, most notably Eric Nelson's trailblazing *The Hebrew Republic*. Yet revolutionary Americans, and following Americans of the early republic, developed new discursive modes through which they made use of the Bible as a political and constitutional text.[7]

Repeated analyses of the constitutional history of the early Israelite polity, the governmental structures in its "republican" phase before it transformed into a monarchy, stood at the center of a remarkable political discussion in America. That history was conveyed mostly in the Old Testament, narrated in the books of Deuteronomy, Joshua, I and II Samuel, and Judges, as a narrative of the relationship between God and his chosen people. Historians, political scientists, linguists, and literary scholars are still in the process of assessing the varieties of the political language of the Bible, and have been able to identify the emergence of a deep Christian interest in the Old Testament as a political text that evolved at the dawn of the modern age. That newfound Hebraism was part of a wider European attempt to reformulate a political theory that would address questions of authority, legitimacy, and the relations of church and state in the wake of Christendom's rupture and the catastrophic devastation of the Wars of Religion. It thus reflected and was defined by Renaissance and humanist methodologies (namely the critical and philological approach to ancient texts) and sensibilities (a new historical consciousness that stemmed out of the work of antiquarians), as well as a Protestant theology that emphasized the authoritativeness of the Bible.

Scholars are consequently delineating the rise and decline of political Hebraism from the mid-sixteenth century until the end of the seventeenth, a period characterized by a broad commitment to addressing the history of the ancient Israelites in the political context. This constitutional context had a particular appeal for European political thinkers who between 1546 and 1710 produced at least twelve major works on the subject. Such biblical sensibilities resonated especially in Protestant circles across Europe. Among Reformed Protestants Hebraic Biblicism struck such a powerful chord that it became an integral part of their theo-politics and was intensified by "a strong sense of identification with imagined Biblicism, piety and intermittent suffering of the ancient Hebrews." Calvinists more than other Protestant sects emphasized the political readings of the Old Testament in their political theology; consequently, Calvinist populations across Europe and the Atlantic, from Germany to New England, fashioned themselves as "new Israels."[8]

By the early seventeenth century biblical Hebraism had developed into a pan-European phenomenon, but one of its earliest manifestations as a popular political idiom had appeared decades earlier, in fashioning the newly born Dutch republic along the lines of the biblical narrative of Exodus. Paralleling the Dutch experience with that of the Hebrews remained "a recurrent motif in Dutch cultural politics . . . throughout the seventeenth century." The Dutch's widely acknowledged appeal to Hebraic models for political inspiration produced some of the most impressive contemporary Hebraic texts, such as Petrus Cunaeus's *De Republica Hebraeorum* (1617). The historian Adam Sutcliffe notes that in the decades around 1600 the intellectual commitment to Hebraism was as strong in England as it was in the Dutch Republic, "the two states that were most heavily invested in the formation of new theological-political identities." That great tide of political-minded Hebraism may have peaked in mid-seventeenth-century England, when jurists such as John Selden, and political thinkers of all convictions—from absolutists such as Thomas Hobbes, protoliberalists such as John Locke, and republicans such as James Harrington and John Milton—invoked and painstakingly analyzed the politics of the Hebrew commonwealth in their scholarship. Underlying this fascination was the robust identification of England as a "second Israel," perhaps first expressed in John Foxe's immensely popular martyrology *The Acts and Monuments* (1563) and peaking during the Interregnum, a time when England was "a culture saturated with the Bible." In those years English scholars "closely studied the Old Testament, and the political structures of the republic of the Hebrews in particular."[9]

Some of the great political thinkers of seventeenth-century England showed particular interest in the Hebraic republic. Hobbes, for example, who was no Hebraist per se, demonstrated a genuine interest in the political history of the Jews, significantly in the third book of *The Leviathan* (1651), in which he dwelled in great detail on the political organization of the ancient Israelites. The Israelite commonwealth thus stood "as the original and perfect paradigmatic example of the Hobbesian commonwealth." Some English thinkers who would hold particular sway in eighteenth-century America were preoccupied with Hebraic politics. James Harrington thus singled out the Mosaic republic for particular attention in *The Commonwealth of Oceana* (1656), as did John Locke in his *First Treatise on Government* (first published 1689). Algernon Sidney (1623–1683), another major figure in seventeenth-century England, elaborated his political reasoning in light of the Hebraic republic while responding, like Locke, to Robert Filmer's *Patriarcha*, a promonarchic and absolutist treatise, itself grounded in biblical reasoning. Sidney, the republican martyr and author of *Discourses Concerning Government* (1680), was particularly dedicated to a repeated appeal to biblical political history. His biblical constitutionalism deserves a closer look, because it is an impressive seventeenth-century manifestation of Hebraic erudition, but especially because his interpretation of the Mosaic constitution deeply influenced readings of that biblical government in revolutionary America.

Sidney was a central figure in eighteenth-century Whig rhetoric on both sides of the Atlantic, and gained particular prominence in American revolutionary republican culture.[10] American revolutionaries, according to Bernard Bailyn, "referred to the doctrines of Algernon Sidney" more than to any other luminary, making the *Discourses*, in the words of Caroline Robbins, a "textbook of revolution." The *Discourses* devoted large sections to historical polities such as the classical societies, but dedicated even larger portions to the analysis of the historical government of biblical Israel. The *Discourses*' declared objective was to refute Filmer's views on monarchy, specifically his notions of divine right and of monarchy as a God-sanctioned biblical institution. Sidney's main preoccupation was thus to demonstrate that biblical kingship was a sin in the eyes of God. He also elaborated on the form and content of Hebraic republicanism before its transformation to monarchy and its exemplary, God-ordained government. That republic, according to Sidney, had "a chief magistrate, who was called judge or captain, as Joshua, Gideon, and others." The complementary institutions of the Hebrew commonwealth were "a council of seventy chosen men, and the general assemblies of the people." While the magistracy was an occasional office, "like the dictators of Rome," the council, "known by the name of the great Sanhedrin... [was] instituted by Moses according to the command of God," and continued uninterrupted for many centuries. The popular assembly, the third leg of the Mosaic constitution, gathered according to Sidney on such a frequent basis "that none can be ignorant of it, but such as never looked into the Scripture." Sidney did not elaborate on the exact mode of operation of those bodies, but specified only that "a Sanhedrin of seventy men chosen out of the whole people, are to judge such causes as relate to themselves, whilst those of greater extent and importance are referred to the general assemblies." The Hebrew republic seemed to have adhered to European notions of rule of law, since no man in Israel could "be raised above the rest unless he be called by God." When such a man (like Moses or Joshua) died, "his children [could] have no title to his office."[11] Judgeship was no kingship. Sidney followed the classical maxim that "there never was a good government in the world, that did not consist of the three simple species of monarchy, aristocracy, and democracy." The Hebrew government was thus godly, but also conformed with good republican political form and stability; it balanced "the one" in the form of a judge, "the few" in the form of the great Sanhedrin (occasionally spelled Sanhedrim), and "the many" in the form of the general assemblies of the people.

Sidney's ideas were disseminated in the rebelling colonies through such media as the 150-page English pamphlet *The Judgment of Whole Kingdoms and Nations*. Entire sections of the pamphlet, which was signed by Lord Summers but attributed to Daniel Defoe and John Dunton and published in America in at least three editions during the revolutionary early 1770s, were verbatim transcriptions of Sidney's passages on the Hebrew republic. Sidney's exegesis of biblical Israel's constitutional form had an even more direct influence on revolutionary Americans. For example, a Pennsylvanian calling himself Cato recalled in the *Pennsylvania Ledger* on April 27, 1776, that "the great *Sydney* ... says *God* ordained a mixed Government, answering to this in all its parts, and consisting of a single Judge, or chief Captain, (we contend not for names,) a Council of seventy chosen men, or Sanhedrim, and the General Assemblies of the People. Is not this our own form complete?" A decade after Cato, John Adams in his erudite and long-winded *Defence of the Constitutions of the United States* (1787) provided an example of Sidney's analysis of the Hebraic government's continuing influence: according to Sidney, Adams pointed out, "the government of the Hebrews, instituted by God, had a judge, the great Sanhedrim, and general assemblies of the people."[12]

The structure of governance of biblical Israel did not support exclusively an ardent republican, antimonarchical rationale in colonial British North America. On the contrary, in the decades preceding the Revolution, American republicanism had not yet experienced what Eric Nelson dubbed a biblically inspired exclusivist turn into an ardent antimonarchical stance. With republicanism in America still a relativist, monarchy-tolerating creed, the Hebrew constitution provided justification for an authoritarian and patriarchic government. Hence in 1750 Samuel Phillips (1690–1771) appealed in a sermon before Massachusetts Bay's House of Representatives for such a cause. Phillips lectured his audience on the angel who appointed Moses "to lead his people out of Egypt," and later assigned Joshua to guide "the several Tribes into Canaan, and [to make] room for them there." Following these two revered leaders, "several Judges being authorized from Heaven, presided over Israel successively." However, the Jews' divinely sanctioned government, which Phillips saw as a commander in chief or judge and a national council called the grand Sanhedrin, consisted in his view of anything but the republican structure that the revolutionaries would later envision. Rather, Phillips stressed not the commonwealthean attributes of the Hebraic government but the "Succession of Kings" that followed the reign of the Judges "by the express Direction and Appointment of the most high." The political moral that the tale of ancient Israel revealed was thus one of subservience. Men, Phillips concluded, should be "under the Government of Men." Once Americans began to speak the language of revolutionary liberty, however, a drastically different view of the nature of the Mosaic constitution emerged. When the Revolution finally came, Americans happily adopted what Nelson has identified as a rabbinically inspired "exclusivist turn" in early modern republican thought. They no longer tolerated monarchy but rather saw kingship "not as a [godly] command, but as a fierce punishment."[13]

Once the Revolution became a reality, many Americans, particularly New England pastors such as Nathaniel Whitaker, saw biblical Israel as "a free, Independent commonwealth," as the discussion of the Hebrew republic continued to adapt to changing circumstances, and spilled from formal sermons to newspaper articles. Thus, for example, an anonymous author in the *Connecticut Courant* of February 19, 1776, pointed out that the Hebrews enjoyed a "kind of republic administered by a judge and the elders of the tribes." Commentators also began to turn their attention to particulars of the model that the Mosaic constitution offered. But the patriots who appealed throughout the Revolution to the Mosaic constitution as a model for a mixed government of the one, the few, and the many encountered an inherent tension: on the one hand ancient Israel seemed to provide an example of a historical entity, much like Greece and Rome, from which lessons political and moral could be derived. Under such an exegesis the demise of the Hebrew commonwealth was often explained in the republican idiom of classical-like corruption. On the other hand, ancient Israel seemed a misfit in secular history, as it had its origin in God, and was thus in the eyes of contemporaries "the only form of government expressly instituted by heaven"; it was also the only polity ever to be "entirely in the hands of Jehova, who was Israel's supreme king and legislator."[14] Ancient Israel seemed to consist of an oxymoron: it was "a perfect republic." But if republics were bodies politic doomed from the start to succumb to the secular forces of *fortuna*, what would be the meaning of a republic instituted, perhaps even administered, by God? What lessons could Americans derive from this perfectly historical, or rather historically perfect, polity?

Gad Hitchcock (1718–1803), a Massachusetts pastor and patriot, was among the first to seriously treat the Israelite nation as a republican political model. In a sermon he delivered on December 22, 1774, in Plymouth, still months before the imperial impasse erupted into an armed confrontation, Hitchcock observed that after the Israelites fled out of Egypt, "God saw fit to institute a certain form of mixed government among them, under which they were to be restored to the knowledge and practice of true religion, and the possession of their natural rights and liberties." Mixed government, true religion, and rights and liberties would be henceforth repeatedly identified as the hallmarks of the Jewish republic. Patriot commentators also characteristically saw this biblical government as "in all aspects free" and one to which the Israelites "gave full consent." But not only did "the spirit of liberty" breathe "in every part" of that government. Hitchcock saw already in the early stages of the rebellion what would be a major source of interest in the Israelite government, namely that that government kept "the balance of power among the several tribes, the security of liberty of the body of people, and the rights of each individual." The Israelite government was thus not only republican but also tribal. In other words, Israel's was a federal government. Others would confirm this view and underscore its perceived merits, including a Connecticut newspaper commentator who pointed out that the political confederacy "enabled the twelve tribes of Israel to withstand the attacks of numerous and mighty enemies, and to vanquish every opposing foe."[15]

Samuel Langdon (1723–1797), Harvard's incumbent president, elaborated further on the form and function of the Hebrew constitution in a sermon he delivered in May 1775. At this early point in the Revolution, barely a month after hostilities had commenced on Lexington Green, much of Langdon's discussion of biblical history concentrated on political degeneration and the need to remove corrupt officers from their posts. At a time when the formation of republican governments was not yet urgent, Americans were preoccupied with exposing the corruptness of the British monarchy. This might explain why the only Hebrew officers Langdon chose to mention were "councilors" and "judges," while other intricacies of the Hebraic constitution were disregarded. Further, unlike in a sermon Langdon would deliver during the ratification of the Constitution thirteen years later, he refrained from extensively foraging through the biblical narrative. Preaching while the colonies were at war with the British but still nominally a part of the Empire, Langdon read the Bible in the tradition that Eric Nelson has dubbed "exclusive republicanism," that is, as an antimonarchical text. "It was a high crime for Israel," he pointed out, "to ask to be in this respect [kingship] like other nations." When God provided his people with a king, through his prophet Samuel and in the guise of Saul, "it was rather as a just punishment of their folly, that they might feel the burdens of court pageantry." Yet Scripture provided Langdon with more than an antimonarchical, "exclusivist" logic. Even before state constitutions and independence were seriously contemplated, Langdon already took interest in the biblical Hebrew constitution.[16]

Langdon turned to consider "the Jewish government . . . merely in a civil view." Although it was a political structure that none could deny, as Langdon would not, was "divinely established," the Hebrew constitution provided a model of "a perfect republic." This remarkable dichotomy, an earthly (and thus corruptible) polity established by God, characterized the mainstream American attitude to the Hebrew commonwealth. The magistrates of that divinely civic polity were the heads of the tribes and elders of the cities of the Israelites, and even if Langdon did not specify the way they were elected (or selected), these officials represented the public good, in a manner suspiciously reminiscent of an ideal representation of his own commonwealth's selectmen. Since it was early in the Revolution, the Continental Congress still functioning as a provisional institution and the colonies imagined as thirteen separate "clocks," Langdon may have chosen in his description on the separate tribes and cities not to focus on the "national" aspect of the Hebrew government. While "the heads of their tribes, and elders of their cities, were their counselors and judges," the Hebrews "called the people together in more general or particular assemblies, took their opinions, gave advice, and managed the public affairs according to the general voice." Yet this pristine and rudimentary republic diverged conceptually from the British political tradition: the Hebrew magistrates encompassed "all the powers of that government, for there was no such thing as legislative authority belonging to it." This emphasis on the lack of a legislative branch, which probably stemmed from Langdon's aversion to parliamentary supremacy, was explained, and justified, through the fact that the Israelite's "complete code of laws [was] . . . given immediately from God by the hand of Moses." The supreme ruler of the universe was the republic's supreme legislator. His articulation was meager compared with later ones, but Langdon already assessed in 1775 that "the civil polity of Israel is doubtless an excellent general model." That excellent model, prescribed, we recall, directly by God, could be copied, at least in principle and "to great advantage," in modern societies. While Langdon, as we shall see, returned to these issues at much greater length and elaboration years later, when a federal constitution was at stake, his and his contemporaries' basic attitudes would not change: Americans often pictured the Mosaic political configuration as a static structure, not as a historical artifact that underwent significant changes over time.[17]

Like Samuel Langdon, Thomas Paine was an exclusivist republican, rabidly antimonarchical and engaged with biblical themes in the era-defining pamphlet *Common Sense* (1776). The historian Nathan Perl-Rosenthal has illuminated how Paine used the biblical text to make a powerful case against the legitimacy of monarchy. Even in the context of attacking monarchy, which was not meant to provide a detailed constitutional program for the British North American colonies, Paine made clear in a passing remark that he too believed the Hebrew polity was a republic: the Israelites had no kings, and "it was held sinful to acknowledge any"; also, their form of government was "a kind of republic administered by a judge and the elders of the tribes." In the following years Americans were to fully elaborate on the republican nature of the ancient Hebrew form of government and its correlations to its American counterpart. Although most revolutionaries who inquired into such investigations were, unlike Paine, New England divines and preachers, their reading of the biblical text was to be as republican as Paine's.[18]

Remarkable articulations on the Hebrew republic emerged after independence. James Dana was impressed in 1779 with the Hebrew government, "the only form of government expressly instituted by heaven," and its pertinence to the American situation. "Their's," Dana pointed out, "was a confederate republic with Jehova at the head," which "consisted of twelve distinct states; each sovereign in the administration of justice within itself." In each of those semisovereign polities, "councils and force were united in whatever concerned them all." Like the United States, the Hebrew republic was structured "for the better security of their common and particular rights." A year later, with independence long established, the war already raging for five years, and the colonies-turned-states unified under the (yet to be ratified) Articles of Confederation, the state of Massachusetts was finally able to endorse a constitution. Samuel Cooper (1725–1783) recounted, in a sermon preached in front of both of Massachusetts's houses, what he, and indeed many contemporaries, found as striking similarities in the circumstances of the "antient Israelites" and the American people: the two chosen nations rose from oppression and emerged "from the house of bondage"; both were pursued through the sea and were led into the wilderness as a refuge from tyranny and as a preparation for the enjoyment of civil and religious rights. As in sermons from earlier phases of the Revolution, Cooper continued to attack manifestations of despotic power, which was "guided and inflamed by . . . lusts of the human heart."[19] But now, with independence established, biblical tyrants such as the Egyptian Pharaoh or the Babylonian king Nebuchadnezzar, who correlated in pre-1776 sermons with King George III, were no longer the focus of Cooper's discourse. On the occasion of the commencement of Massachusetts's constitution the preacher expanded on the political structure of the biblical Hebrew nation.

Cooper opened his sermon with the prophecy in Jeremiah 30:20–21: "Their Congregation shall be established before me: and their Nobles shall be of themselves, and their Governor shall proceed from the midst of them." This prophecy seemed to Cooper "to have been made for ourselves," but also to embody the biblical spirit of "that essential civil blessing" of the Mosaic constitution: it seemed to confirm the ideal characteristics of a commonwealth, led by a natural, nonhereditary aristocracy bred from its midst. In concurrence with Langdon, Dana, and others, Cooper pointed out that Israel was a well-ordered nation with a balanced constitution, but also a "free republic, over which God himself, in peculiar favour to that people, was pleased to preside." Cooper attempted to explain that paradox through Israel's "charter from heaven," which seemed to declare that the Jewish people themselves, not God, would manage their polity. Cooper understood ancient Israel not as a theocracy in the form of a republic but as a true republic with divine characteristics.[20]

Like in other contemporary depictions, Cooper portrayed the Hebrew polity as consisting of three parts: a chief magistrate called a judge, a council of seventy chosen men (the Sanhedrin), and the general assemblies of the people. This neat division into the prevailing concepts of contemporary political theory of "the one," "the few," and "the many" was not to be found so clearly in the Bible. Nevertheless, as the political scientist Daniel Elazar pointed out, the system of the separation of biblical political domains, one that could combine or separate the authority and powers of the executive, legislative, and judicial spheres, depending on a given situation, was "roughly similar to Western separation of powers in certain respects, but profoundly different in some critical ones."[21] The Bible was first and foremost a religious text in which matters of secular politics and history were secondary to and derivative of theology, and as such were often confusing and inconsistent. Cooper, like other American exegetes of the Hebrew republic, had to search the scriptures explicitly for constitutional notions. His findings were remarkable.

Cooper, like Langdon before, inferred that the assemblies were of a more "essential and permanent" nature than the chief magistracy, the judgeship. The Sanhedrin "remained with but little suspension, through all the vicissitudes they experienced, till after the commencement of the Christian æra," while the assemblies of the people "were frequently held by divine appointment, and considered as the fountain of civil power." Those powers were exerted through decrees and other channels that they judged "most conducive to their own security, order, and happiness." The chief magistracy, the judgeship, on the other hand, was of a more occasional nature. Such understanding of the Hebrews' political system was somewhat anachronistic, interpreting it as driven by modern notions of popular sovereignty. Consequently, Cooper insisted, even the law that God himself delivered to Moses on Mount Sinai was not imposed on the Israelites against their will. That legal code was "laid open before the whole congregation of Israel; they freely adopted it, and it became their law ... by their own voluntary and express consent." To illustrate this interpretation Cooper cited the renewal of the covenant of the Hebrew tribes in Shechem under Joshua's leadership, whereby they voluntarily reestablished their acceptance of their godly constitution. In this voluntary act of confirmation of their governing laws and statutes "the Hebrew nation, lately redeemed from tyranny, had now a civil and religious constitution of their own choice." Such an account underlay federal theology and notions of covenant, but was especially illuminating in the context of republican thought. Biblical covenant ideas and civic humanism thus merged into a novel amalgam of Hebraic republicanism, which was particularly instrumental in articulating a historical genealogy for American constitutionalism. Cooper concluded that the biblical history of the children of Israel pointed to the kind of government that "infinite wisdom and goodness would establish among mankind."[22] Such a government would be a republic, perfectly balanced and divinely ordained.

A year later, in 1781, in a sermon preached at Coventry, Connecticut, Joseph Huntington proposed similar readings of the Hebrew constitution. Like Cooper, Huntington believed that God provided the Israelites with "the most perfect form of Civil government." That ancient constitutional plan had "no king, no despot, no emperor, no tyrant, no perpetual dictator allowed for." Yet Huntington's interpretation of the biblical constitution was much more elaborate than the readings we have examined thus far. If the exegeses up to Huntington were mainly interested in the republican character of the Hebrew government, thus reflecting the seventeenth-century European discourse of political Hebraism, Huntington introduced a new set of problems to the discussion that would define the way in which contemporaries would understand the Hebrew republic in decades to come. Deliberating over the seemingly federal nature of the Hebrew nation, Huntington and his followers confronted the fundamental paradox of the American founding, namely, that the United States was a plurality of distinct states that supposedly spoke in a single national voice.[23] Ancient Israel, a nation comprising distinct tribes, would provide hereafter a historical example and divine sanction to the novelties of the American federal experiment.

Huntington understood each Hebraic tribe, which he alternately referred to as "states," thereby underscoring their similarity to the American states, as a discrete administrative unit. All these tribes, according to Huntington, "managed their internal police within themselves; had each of them their legislative body, for their own state or tribe; also their judges, and courts of justice." Each tribe, then, had a general congress headed by a "president"—the use of the American nomenclature is of course telling, and a Sanhedrin (as opposed to the national Great Sanhedrin). Their officers, called "the elders of the tribes," governed the particular tribe or state they were set over; they were elected by the people or appointed by divine decree. Huntington understood these two ways as equal, since the voice of the people, he believed, manifested the voice of God. Equating godly decrees to democratic resolutions and popular sovereignty was another innovative way to resolve the problem posed by a republic that was perfect through its relation to God, as well as to alleviate the apparent contradiction of terms, of legitimizing a complex distribution of authority among jurisdictions.[24]

As long as this order endured, the constitution "united and cemented" the Hebrews through the general "congress," which had originally been appointed in the wilderness of Sinai and whose mission was to advise and direct the elders of the tribes and general assemblies. The Hebraic constitution, in accord with God's own will and adapted to mankind to secure "the privileges of the subject," made the children of Israel "far the happiest nation under heaven." That liberal version of national happiness prevailed, however, only from the time of Moses to the time of the prophet Samuel. At that point, "the constitution was subverted" as the children of Israel requested, and were subjected to, a king.[25]

Huntington found the similarities between Israel and America striking. Both were federal republics and both consisted, according to the Connecticut preacher, of the same number—thirteen—of political parts: the United States of thirteen states, the Israelites of thirteen tribes. Huntington explained this unconventional and deliberate count—the Hebrew nation being conventionally taken to consist of twelve tribes, the progeny of Jacob's twelve sons—through the subdivision of the tribe of Joseph into the tribes of Ephraim and Mannasseh; these thirteen tribes, like America, consisted of "thirteen united, *free and independent states*." It was thus "really worthy of notice that our number should be exactly the same, even in the first establishment of our independency." So the preacher force-counted the tribes as thirteen, but he also repeatedly, and intentionally, confused the biblical and contemporary nomenclature of "state" with "tribe" (and vice versa) as well as "Congress" with "Sanhedrim." Huntington found further striking symbolism in the composition of the two republics: America's "Sanhedrim," he claimed, answered in "substance to the seventy elders of Israel that were over all the tribes as their supreme council." (It was quite common to conclude, as John Murray did in a sermon from 1784, that "those seventy [Israelite] worthies" correlated with the American Congress, that "august and venerable Council nearly of the same number.") Even in the federal nature of the two polities the preacher found remarkable similarities: "We have a General

Assembly, in each of our States, the same, for substance, with the elders of each tribe or state in Israel of old." In their assemblies, but also in the nature of their offices and magistrates, the ancient and modern polities were similar: "We have our courts, judges, and teachers formed on the same general plan, varying only in a few circumstances." Further, Huntington pointed out that in the United States and in the tribes of Israel officers were elected by "the people at large" or "by those to whom the people delegated power for that purpose." Even in their religiosity the ancient and modern republics correlated, since both had "the same rule to walk by . . . the perfect word of God." Both ancient Israel and America had, in short, "in a civil and political view . . . the best regulated commonwealth that ever the wisdom and goodness of God formed."[26]

Three years later, in 1784, Huntington once again preached the merits of the Hebraic constitution, this time before both houses of Connecticut's legislature. With the war now over, a new era seemed to have been ushered in. According to the preacher, God had provided America "a land as fertile as the land of Canaan, and of much larger extent," which was ruled by "the best civil constitution now in the world, the same in the general nature of it, with that he gave to Israel in the days of Moses." The constitution he referred to was not the still to be conceived federal constitution of 1787 but the loose Articles of Confederation, finally ratified in 1781. These articles put in place a Congress which was like ancient Israel's "supreme council . . . chosen, by delegates from each [tribe], often called their Sanhedrim." Yet now, with the war over, Huntington found even more reasons to revel in the similarities of the ancient and modern constitutions than a few years earlier. Not content with his novel conclusion on the thirteen "tribes" of both America and Israel, he determined that "our number of people is about the same with their's in the days of Moses—i.e. about three millions." Huntington did not divulge his source for this figure, but the conforming number of Israelites and Americans underscored even more boldly the alleged similarity of the ancient and modern constitutions: the number of states-tribes (thirteen), the size of the populations, and the federal nature and form of administration of the discrete parts of both polities—all matched.[27]

Republican numerology was followed by nomenclature. Huntington continued to insist that regardless of "the difference of names, titles and phrases," a nuisance he handled, as we have seen, by ignoring conventional terminology, claiming that the "substance of things is the same." By this he meant that each tribe (or state) "managed its own internal police, each had a General

Assembly, composed of their best men, at the free election of the people," and that "they had their executive courts and officers in various stations, for substance answering to ours." If Canaan was the Hebrews' inheritance, Columbia, whose "southern dominions cover the same climate in which [the Israelites] dwelt," was the Americans'. Huntington further provided a solution to the perennial ill of republics, those bodies politic doomed to corrupt in time: all Americans had to do was "keep the commandments of our God. This will secure to us every blessing, and make us 'high above all nations.'" The republic would avoid political and moral degeneration, widely referred to as "the Machiavellian moment," through a Mosaic moment of godly republicanism.[28]

As Massachusetts braced itself to vote for the ratification of the federal constitution in early 1788, Samuel Langdon returned to the issue of the Jewish republic after more than two decades. He provided, on the eve of his state's eventual adoption of the Constitution, a remarkably elaborate analysis of the Hebrew constitution and its relevance to the United States' system of governance. As the title of his sermon indicates, Langdon believed that the republic of the Israelites provided "an example to the American States." Moreover, not only America could benefit from the example of "every thing excellent in their constitution of government." Rather, although the Israelites had "the advantage of applying to the oracle of the living God," the Mosaic constitution still provided a civic law and could thus "be considered as a pattern to the world in all ages." They were the first nation to establish government by law: other nations traditionally saw kings' ruling as "their will ... as a law," or "the capricious humour of the multitude" ruling, or "senators and judges ... left to act according to their best discretion." The first to balance the one, the few, and the many, the Hebrews were also the first to instill the rule of law. For these reasons Langdon believed that Israel was a better example than the one provided by the revered classical societies, thus reversing the common wisdom of eighteenth-century political discourse: while Lycurgus provided the Spartans with a code of laws, that system was six centuries younger than that of Moses, "imperfect," and in some instances even "absurd." Six centuries after the Spartans, the laws of the Roman Empire, even at the height of its glory when its complex and effective legislation was "carried to great perfection," were "far from being worthy to be compared with the laws of Israel." Langdon went on to charge Great Britain's laws with "tediousness, voluminous bulk, intricacy, barbarous language, and uncertain operation of many of them as to equity." The laws of Israel antedate these and other exemplary systems by centuries and millennia (an especially important attribute in a culture still saturated with the legalistic language of "usage"), but were also inherently superior, politically and morally, to any judicial code, ancient or modern. Yet the Israelite republic offered America much more than a superb and time-proven legal code; ancient Israel, which was according to a modern student a "tribal federation in which the tribal leadership play[ed] a vital role," rendered a model federal constitution, which was especially instructive to Americans about to adopt the innovative governing system that was proposed by the delegates to Philadelphia in the summer of 1787. Langdon thus proposed to "look over [the Israelites'] constitution and laws, enquire into their practice, and observe how their prosperity and fame depended on their strict observance of the divine commands both as to their government and religion."[29]

Appropriately, issues of state formation were the focus of Langdon's sermon, delivered at the moment of American political and legal reorganization. Langdon noted that when fleeing from the Egyptians into the wilderness, the Israelites were merely an unruly multitude "without any other order than what had been kept up" during their captivity. Yet the fleeing Hebrew multitude was "suddenly collected into a body under the conduct of Moses." Like the Americans who declared independence from their oppressors, the Israelites were reduced in a short space of time after they had passed the Red Sea "into such civil and military order . . . [and] adapted to their circumstances in the wilderness while destitute of property." That martial order was further enforced by able men being chosen out of the tribes, and made "captains and rulers of thousands, hundreds, fifties and tens: and these commanded them as military officers, and acted as judges in matters of common controversy." The Israelites' quick progress "from abject slavery, ignorance, and almost total want of order, to a national establishment . . . from a mere mob to a regulated nation," impressive, perhaps even miraculous as it was, was only half the tale. So was the history of the American Revolution before the adoption of the Constitution.[30]

A people mobilized for war, as were both the Israelite tribes in the wilderness and the revolutionary American states, did not satisfy the civil dimensions of society. Langdon recounted how God commanded Moses to bring seventy men, "chosen from among the elders and officers, and [to] present them at the tabernacle," so that they might share the burden of government with him. Thus, the American preacher concluded, a "senate" was constituted, "as necessary for the future government of the nation." Like

Huntington before him, Langdon purposely conflated the American (or rather Latin) and Hebrew nomenclatures, "senate" with "Sanhedrin." Yet Langdon's conflations were conceptual too. Conceding that changes have taken place over the centuries in political theory and practice (in biblical times, he pointed out, "the people in all republics were entirely unacquainted with the way of appointing delegates to act for them, which is a very excellent modern improvement in the management of republics"), he went on to underscore the similarities in the procedure of the election of the Hebrew "senate" and the way in which modern assemblies were elected: even if they did not actually elect their representatives, Langdon declared, "doubtless the [Hebrew] people were consulted as to the choice of this senate." The preacher indeed believed that they had a voice in public affairs "from time to time," when the "whole congregation [was] . . . called together on all important occasions." The conclusion of this constitutional exegesis was foreseeable: the Hebrew government was "a proper republic."[31]

That biblical commonwealth, however, was not a simple republic but a federacy. "Every tribe," Langdon pointed out, "had elders and a prince . . . with which Moses did not interfere." Those tribal leaders had an acknowledged right to meet and consult together and "with the consent of the congregation do whatever was necessary to preserve good order, and promote the common interest of the tribe." In short, according to Langdon's interpretation, the tribes resembled the American states under the Constitution: they were autonomous and semisovereign entities. As in the United States, the local governments of the Israelites' tribes were structurally "very similar to the general government." Each had "a president and senate" at its head, while the whole of the Hebrew people "assembled and gave their voice in all great matters." The arrangement of the Hebrew courts, too, resembled the American federal solution. The civil government of the Israelites included, after the settlement in Canaan, courts "appointed in every walled city," in which elders "most distinguished for wisdom and integrity were to be made judges, ready always to sit and decide the common controversies within their respective jurisdictions." The people of the separate tribes could appoint "officers as they might think necessary for the more effectual execution of justice." As in the proposed Constitution, from the provincial Israelite courts "an appeal was allowed in weighty causes to higher courts appointed over the whole tribe, and in very great and difficult cases to the supreme authority of the general senate and chief magistrate." This Hebraic hierarchy of courts supposedly mirrored the complex and layered judiciary branch of the proposed Constitution. The Hebrew republic, in short, provided a blueprint of the United States' federation. Its constitution was "concise and plain, and easily applicable to almost every controversy." It rendered a laudable governmental structure which was God-given. On the eve of the adoption of the Constitution, the Hebrew political structure provided a historical example of division and balance of powers in the magisterial, legislative, and judicial spheres between periphery and center that reflected the expectations (at least Federalists' expectations) of the proposed Constitution of the United States. The "perfect republic" could indeed be both faultless and republican not because it was God-given; rather, because it was God-given it was "founded on the plain immutable principles of reason, justice, and social virtue," which perfected it to the utmost.[32]

The revolutionary- and constitutional-era discourse of the Hebrew republic did not generate a new political philosophy. However, the repeated reference to and use of the constitutional history of biblical Israel demonstrates how New Englanders attempted to reconcile their biblical commitments with the novel politics of revolution through understanding America in light of the Hebrew republic. This biblical republicanism, which, in the words of a contemporary, provided an "Israelitish" exemplum of a mixed, godly, and federal government, was especially appealing since the American confederacy and the Constitution could be seen as preceded, and sanctioned by, a godly Hebrew constitutional arrangement. These biblical conceptualizations were not severed from preexisting ideological commitments or discontinuous with other explanations of the Revolution or Constitution, but were rather framed by a growing sense of a nationhood and constitutionalism that were regardless already on the political horizon. The Constitution was becoming a reality, shaping Americans' lives and culture, and that reality necessitated intellectualization and justification. Providing what contemporaries saw as "an example," and "a general plan" of the "same in the general nature" as their own revolutionary endeavor, the Hebrew republic addressed those urgent needs.[33]

The main tenets and features of the revolutionary- and constitutional-era interpretation of the Hebrew republic and its presumed relevance to the American political endeavor continued to characterize the discussion in the decades following the founding of the republic. Throughout the first half of the nineteenth century, numerous commentators analyzed the political foundations of "the nation of Israel," which, in the characteristic words of a pseudonymous Historicus, "consisted of twelve tribes, united under one head," a federalism that provided Israel—and thus, it was to be hoped, the United States—with a powerful "sense of national independence."[34] Nevertheless, as the Hebrew republic would henceforward be employed by public speakers who were not necessarily New Englanders, ministers, or clergymen (or even Calvinists), the nineteenth-century discussion, as we shall now see, transcended its former northern geographical confinement. In a country that was rapidly spreading westward, it became a discourse of national scope reflecting the steady formation and consolidation of a national culture (and one upon which New England had a disproportionate bearing).[35]

Nevertheless, even in the nineteenth century many (yet definitely not all) of the elaborate and extensive contributions to the discussion and analysis of the Hebrew republic were still produced in New England, suggesting a strong continuity with the late-eighteenth-century discourse. A few of these texts, with their extensive citations, comments, and references to Israel's political constitution, stand out in their scope, as well as in their reflection of the transformation of contemporary political culture and sensibilities. Works such as David Tappan's *Lectures on Jewish Antiquities* (1807), Lyman Beecher's lecture on "The Republican Elements of the Old Testament" (published 1852), and E. C. Wines's aforementioned *Commentaries on the Laws of the Ancient Hebrews* (1853), among others, were remarkable attestations to the enduring appeal of the Hebrew republic and its pertinence to the United States as well as to the new political sensibilities that had emerged in tandem with the rise of the American democracy.[36]

Virtually all nineteenth-century treatments of the Hebrew republic reasserted Israel's federal nature as well as its relevance to the United States. David Tappan, writing in the first decade of the century, but conforming with earlier assessments, pointed out that in biblical Israel "the rulers of no one tribe had a superiority over those of another; but each portion of the confederacy, like the several states of America, possessed a loyal and independent sovereignty"; Tappan concluded that "their general or national government was that of a complex or confederate republic." Decades later Lyman Beecher (1775–1863) agreed, calling "the civil constitution of the Old Testament a federal republic." "Each tribe," Beecher explained, "as to all purposes of government within itself, was perfectly independent. . . . They regulated all their own peculiar matters, and the national government did not intermeddle with them. So the tribes, were each governed by their own laws; and those laws were as full of liberty as it is possible for laws to be, and still retain any force at all." Beecher was particularly concerned with making the similarities of the biblical and American polities even more explicit, as he found the correspondence between the two federations striking: he mentioned, among other parallels, the "doctrine of appeals from the lower to the higher courts" in which an "appeal might travel up from the lowest to the highest courts in each tribe . . . similar to the United States Supreme Court," as well as the way in which the Israelites "accepted and adopted their constitution . . . as truly as the constitution of this country was adopted by the people." Like in the United States, each Israelite tribe, "as to all purposes of government within itself, was perfectly independent, as each state is in our Union." Beecher concluded that "the Mosaic institute comprehends, in a high degree, all the elements and outlines of a federal national republican government, more resembling our own than any government on earth ever did, or now does."[37]

In the decades-long discussion of the Mosaic constitution in America, Enoch Wines's monumental study stands out as a most profound, ambitious, extensive, and definitive of American treatments of the subject. Throughout the book Wines concurs with the view that the Hebrew republic, like America, was "a confederacy in which each of the Israelitish tribes formed a separate state, having a local legislature and a distinct administration of justice." As in the United States, "the power of the several [Israelite] states was sovereign within the limits of their reserved rights. Still, there was both a real and a vigorous government." As in the American federation, "the Hebrew tribes were, in some respects, independent sovereignties, while, in other respects, their individual sovereignty was merged in the broader and higher sovereignty of the commonwealth of Israel. They were independent republics, having each a local government, which was sovereign in the exercise of its reserved rights; yet they all united together and formed one great republic, with a general government, which was sovereign in the highest sense."[38]

Wines saw clearly that Israel's constitution had "a similitude to our own, which will strike every reader." By the 1850s Wines could analyze Israel with the hindsight of decades of deliberations and crises regarding the proper sphere and sovereignty of the states vis-à-vis the federal government. He thus compared the United States to a biblical federation that he believed worked exceptionally well: "All the tribes together formed a sort of federative republic, in which nothing could be done or resolved without the general consent of their respective representatives, and in which each individual tribe had a constitution formed upon the model of the national constitution. So similar did America and Israel seem, that Wines concluded that "the nation might have been styled the united tribes, provinces, or states of Israel"![39]

This widespread view of American federalism as modeled on the Hebrew republic was thus not fleeting or temporary but a significant and persistent interpretive mode of American political thought. What may have begun as an expedient revolutionary-era measure had developed by the nineteenth century into a full-blown ideological justification. The interpretation of the United States in light of the Hebrew republic still held sway during the Civil War, a century after its initiation in America, proving that it was well suited to the evangelical landscape as well as to the now matured belief in America as a Second Israel. Such prolonged readings of American and Hebrew federalism reflected persistent anxieties about the viability of the American political experiment, which resulted in recurrent attempts to situate American federalism in its theo-historical context.

Like their revolutionary-era predecessors, nineteenth-century American students of the Mosaic constitution continued to wrestle with the meaning of a Hebrew polity that had godly origins, indeed, one that they now tended to agree was a theocracy. Nineteenth-century answers to the exact implications of a theocratic republic varied and cannot be dealt with here at length. Suffice it to note that it was quite common to believe that while "there was a strong infusion of the theocratic element in the Hebrew constitution," contemporaries agreed that biblical Israel was not "a pure theocracy"; rather, theocracy was a mere "element in [its] government." Hence the Israelite republic may have been a theocracy, "but . . . in a restricted sense." Characteristically, nineteenth-century commentators viewed even that theocratic element in terms of modern notions: "Jehova was made the civil head of the Hebrew state . . . *by the free choice of the people*." The implication was that "the lawmaking power and the sovereignty of the state were, *by the popular suffrage*, vested in him."[40] Theocratic or not, the Hebrew republic corresponded with the democratic sensibilities of the Jacksonian Era.

Antebellum commentators were more confident when projecting their nineteenth-century sensibilities on the Hebrew republic's political and social characteristics than when commenting on its theocratic elements. The resulting image was modern and recognizable, as biblical Israel became in their political fantasy a Jeffersonian polity, imagined as a democratic and egalitarian nation of virtuous yeomen. This recurrent interpretation painted the Hebrew republic in the colors of a Jeffersonian Empire of Liberty, as an ideal cultivated state in which independence was secured by a middling class of upright and landowning farmers. Although a committed Federalist, Lyman Beecher described nonetheless the republic's fundamental and defining characteristic—its "admirable trait"—in Jeffersonian terms, namely its "distribution of land, which made every adult male a land-holder; not a tenant, but the owner of the soil on which he lived." Such distribution of land among independent citizens, as students of the classical polities had known for millennia, was "the great spring of civil liberty, industry, and virtue. By this simple arrangement, the great body of the nation were elevated from the pastoral to the agricultural state, and were at once exempted from the two extremes most dangerous to liberty—an aristocracy of wealth, and a sordid, vicious poverty." This "single principle of universal ownership . . . of the soil" in the Hebrew republic could thus secure "intense and universal patriotism, indomitable courage, untiring industry, and purity of morals." The Hebrew state was thus one of a middling republicanism, in which "neither an hereditary nobility, nor a dependent peasantry, nor abject poverty, could exist." Beecher concluded that the Hebrews' republic was "compact, intelligent, and efficient," and conformed with the Jeffersonian ideal of "a nation of land-holders, owners of the soil by a tenure which excluded alike a voluptuous nobility, and a landless, reckless poverty,—the most terrific material of republics."[41]

Enoch Wines provided an even more elaborate representation of the Hebrew republic as an ideal Jeffersonian-like polity. Like Beecher, Wines believed that "no part of the Mosaic legislation is more excellent or admirable than the statute respecting the distribution and tenure of lands." Israel's Jeffersonian and democratic essence thus stemmed from the fact that "the whole nation constituted a republic of freemen, equal originally even in property, equal in political dignity and privilege, equal in their social standing, and equally entitled to the care and protection of the government." Such modest and restrained land holding by independent yeomen ensured that the Hebrew government would be "instituted for the good of the many, and not of the few, for the happiness of the people, and not the advantage of the prince and the nobles." Echoing the spirit of the Declaration of Independence and foretelling Lincolnian notions, Wines asserted that the Israelite republic was constituted to make sure that "the life, liberty, and property of no citizen should be infringed, but by process of law . . . that every man who obeys the laws, has a right to their protection; that education, embracing a knowledge of the laws, the obligations of citizenship . . . should be universal." These liberal traits were "the paramount objects of the Hebrew constitution"; more important, they were features that "mark its kindred to our own."[42]

Israel's egalitarianism seemed to have originated in its founder, as Moses' legislation was thoroughly "impregnated with democratic principles." Wines understood Moses as committed to a "hatred of tyranny," and to advancing a Lockean understanding of "the rights, the liberty, and the happiness of man." Others concurred with this anachronistic view of the Hebrew legislator, seeing in Moses' legislative code "the most liberal theory of the rights of man." This perceived Mosaic commitment to democracy and rights ensured that the Hebrew republic would manifest "agriculture, universal industry, the inviolability of private property," and even "the sacredness of the family relation . . . universal education, social union." It must have been gratifying to interpret biblical Israel as a republic manifesting "a strong democratic tendency" through an American-like realization of "the political equality of the people, without either nobles or peasants properly so called." A state for social justice, the Hebrew republic seemed to have provided for "the poor and the weak," who were "not to be the victims of the rich and the strong. The small as well as the great were to be heard, and equal justice awarded to all."[43]

Enoch Pond remarked in a similar vein that the Hebrew republic's laws protected the poor against the rich, as well as "the weak against the strong; the needy and the stranger were provided for; the ungodly and injurious were restrained; and popular liberty, with no checks but those of the most obvious necessity, was secured." Even southerners, such as the early-nineteenth-century "Demophilus" publishing in the *Carolina Gazette*, joined this Hebrew democratizing and leveling choir, pointing out that democracy was "the only constitution of government that God ever sanctioned." This Greek-styled "lover of the people" lauded the "Israelitish government" because its "perfect balance of powers in the state, on one side, to guard against anarchy, and on the other, against oppression, are all such characters of a perfect government"; biblical government was "a true representative democracy." There were, according to the southerner, "no ranks of nobility in the state. . . . There is no term in the Hebrew language to express what we mean by aristocracy. . . . The wants and conveniences of the people at large are alone consulted." Furthermore, like his northerner compatriots, Demophilus did not deem the Hebrew democracy merely as politically democratic; rather, it also seemed socially leveling. According to Demophilus, "governments in general, take no notice of the poor," it was "far otherwise in the Jewish constitution. . . . The common people [were] members of the community, equally with the rich." Demophilus concluded that the Jewish constitution had a strong "obligation of humanity" and an "unequalled regard . . . to the most helpless and pitiable part of the human race." Yet again Americans unearthed Hebraic traits and ideals that they wished to attribute to their own society. These admired aspects of the Israelite nation pleasingly reflected their own American Israel. Such discoveries with regard to the only "form of polity" on which God distinctly revealed his "will on the subject of government" provided them with powerful historical vindication for their own political endeavor.[44]

The aforementioned Demophilus was not the only southerner to engage in the analysis of the Hebrew republic. Other obscure southern authors, such as an anonymous writer in the *South Carolina State Gazette and Timothy's Daily Advertiser*, occasionally alluded to the Hebrew form of government, which was "a kind of republic, administered by a judge and the elders of the tribes." During the 1830s more prominent southerners stepped forward to examine the Hebrew republic on the national stage. John C. Calhoun was interested in the Hebrew republic's federal nature, particularly how its government distributed powers between the center and the periphery. The politician Calhoun's interest stemmed from pressing political matters. Reacting to the Force Bill, and no longer constrained by his position as vice president, which he had recently resigned, in February 1833 Calhoun delivered a two-day speech to the United States Senate, in which he rejected the federal government's authority to coerce southern states, particularly his home state of South Carolina, into paying the "tariff of abomination," which supposedly served northern industrial interests and hurt the South. Calhoun analyzed in his speech the state of the Union, which was already manifesting the ominous sectional tensions that would eventually lead to civil war. The question Calhoun confronted was "whether ours is a federal or a consolidated system of government." Thinking historically, he found "centralism or consolidation . . . the pervading principle in the Asiatic governments, while the federal system, or, what is the same in principle, that system which organizes a community in reference to its parts, has prevailed in Europe." Nevertheless, "among the few exceptions in the Asiatic nations, [was] the government of the twelve tribes of Israel, in its early period." "Their government," Calhoun pointed out to his senatorial audience, "was a mere confederation without any central power, till a military chieftain"—was he thinking of the American president, Andrew Jackson?—"with the title of king, was placed at its head."[45]

The Hebrew republic continued to provide a model for analyzing American federalism as the tensions between north and south intensified in the following decades. Moses Stuart, a leading northern theologian who attempted to solve the moral dilemmas stemming from a federal slaveholding republic, exemplifies this practice. In an apologia for the act of returning runaway slaves to their southern owners (actually, for the institution of slavery in general, if not for the way it was practiced in the South), Stuart asserted that "we of the North are only other tribes of the same great commonwealth" as American southerners were, and thus "cannot sit in judgment on cruel masters belonging to tribes different from our own." While northerners might justly "pity the restored [black] fugitive," Stuart reminded his audience that "the mosaic law does not authorize us to reject the claims of our fellow countrymen and citizens, for strayed or stolen property." As among the different Israelite tribes, so in America, southern slaveholders were still "brethren and fellow citizens of the great community."[46]

Native Americans were another politically marginalized people who were contemplated and imagined through the Hebrew republic. In a defense of the American Indians (and as we shall see in a later chapter, in an attempt to prove that they were the direct descendants of biblical Israelites), Elias Boudinot, a New Jersey signer of the Declaration of Independence and founder of the American Bible Society, claimed that the American natives were "perfect republicans," who would admit "of no inequality among them." Even more remarkable than their republicanism was the Indian republicanism's character: "As the Israelites were divided into tribes," Boudinot pointed out, "and had a chief over them, and always marched under ensigns of some animal peculiar to each tribe, so the Indian nations are universally divided into tribes, under a sachem or king, chosen by the people from the wisest and bravest among them."[47] The likening of Indian federalism to the Israelites' in an era during which such interpretations of American federalism were common, is a testament to the central role of the model of the Hebrew republic in the antebellum American political imagination.

Mordecai Manuel Noah's (1785–1851) failed attempt to establish a Jewish biblical government in upstate New York sheds further light on the dynamism of the public discussion on the Mosaic constitution in the early republic. Ararat, Noah's proposed Hebrew city that will be further discussed in a later chapter, demonstrates convincingly the way in which the Hebrew republic functioned in the public sphere in the early American republic, so much so that it merits discussion at some length. Noah wished to establish Ararat, which he designated as a Hebrew city of refuge, on Grand Island in the Niagara River a few miles downstream from Buffalo. Thither Noah wished the Jews of Europe and the Levant to escape from the persecutions they were suffering in their own countries. In the dedication ceremony that he organized on September 15, 1825, Noah, as Ararat's founder, proclaimed himself "judge of Israel" and promised to "revive, re-new and reestablish the Government of the Jewish Nation" in America "under the constitution of the United States." Thereafter, Noah unfolded an ambitious but ultimately futile political plan that deeply engaged in and derived from the ongoing interest in the Mosaic constitution as a political model for American republicanism. In fact, by seriously contemplating the early United States as a place in which a neobiblical polity could be constituted, Noah's Ararat may have taken the interest in the Hebrew republic to its farthest logical extent.[48]

Ararat was not conjured up on the spur of the moment. Indeed, Noah contemplated and planned his colonization scheme for several years. In early 1820 he asked the New York legislature to sell him Grand Island to serve as a colony for the Jews of the world. Noah's petition sat idle for four years, but the legislature's decision to survey and sell Grand Island finally came in April 1825. The subsequent sale of tracts of the eight-mile-long island to various purchasers, among them Noah, spurred the Jewish entrepreneur to action. By early September 1825 Noah was ready to announce to the world his scheme to reconstitute a Hebrew government in America. He orchestrated a solemn ceremony and arranged for a large cornerstone. The spectacular "Masonic and military ceremonies" that ensued on September 15 were advertised in advance and later reported in detail in many newspapers across the nation. The line of procession lined up at 11:00 A.M. and marched through the streets of Buffalo. (There were not enough boats to ferry the crowds across to Grand Island, nor was the island suitable for staging the elaborate ceremony that Noah planned.) The pageant consisted of a band playing the grand march of Handel's *Judas Maccabeus* (commemorating the Jewish Maccabean revolt against the Seleucid Empire that reestablished Jewish independence in Judea), militia companies, civil and state officers in uniforms, and marchers representing various professions and churches. Then followed Noah, the self-proclaimed "judge of Israel," in "robes of *crimson* silk, trimmed with ermine, wearing a medal of embossed gold." The spectacular procession approached Saint Paul's church, wherein on top of the communion table lay the cornerstone. A portion of the inscription was in Hebrew and read: "Hear,

O Israel, the Lord is our God, The Lord is one." The remainder of the inscription, rendered in English, read: "Ararat, a City of Refuge for the Jews, founded by Mordecai Manuel Noah, in the month of Tishri, 5585, September 1825, and in the 50th year of American Independence." After reading a "Proclamation to the Jews" (of whom, as the historian Richard Popkin points out, there could not have been many in the audience), a grand salute of twenty-four cannons was fired and the band played "patriotic airs." "A finer day," reporters remarked, "has not been known on any similar occasion."[49]

Noah laid out his vision for Ararat's political structure in the "Proclamation to the Jews" and the speech that he delivered the following day; both were published in numerous newspapers across the nation in the weeks after the dedication. Although the plan Noah proposed was embryonic and rudimentary, it is remarkable in its powerful demonstration of contemporary preoccupation with the Mosaic constitution. Scholars have studied various aspects of Noah's plan of the Hebrew-American city, from its grappling with tensions pertaining to Jewish identity to the influence on Noah of ideas circulating in postrevolutionary France.[50] However, Noah also engaged deeply in the imagination of a Hebrew republic functioning in the United States, under the American Constitution.

Noah's political plan for Ararat, although fragmentary and incomplete, drew extensively on and participated imaginatively in the contemporary discourse of the biblical Hebrew republic. If the biblical Israelite state had been disbanded and its people dispersed two thousand years before, Noah intended to reestablish the Hebrew government as it existed in biblical times. That this revival was to be in the land of a nation that was constructing its image as the Second Israel was, naturally, deeply meaningful. The very name of the planned city, Ararat, was emblematic, associated with the name of the city's founder: Mount Ararat, the highest mountain in what is now Turkey, is the place where Noah's Ark comes to rest when the flood recedes in the book of Genesis. Mordecai Noah's choice of the name, and of himself as "judge of Israel," may hint at excessive self-grandeur; yet those titles also manifest the biblical cosmology that shaped his call for action. However, although he invoked God to fulfill "the promises made to the race of Jacob . . . his chosen people," Noah's call relied not on divine but on human agency and action, advocating pragmatic, if far-fetched, political measures. Though he was a utopian schemer, his advocacy and pursuit of an "expedient" attempt to "reorganize the [Jewish] nation under the direction of the judges" was a sensible if visionary effort based on (gentile) contemporary acquaintance with and appreciation of the political qualities of the Mosaic constitution. Ararat was hence a practical, if stillborn, political project, fashioned to cater to contemporary sensibilities.[51]

The biblical judges, the magistracy that Noah co-opted to govern Ararat (and to act out himself, attired in a theatrical robe), ruled the Israelites after Joshua's death until Samuel's ascendancy, which ended with the institution of hereditary kingship. Their purview embraced, as Mordecai Noah recognized, "all religious, military and civil concerns." However, while the judges "were absolute and independent like the Kings of Israel and Judah," they lacked "the ensigns of Sovereignty." The biblical judgeship thus accorded with Noah's plans: an ancient, powerful, and revered office, it would not threaten, Noah believed, the sovereignty of American state and federal magistrates. However, as Noah recognized, reestablishing a Mosaic constitution created practical problems. An example was how to decide in nineteenth-century America "with certainty on the manner and forms adopted in choosing the judges of Israel," since "most of the distinguished men who had filled that station were 'raised up' by divine influence." The problem of creating a secular government based on a model that time and again enjoyed divine revelation (and that by many contemporary accounts, as we have mentioned, was a theocracy) was troublesome. One option, of course, was to select a judge by democratic (hence human) election, as opposed to godly appointment. But since the Jewish nation was currently dispersed, there was "no possibility of concentrating the general voice" to choose a judge by ballot. Noah came up with an extrajudicial solution: paying lip service to the "general consent and approbation" as well as—why not?—to "divine permission," Noah proclaimed himself "judge of Israel," declaring that he would "always be sustained by public opinion." If Ararat's first judge was to be appointed, not elected, he would still be judged by a democratic appeal to public opinion.[52]

Noah rightly expected that his innovative plan for Hebraic revival would draw harsh criticism. Even sympathetic contemporaries who had "no doubt of the genuineness of Noah's Proclamation to the Jews" still thought that some would surely suspect his motives and that Noah should anticipate "a little *badinage*."[53] Noah attempted to preempt such censure by elaborating the extent to which Ararat was compatible with the contemporary American political and constitutional modus operandi. Yet a deep political and constitutional dilemma lay at the heart of the Ararat venture: what did Noah's call for a Hebrew city of refuge on the Niagara "under the constitution of the United States" *mean*? To be sure, Noah stated that the Jewish government he was reviving was "under the protection of the United States" or, as he put it elsewhere, "under the auspices and protection of the constitution and the United States." He also made clear that Ararat and the U.S. Constitution and laws "conformed" with each other. Noah, a veteran of New York's nascent Democratic machine, conflated his neobiblical plan with the available political idioms of the day as he skillfully employed the republican and democratic language available to him. He dubbed his proclamation, for example, "a declaration of Independence." Like Thomas Jefferson, who in his revered Declaration addressed "a candid world," Noah proclaimed that "the world [had] a right to know what inducements have led to this declaration of independence" in Ararat. Noah was well aware of the strength of the patriotic chords such representation could strike in American hearts, just a year after the jubilee of independence and Jefferson's passing. Beyond positioning his proclamation within a contemporary discourse of "rights and privileges" and fashioning it as a declaration of independence, Noah further described the Ararat judgeship in terms of a republican magistracy. Like its biblical counterpart, judgeship in Ararat would stem "immediately from the people" and would not be hereditary. This latter-day judgeship would resemble the position of "that of Chief Magistrate" to the American presidency. If Noah were appointed Israel's first judge, it would only be out of necessity: Ararat's institutions and its governing body were not yet in place, and the Jews had not yet convened in America. Noah's successors would be elected in good republican fashion: like the American president, "A Judge of Israel shall be chosen once in every four years." The judge would be elected "by the [Jewish] Consistory at Paris," which again, like the Electoral College, would receive at the time of the election "proxies from every congregation."

It is easy to see why Noah readily believed that Ararat's judgeship would not offend American sensibilities, for it was in essence a republican institution: Judges were not hereditary magistrates but an executive branch that stemmed "immediately from the people, mingling in their deliberations, directing their energies, commanding their armies, & executing their Laws." The republican, if not fully democratic, nature of judgeship in Ararat, reminiscent of the American presidency, would, Noah hoped, be "in accordance with the genius and disposition of the people of this [American] country."[54]

However, Noah had to streamline the problem of *imperium in imperia*, as Ararat was bound to fail if it threatened the sovereignty of existing American magistracies and institutions. In fact, it had to operate within a multiplicity of overlapping sovereignties, in a federal political environment. Theoretically, Ararat could operate as part of the American union of semiautonomous states, which by 1825 was already experienced in handling different spheres of sovereign power (as we have seen, the Hebraic federal system was itself admired for its alleged genius for dividing authority among distinct levels of government). That Noah presented himself as "*governor* and judge of Israel" is crucial to understanding how he imagined Ararat's functioning or even existing within the American state system. Regardless of the symbols of self-government in Ararat, such as a flagstaff "erected for the Grand Standard of Israel," Ararat was not meant to constitute a politically autonomous community or a sovereign nation. Noah intended it to reside under the auspices of the government of the United States; Ararat would merely be an additional tribe in the American Union of states-tribes. This must have made sense to Americans who by 1825 had already been discussing for half a century the federal nature of the Hebrew government, as well as its apparent similarities to the American political system. Unfortunately, since Ararat never materialized, it remains unclear exactly how Noah's proposed plan of Hebraic revival would have worked within the intricacies of the American federal system and in relation to the dynamics of a vigorous democratizing culture.[55]

So careful was Noah not to overstep American sovereignty that he made clear that the era of biblical Jewish independence would not be repeated (the proclamation being a Jewish "declaration of independence" nonetheless). Israel, according to his plan, would experience in America a postheroic existence: as a subservient national entity under the government of the United States, Israel would likely not "have again such generals as Joshua, David and Maccabees." However, "in blending our people with the great American family," Noah wished to see the children of Israel sustaining their "honor with their lives and fortunes." Here was a conscious, if moderate, Jewish reformulation of the sacred American trinity of life, liberty, and the pursuit of happiness.

Ararat's failure (nothing happened after the impressive ceremonial dedication) should not obscure the fact that a savvy political operator like Noah conceived of such a plan in the first place, and believed that his contemporaries would share his enthusiasm. The crowds in Buffalo on September 15, 1825, and the thoughtful nationwide discussion that followed, seemed at least initially to confirm Noah's conviction. Even though Americans eventually rejected Ararat and deemed it incompatible with their federalism, they were wholly familiar with the assumptions and historical knowledge that underlay its conception. The early American republic, where a discussion of and comparisons with the Hebrew government had been ongoing for decades by the time of Ararat's dedication, was the only country where such a plan would have been culturally permissible, indeed sensible. Only decades later, at the beginning of the twentieth century, would an Austro-Hungarian Jew by the name of Theodore Herzl envision a similar plan. Unlike Noah's scheme for the New Israel, Herzl's would be successfully implanted; indeed, it would eventually lead to the creation of a new and modern state of Israel.

Scholars have widely acknowledged the use made by early Americans of the polities of the classical world as historical models to guide them in creating and substantiating the republic. It is thus remarkable that a string of articulate late-eighteenth- and nineteenth-century Americans saw the origins of their republic as rooted not in the classical political tradition but in biblical Israel. Lyman Beecher asserted, for example, that the American Constitution did not originate in "Greece or Rome" but "from the Bible." Beecher acknowledged that even "where we borrowed a ray from Greece or Rome, stars and suns were borrowed from another source—the Bible." He mused, "As the moon borrows from the sun her light, so our constitution borrows from the Bible its elements, proportions, and power." In a similar vein David Tappan underscored the chronological primacy of the Hebrew polity, which manifested "a popular or representative assembly, an advising senate, and a presiding judge or executive magistrate," which were "the best features of the most perfect constitutions" which were afterward established in Greece and Rome. Tappan added that they were "at present in United America" too. Others asserted that it was Israel, not Athens, that "imbodied, for the first time in the world's history, the rights of the people," and Israel, not Rome, that "gave to the human race that perfect and beautiful model of a republic." Hence it was a Hebraic, not a classical, model that "was afterward to be realized in a far distant land, over the blue waves of the ocean."[56]

The leaders of the American Revolution and their successors did not draw on a biblical precedence for a constitutional outline or blueprint. Instead, they articulated a particular and effective mode of political rationalization and legitimization. In light of those contemporary views we need to seriously consider an intellectual framework that traced the origins of the American republic to a biblical model. We should add the biblical Jewish state, perceived as a republican and federal polity that had its roots in God, to the sources that nourished the American political and constitutional tradition in its formative era.[57] Generations of Americans expressed and articulated their republicanism and constitutionalism through the biblical history of the Hebrew republic in an attempt to reconcile their potentially contradicting commitments, namely the authority of the Bible with the public politics of the times. (They would continue for many decades to render thus the tense duality inherent in the Hebrew republic: a self-governing body politic that originated in, and according to some was also headed by, God.) This remarkable mode of thinking about politics sheds light on unnoticed aspects of Americans' conception of their relation to biblical Israel: both nations were not only believed to be chosen and favored by God, they also seemed to share a unique political structure, namely federal republicanism. The discourse of the Mosaic constitution enabled Americans for decades to frame and conciliate notions of chosenness with the emerging American federacy, of divine sanction with worldly politics.

While not necessarily consisting of a new political philosophy, in the early decades of Americans' national existence the republican reading of the history of the ancient Hebrews provided its adherents with a language to conciliate their desire for biblical sanction and their modern republican federation. Seeing the American federal republic as historically and structurally connected to the ancient Hebrew republic could alleviate anxieties and legitimize their federal and republican modus operandi. Such framing was especially significant due to the apparent paradox of the American founding, the tension between the *pluribus* and the *unum*, the union and its parts, which other contemporary political idioms seemed at pains to accommodate. Americans, who constituted themselves as a people of peoples (or states), eagerly read the history of the Israelites as that of a federal nation comprising tribes. It is rewarding to acknowledge this discursive tradition at a time when Hebraic political studies is experiencing a scholarly renaissance, particularly in its early modern European context. Applying the discourse of the Hebraic constitution to its American context lends an American dimension to the study of political Hebraism, just as political Hebraism adds a Hebraic dimension to the history of the formation of the American republic. In the following chapters I continue to draw on this fruitful tension.

3
"A Truly American Spirit of Writing"
Pseudobiblicism, the Early Republic, and the Cultural Origins of the Book of Mormon

> 1. And it came to pass in those days, that there was no King in all the land, even in all Columbia, but every one walked after the imagination of his own heart.
> 2. And the people said one to another, "We will choose from among our own numbers Elders to rule over us; even discreet men, out of all the land of Columbia from the borders of the Great Lakes, Northward, till thou comest to the plains of the South, which abounds with Oranges, Pomegranates and Figs.
> 3. "And let all the Elders meet together in the great city, even the city of Philadelphia, and make laws for us, for why should our goodly heritage be given up to strangers?"
>
> —THE 1ST BOOK OF THE CHRONICLES OF JOHN, chap. I (1812)

The text from which the epigraph above is taken is a partisan Democratic tract published originally in the *Richmond Enquirer* and reprinted in the South Carolina *Investigator*, encouraging Americans during the early stages of the War of 1812 to support France ("Gallia") in the hopes of bolstering President Madison's war against Britain ("Albion"). Its language is recognizably biblical, while its content is clearly American, describing an early episode of the late Revolution. *The Book of Chronicles* went on to illustrate in two chapters containing twenty-nine verses that "John," an American patriot elected through the ancient method of casting lots, represented the true interests of the republic (that is, siding with the "Gallians" against the "Albionites") before "the Elders assembled together, even in the city of Philadelphia." By the end of the book "the Elders heard the words that John had spoken, [and] said one to another, 'What manner of man is this? For behold he speaketh the words of truth.'"[1] However eccentric such a rendition may seem to us today, numerous similar tracts were written in America after 1740 for more than a century until the onset of the Civil War, peaking from approximately 1770 to 1830. This unique and previously unfamiliar American tradition of writing "in the style of antiquity" opens a window onto a lost early American world of biblical imagination.

The language of the King James Bible was as strange and foreign to late-eighteenth-century and nineteenth-century Anglophones as it is to twenty-first-century English-speakers. The paratactic rhythms confined in short and numbered verses, the repetitive use of phrases such as "and it came to pass," and the use of verbs with suffixes such as "-eth" had been long gone from the spoken language by the second half of the eighteenth century. Nevertheless, generations of Americans reverted to that language and its accompanying structures and forms to discuss their difficulties and represent their achievements, past and present. Surprisingly, this was not a predominantly religious idiom, as Providence was notably absent from those texts as an active agent.[2] Rather, American authors and commentators used this ontologically privileged language as a means to establish their claims for truth, as well as their authority and legitimacy in public discourse.

The distinct use of biblical language for a broad range of topics, notably political issues across the ideological spectrum, thus presents an ideal vantage point from which to appraise and better understand a unique mode of expression that coincided with the emergence of the United States. The nexus of biblical language and politics in early America, or rather the discursive ability to mold the world into revered and well-known structures, provides an indication of the ways in which Americans attempted to understand their role in history in a fast changing world. Through commenting on their experiences in biblical language, Americans perpetuated such practices as typological exegesis and reaffirmed their national role as a second Israel. While the language of the Bible reiterated Americans' understanding of their collective mission, it also positioned politics as the new religion of the republic, a medium that sanctified the nation and articulated Americans' perception of chosenness. Americans were also applying a strict and genteel language in a world that still valued formal and refined forms of expression. Once the United States was overwhelmed by forces unleashed by the market revolution, plain democratic forms of expression repeatedly replaced "aristocratic" discursive modes. A formalistic language that invoked its authority from traditional sources, in the end it could not withstand the democratic onslaught of stump speeches and plain talk.

The Protestant Reformation reinserted the Bible into the lives of millions of believers by declaring *sola scriptura*, "by scripture alone." The implication was clear: believers should read and comprehend the Bible with the external mediation of Church or priest, if not discarded altogether, submitted to the supreme authority of the biblical text. That doctrine drove throughout the sixteenth century massive projects of biblical translation into vernacular languages, notably German and English, from the original Hebrew and Greek. Translation into spoken languages allowed Protestants to take possession of the Bible and thus to become their own authority in light of the truths they revealed in Scripture. One of the monumental outcomes of that drive was the translation known as the King James Bible. James I of England (1566–1625) in 1604 established a fifty-four-member committee working in six companies at Westminster, Cambridge, and Oxford to produce a new translation of the Scriptures; the project was intended to eradicate mistakes and clarify misunderstandings (or inconvenient theological and political interpretations) stemming from earlier versions, particularly the popular Calvinistic Geneva Bible (1560). The translation was completed in 1611 and was to be the last and greatest of the official committee bibles: the flow of early modern biblical translations ceased in England thereafter. The sixteenth-century impulse to articulate the Bible in the vernacular was thus followed by a period of stagnation in the field of biblical translation. Within this context of the textual stability, the King James Version would become after 1700 universally acclaimed both in Britain and in America as the great Bible of English literature.[3]

If the vernacular Bible had bridged the gap between heaven and earth, it had also underscored the human side of the biblical text. Hence, as Christopher Hill has noted, a Pandora's box opened once the Scriptures were translated into the vernacular and mass printed: the vernacular Bible could not but be seen, at least partly, as the product of human labor and art. Making use of biblical texts for contemporary needs was thus seen in post-Reformation England not necessarily as sacrilege but as the continuation of a process which sixteenth-century translators had initiated. Consequently, during the seventeenth century England experienced a spectacular flowering of biblical poetic writing, making the Bible for the first time not only a source of revealed truth but also a spring for poetic art. By the eighteenth century authors such as Isaac Watts accommodated "Protestant Poetics" to the sensibilities of the Augustan age in such works as *Horae Lyricae* (1706), and *Psalms of David* (1719), which were printed numerous times over the next centuries in America. Alexander Pope, Joseph Addison, and other lesser writers similarly produced immensely successful adaptations of biblical texts and narratives to contemporary poetic standards. Works written in this paraphrastic tradition, which abandoned the attempt to preserve the taste of the biblical verse, meter, and rhyme, were consciously crafted *not* to resemble the actual language of the Bible.[4] Indeed, within this broad biblical literary culture, no genre prescribed the use of biblical language. On the contrary, what authors habitually did was strip a known biblical plot of its distinct textual dressing and re-present it in Augustan linguistic fashion. Aside from the Scriptures themselves the language of the King James Bible was absent from English biblical culture until the mid-eighteenth century.

It is surprising that an inspiring idiom such as the King James Bible's English, commonly singled out as a foundational influence on the development of the English language, has achieved its literary grace by accident, rather than design. Its distinctive antiquated language, its rhythms and cadences, meant to evoke a voice of divine wisdom and truth, were already becoming archaic in the standard English of the time it was being produced. The English used in that translation was associated with William Tyndale's (1484–1536) earlier and incomplete translation. Tyndale, the greatest of all English biblical translators and the foremost influence on the royal committee appointed by James I, used a language that was breaking down by the early seventeenth century. That language had become by then more of a metrical convenience than a spoken norm. Yet the King James Bible's translators intentionally retained the forms that were standard in Tyndale's translation because those forms had already come to signify liturgical decorum, which represented the antiquity and dignity James and his committee wished to preserve. The king's translators were specifically forbidden to depart from the language used by earlier translations. Thus the inbuilt conservatism of the translation process, reflecting the concerns of those who commissioned the new Bible, led directly—if unintentionally—to the retention of older ways of speaking in religious contexts by reproducing the English of nearly three generations earlier. The antiquated music and flow of the King James Bible sounds archaic not only to modern ears. That language was almost one hundred years older than the royal translation itself, and was already outdated and sounded conspicuous to contemporaries.[5]

A palpable characteristic of the King James Bible was its use of "thee," "thou," "thy," and "thine" where modern English would simply use "you," "your," and "yours." Similarly, verbal endings such as "-eth," which pervade the King James Bible, had already been mostly replaced with "-s," while the use of "thereof" had been replaced by the possessive pronoun "its."[6] That archaic language was the language eighteenth-century Americans encountered when they opened their bibles, as the King James Bible became the most influential text in the Anglophone world. It conjured up visions of the sacred while signaling American readers to shift register from a colloquial cognitive mode of everyday speech to one of liturgical interpretation.[7] It was also the language Anglophones, notably Americans after 1765, came across in scores of modern political newspaper articles, pamphlets, and books published from the mid-eighteenth century onward.

Although the adoption of biblical language for nonreligious purposes eventually became a distinct American intellectual expression, as in virtually every other cultural respect, colonial British North America followed and imitated the imperial metropole rather than led. The first known text of that kind was a published letter from Horace Walpole to Horace Mann dated July 14, 1742, thus out in the public sphere long after other biblical literary genres were well established. That early piece, titled *The First Chapter of the Book of Preferment*, contained two "lessons" that already demonstrated some of the basic contours that would distinguish that genre in the following century. Named as a quasi-biblical book, the "chapter" was divided into short numbered verses, and used the form of a biblical narrative from its beginning—"Now it came to pass in the fifteenth Year of the Reign of G—ge the king"—thus locating readers temporally according to a monarch's reign, just as in the Bible. The piece itself was a critique of corruption and distribution of places in mid-eighteenth-century English politics. According to the author's testimony, after *The Book of Preferment* was published it became "the original of a numberless quantity of the same kind, which were published upon all subjects for a year or two." Walpole's piece was published in America in at least two newspapers, in New York and Pennsylvania. Another satiric biblical piece, titled "The French Gasconade defeated, and then swept out of Germany," providing a humoristic rendition of European international politics, appeared in the *Boston Evening Post* later in 1743.[8]

The "most successful of English works" in America was published in 1744, a year that represents a turning point in the history of American biblical-style writing. *The Chronicle of the Kings of England, Written in the Manner of the Ancient Jewish Historians*, which eventually was published in America in at least seven editions during the following half-century, constituted a major step forward in the elaboration and sophistication of what was to become a vital tradition in American letters and politics. Self-proclaimed to have been written by Nathan Ben Saddi, "a priest of the Jews," and attributed to Robert

Dodsley, the 1744 edition of *The Chronicle of the Kings* dressed British history in the recognizable biblical style, from the reign of William the Conqueror until that of Queen Elizabeth.[9] The *Chronicle* opened in a familiar biblical format: "Now it came to pass in the Year One thousand sixty and six, in the Month of September, on the eighth Day of the Month, that William of Normandy, surnamed the Bastard, landed in England, and pitched his Tent in a Field near the Town of Hastings." The language, style, and grammar were biblical, the tone ironic, and the text abundant with intentional anachronisms. The traits of a genre were established.

While pieces written in the biblical style were common in America during the 1740s and 1750s, most were reprints of English publications. They were not yet American, in content or in form. The first identifiable American piece in biblical style, produced two decades after the *Chronicle*, was *The Fall of Samuel the Squomicutiti* (1763). That first American pseudobiblical text was a satiric parody, probably composed by Samuel Hopkins or someone from his party in Rhode Island. That piece was followed in 1766 by a short tract in *The Maryland Journal* titled, characteristically, as it would turn out, *Chronicles*, whose author criticized the mismanagement and embezzlement involved in a local lottery project. Although those early-1760s pieces were still sporadic and different in significant respects from future similar texts, they nonetheless demonstrated that the biblical style was present in late colonial publications. The next significant milestone in the life of the tradition of writing in the style of antiquity was passed with the advent of the American Revolution, in the pro-American satire "The Book of America" (1766), published in multiple American reprints.[10]

The Revolution brought the tradition of writing in biblical style to the forefront of patriot polemics. Although written in England, the pro-American *The Book of America* foreshadowed in many respects the distinct genre that was soon to develop in America: its theme was historical and American (it traced English history from the Seven Years' War to the Repeal of the Stamp Act in 1766), its language and form biblical, its tone anachronistic and ironic: the notorious British tax stamps (as "a stamp it is called unto this day"), for example, were written on lambskins, the coin used in America was the Hebraic shekel, and mobs were the biblical evildoers, "sons of Belial." Nomenclature, as in all such texts of the following decades, was thoroughly biblicized: Georgians were "the Children of the land of George," Virginians were "the children of the land of the Virgin," and so forth. Even the most recognizable slogan of the Revolution, "no taxation without representation" was rephrased in biblical fashion: Americans demanded "that they should have their own Sanhedrim, in which they should be taxed."

The revolutionary ferment of the early 1770s, the immediate years before the commencement of hostilities, wrought further transformations in the biblically styled writings. The 1773 and 1774 editions of the *Chronicle of the Kings of England*, for example, added to the prerevolutionary editions an elaborate and reverential section describing the reign of the now deceased George II (the earlier editions had a brief entry about the then reigning monarch), as well as an entirely new chapter concerning the reigning monarch, George III, whose tenure was represented less favorably than those of the other post-1688 monarchs. It did seem to start off on the right foot: the king carried the war "against Lewis King of Gaul" to a most felicitous end, as military victories were sealed with the Treaty of Paris of 1763, which practically ended the French presence in North America. Yet with the conclusion of the Seven Years' War the king listened to his "Evil Counsellors," who asked him in biblical fashion, "if we have found favor in thine Eyes, [to] let a Decree be passed, forbidding any American to take unto himself a Wife, or buy, or sell, or write, or read . . . unless he pay unto us for each Time a Piece of Silver."[11] The reverence shown to earlier monarchs was no longer to be found as the *Chronicle* took a blunt pro-American turn.

These and similar elaborate and extensive pieces (often consisting of dozens of verses and thousands of words) were reprinted across the colonies. They consisted of an Enlightenment-era cultural product, written in a universally known and admired idiom. Rational, paced, and making minimal reference to God, they were not meant to provide providential historical explanations. Although this modern use of biblical idiom could have risen only in a society suffused with biblical language, it stood ambivalently in light of traditional pious sentiment. Surely, only a society that took its distance from biblical language, if not from the religious truths it revealed, could sustain, indeed embrace, such use of sacred language for the needs of the present. The use of biblical language for secular purposes thus underscores that the Bible in late-eighteenth-century America was no longer a self-legitimating text that affirmed itself as God's Word. Although probably none of the writers of texts in the biblical style intended to defame or detract from the Bible, that humans allowed themselves to write such texts reveals the degree to which the Bible had become a "document" open to criticism and scholarship.[12] While biblical authority was reassigned to the world of human beings during the Revolution, the pseudobiblical genre illuminates the permissibility of the intellectual environment in which those texts were written.

One way to understand the extensive use of biblical form to convey modern political messages would be to emphasize the irony stemming from the frisson gained through invoking language still seen as quasi-sacred to describe contemporary reality. Indeed, beyond the mere boldness of using the biblical style for earthly purposes, some of the pseudobiblical texts capitalized on the dissonance between form and content and functioned as outright parodies, often using the biblical style to disparage, mock, and deride political enemies. In such texts adversaries became anything from "Sons of Belial," to usurping biblical kings, and even vivid demonic "beast[s]... having a mouth, speaking blasphemous things, and also an head, but how many horns no one knoweth."[13] Such application of biblical language and form to the political realm was at least implicitly, and often outright, satirical.

The most popular writing in biblical style of the revolutionary era was John Leacock's (1729–1802) *The First Book of the American Chronicles of the Times*, which signified the complete Americanization of the genre; that work was also the epitome of the biblical parody. Leacock, a Philadelphia silversmith and merchant, was a committed patriot from early in the imperial contest. As a Whig propagandist he attempted to advertise the colonial patriot position so that all readers would identify with the positions of middling and upper-class patriots. The immensely popular and anonymously published *First Book* consisted of six chapters and was published serially and reprinted in newspapers and later in several pamphlet editions across the colonies, from Massachusetts to South Carolina, during the fall and winter of 1774–1775. The tract, far too extensive, rich, and complex to analyze here at length, was innovative in significant ways: it was the first long and full-blown exposition of American events by an American author in biblical style, and its richness and parodic nature provided, no doubt, a remarkably amusing read for contemporaries. Characters such as the Indian chief Occunneocogeecococacheecacheecadungo, or the British attempts to make Bostonites "bow down to the TEA CHEST, the God of the Heathen," as well as camels—a biblical vehicle—loaded with cargoes of Tobacco, the ultimate American crop, could not but have raised contemporary smiles.[14]

The First Book consisted of a Whig narrative of the political events of 1773 and 1774 in biblical style. It makes extensive use of biblical nomenclature: all in all it employs a *dramatis personae* of about one hundred, the majority of whom bear either such readily deciphered names as Mordecai the

Benjaminite (for Benjamin Franklin) and Thomas the Gageite (Thomas Gage, the military commander of Boston), or such plain biblical names as Joshua, Ehud son of Gera, and Jedidiah the priest. Some of the names were widely used in contemporary discourse, such as Rehoboam for George III, alluding to the Hebrew monarch who was held responsible for the separation of Israel into two rival kingdoms. The imagery Leacock uses is densely biblical, too, and his idioms often Hebraic. For example, the four great beasts of Daniel's prophecy stand in *The First Book* for four hated imperial magistrates, Bute, Mansfield, Bernard, and Hutchinson, while vessels loaded with Indian tea are biblical "ships from Tarshish." Leacock also repeatedly merges ancient and modern into the kind of anachronism that characterized the stylistic tradition of pseudobiblical writing; repeating II Samuel 1:20, Leacock urges his American compatriots in the lamenting words of David the son of Jesse: "Tell it not in Gath, nor publish it in the streets of Askalon."[15]

In a laudable introductory essay to the modern edition of Leacock's *First Book* the literary historian Carla Mulford, beyond establishing Leacock's authorship, analyzes its consistently anti-British attack on tyranny, militarism, Catholicism, Puritan millennialism, and extreme thought and action of all forms. Mulford identifies as contemporary Americans many of the characters on whom biblical names are bestowed but admits that the identities of other characters are not easily established. Mulford is thus probably the only modern scholar to notice a tradition of writing in biblical style in America.[16] However, her understandable focus on Leacock's *First Book* obscures the fact that, especially elaborate as it was, it was only one among scores of similar texts. Indeed, biblical-style writing neither peaked nor culminated with Leacock's *First Book*; that tradition thrived and evolved for at least half a century after the Revolution.

Still, Leacock's *First Book* was exceptional in significant ways: its length and complexity were unusual, and it featured comic moments few other texts could, or wished to, boast. With the urgent need to create a usable past in the wake of the Revolution, numerous pseudobiblical texts did not present themselves as parodies, at least no more than the Bible itself. We moderns, much less immersed in the Bible than were early Americans, need to be reminded of the extent to which the Bible has its vehemently acerbic instances of irony and contempt, particularly toward wrongdoers. Americans did not inject the Bible with sarcasm, irony, and satire it was devoid of but framed their political views within a biblical outlook that could accommodate their vitriolic and Manichean political culture.[17] Too much emphasis on the degradation and impiety present in the pseudobiblical language might distort and obscure some of the significant cultural meaning that that language implied.

Although the liberal use of biblical language changed the meaning and stature of that language, it did not reflect a straightforward process of secularization, seen as an unambiguous transformation from a pious to a skeptical society, as might be inferred from seeing satire as the sole thrust behind such use. Religion, historians have recently noted, was reconstructed and remade in the early modern period, not undone; presenting a strict dichotomy between the Bible and its traditional uses and the profane application of its language to politics could be misleading.[18] More nuanced processes implying change in religious attitudes, not their demolition, better describe the uses of the biblical language for American ends.

Many postrevolutionary texts adopted a somber tone rarely attempted to crack a biblical joke at a rival's expense, and thus reflect novel pseudobiblical sensibilities. Such seriousness caused contemporaries to depict their political enemies in biblical fashion as "men who had not the fear of God before their eyes," implying that in the writers' own eyes, they themselves, who used the Bible's language for secular purposes, were pious. Significantly, others wished to strengthen Americans' attachment to the Bible by applying the language of the King James Version to describe American history and politics. Gilbert Hunt, the author of one of the most elaborate and protracted texts in the pseudobiblical tradition, stated that he "adopted for the model of his style the phraseology of the best of books," namely the Bible, so that it would induce "the young pupil . . . to study Holy Scriptures."[19] Biblical renditions of American history could thus be seen as constituting a method for drawing young Americans back into the Scripture's sway. That contemporaries did not think that the use of sacred language for earthly ends necessarily degraded or secularized that language demonstrates that such language did not (necessarily) lead to the abandonment of religion. Rather, such use incorporated the political into the religious, and brought the latter more intimately and through new modes into the lives of contemporaries.

"Chapter 37th," published in Boston in 1782, represents the staid, counterparodic end of the spectrum of the pseudobiblical texts. The author of the "Chapter" established the setting in the first verse—"And it came to pass in the reign of George the king, who ruled over Albion, and whose empire extended to the uttermost parts of the earth"—then versified the history of the Revolution in a no-nonsense biblical fashion. The "Chapter" concluded with an American hero singing in biblical fashion, "the song of triumph, saying others have slain their thousands, but I have slain my ten thousands." This and similar texts depicted America, implicitly or explicitly, as a latter-day Israel, a chosen nation in the most earnest terms. The Bible, through the distinct usage of its language, forms, and style, no longer informed early Americans merely of the ancient history of a bygone Israelite society; nor was it solely a typological text that signified, foresaw, and corresponded to the happenings of American society. Through pseudobiblicism the Bible became a living text, an ongoing scriptural venture which complemented and fortified notions of national chosenness and mission. This transformation occurred within a poisoned political culture which created "two parallel imagined communities," namely the two political parties, the Federalists and the Republicans, that denied each other's legitimacy. This disposition, already manifested in the late 1780s, created a political culture governed by a grammar of combat, which entailed a "politics of anxious extremes."[20] It fostered the intense employment and further construction of biblical politics, each side depicting the other as wrongdoing "Adamites" or "Jeffersonites." However, beyond its partisan nature, pseudobiblicism further constructed the United States as a biblical nation. The language of the King James Bible wove the Bible into American life and sanctified the young nation. American politics were transformed, in texts largely devoid of references to God, into the new religion of the republic.

After the Revolution, Americans continued to publish faux-biblical texts at such a rate that attempts to assess them all are futile and pointless. Nevertheless, the pinnacle in the history of the tradition of writing in biblical style, particularly in the earnest and nonsatiric depictions of America as a latter-day Israel, was reached in 1793, with the publication of Richard Snowden's (1753–1825) *The American Revolution; Written in the Style of Ancient History*. Snowden's history must have touched an intellectual nerve in fin de siècle America. The history, which occupied two protracted volumes, was also published serially as dozens of chapters appearing in newspapers throughout 1794–1795 from Vermont in the north to South Carolina in the south. Additionally, Snowden's history would spawn decades after its publication at least one intellectual sequel in the form of a similarly biblicized full-scale history of the War of 1812. Popularity aside, there was nothing especially innovative either in Snowden's style and use of language, or in his retelling a history rather than commenting on current events.[21] His history is important in its being the first full-blown, thorough, earnest, and mature attempt to biblicize the United States and its historical record. Its reverence for America's revolutionary past was wholly sentimental and Whiggish. In other words, it was a distinctly novel American cultural production.

As in the vast majority of writings in biblical style, Snowden did not provide his readers with a history of the Revolution driven by divine intervention in which Providence played a central role. The fact that Snowden wrote "in the style of ancient history," which could have easily meant classical, not biblical, history, indicates that he emphasized the historical aspect of the biblical narrative. Indeed, God is virtually absent from Snowden's history, a curious fact if only because many other contemporary American historians of the Revolution—who were not committed to biblical style—could assign Providence a more significant role than Snowden did. According to the genre's conventions, throughout the history's volumes Snowden used relatively short and numbered verses. As in the other texts belonging to this tradition, the versed staccato was hardly the entire antique array. Snowden employed archaic English throughout, everywhere using constructions such as "spake" and "thou." He antiquated his vocabulary, nouns, and narrative style, as well as the American nomenclature. For example, throughout his history Snowden replaced modern cities' and nations' names with ancient equivalents. Hence London became Lud (an ancient Hebrew city), while Ireland was alluded to by its Latin name, "Hibernia." Even when the author preserved a nonbiblical name, he attempted to provide it with an antique flavor, for instance, "that ancient river, the river Rhine." Following the example of earlier texts in the biblical style, Snowden particularly antiquicized American names. The town of Concord became "Concordia," Virginia "the state of the Virgin," and America the "Land of Columbia." These and numerous other names, used consistently throughout Snowden's protracted narrative, biblicized the mental geography and imagined landscape of the American Revolution. As in the Bible, and contrary to modern identification which relied mostly on family names, the author identified historical actors almost solely by their first names. He reviewed, for example the names of the Continental Army's commanders (whom he called "captains," as in biblical-era armies, not generals as in modern forces): "And the names of the captains [of the Continental Army] were these, Artemas, Charles, Philip, Israel, Horatio, Seth, Richard, David, William, Joseph, John . . . ," referring to generals Ward, Schuyler, Putnam, Gates, and so on. In the absence of family names, Snowden frequently had to revert to footnotes to clarify to whom exactly he was referring, demonstrating once more that biblical style and simplicity were frequently not compatible. In line with the tradition within which he wrote, Snowden biblicized institutions: Congress (as in numerous other texts) became "the great Sanhedrin"; smallpox was "the leprosy of uncleanness," alluding to the Bible's most cursed ailment; and rum was "the strong water of Barbados." Snowden made extensive use of Hebraic idioms and figural language. Thus Lord North's counsel was "as the counsel of Achitophel in the days of David king of Israel," Achitophel having been the king's adviser who counseled him against his own interest; American courtiers, "like the locusts of Egypt, ... devoured every goodly thing."[22]

Like other writers in the pseudobiblical style, Snowden often concluded chapters in the repeatedly used words and format of the biblical canon (favored also by other texts in the tradition of writing in ancient style): "And the rest of the acts of Dunmore, and all that he did ... are they not written in the book of Ramsay the scribe?" Here David Ramsay, arguably the most contemporarily recognized of the revolution's historians, was himself portrayed as a biblical chronicler. Similarly, Snowden could conclude an episode: "And the rest of the Acts of the people of the [American] provinces, [and] how they warred ... are they not written in the Second Book of the Chronicles of the wars of the king of Britain with the people of the provinces; and recorded by the Scribe of Columbia, in the books of the great Sanhedrim?"[23] This quotation, typical of Snowden's style, demonstrates the extent to which pseudobiblicism enabled Americans to merge and sanctify the political realm, in Snowden's case that of the American Revolution, through the use of historical anachronisms (a modern revolution "written in the Second Book of Chronicles"), and of ancient signifiers (an American "great Sanhedrim" and a historian filling the role of a "Scribe of Columbia").

To complete the ancient vision Snowden articulated, he wrote as if he himself were actually addressing an ancient audience, devoid of knowledge of things modern. Since Snowden had committed himself to an ancient fantasy, like other writers in biblical style he found it necessary to reconcile eighteenth-century devices with a biblical-style narrative. Hence he repeatedly describes British warships as "armed with engines," meaning guns, "as were not known in the days of old: fire and balls issued out of their mouths.... They were inventions of Satan." Continuing to be amazed by inventions already hundreds of years old by the late eighteenth century, Snowden describes gunpowder as "black dust which they put into their engines.... Without it the engines could do nothing." To complete the estrangement from the present Snowden refers to "those days" when alluding to the Revolution, as if he were actually discussing a distant and fundamentally altered reality. The list of Snowden's stylistic measures, as in numerous other texts written in biblical style, is too elaborate to treat exhaustively. But the picture is clear: Americans, by the closing decade of the eighteenth century, could describe their experiences past and present as if they were occurring in a world of biblical heroes and villains, governed by a Manichean cosmology in which the division between good and bad was clear. Snowden, who as we shall now see had a patriotic-didactic objective in mind while writing his history, constructed the United States as a chosen nation, a second Israel. Federal-era America never seemed so biblical.

Snowden was among the few authors who reflected on their choice of biblical style, pointing out that his patriotic history targeted schoolchildren as its intended audience. "The style of ancient history was chosen," for narrating the Revolution, Snowden confessed, "both for its conciseness and simplicity, and therefore the most suitable to the capacities of young people." Snowden trusted that his young readership would decipher his pseudobiblical text because early Americans were conditioned from young age to reading biblical English. As historians of early American education noted, the Bible was a principal text for teaching reading and writing in eighteen-century schools, and was still the common reading book in early-nineteenth-century schools. There is reason to doubt, however, whether readers, especially the young, grasped Snowden's history as effortlessly as the author would have liked. Short biblical-style verses did tend to focus on action rather than on the psychology of heroes, and thus enabled Snowden to condense complex plots. However, the author's frequent use of notes to explain numerous cumbersome biblical descriptions of American objects, people, and events testifies that his biblicizing necessitated clarification. The fact that young eighteenth-century readers were commonly presented with the actual biblical stories stripped from their distinct language in order to "familiarize tender age," or were rendered as biblical dramas "intended for young persons" in contemporary language attests that biblical language was commonly *not* perceived as the most simple of communication forms. Indeed, one of the most popular contemporary biblical texts for the young was *The Holy Bible Abridged*, intended to "give children such a taste of the writings of the holy penmen" in ordinary prose.[24] Evidently, for the sake of "simplicity," if not "conciseness," young readers occasionally needed biblical language simplified, not American history biblicized. Snowden's extensive history written in biblical idiom must have built then, at least in part, not on readers' training in biblical

English but rather on the conditioning of American audiences in reading American texts written in biblical idiom.

Although the pseudobiblical style was Americanized even before the Revolution ended, there is no escaping the fact that the predominant narrative style through which Americans chose to understand and communicate the nation's founding era originated in Britain, employed Elizabethan-age English, and was associated with a British monarch, James I. This collective choice had several causes. One was the cultural supremacy in America of the King James Version, which was not responsive to political changes; another was the lack of real alternatives, since American translations of the Bible were to emerge only in the Jacksonian era. The choice also underscores the extent to which the Revolution was, in the words of the eminent historian Jack Greene, a "settler rebellion," a rather conservative affair that could not untie many of the existing cultural bonds.[25] Only when the democratic impulses of the antebellum era were unleashed did novel American idioms replace the pseudobiblical style. In the intervening generations until then, the King James Bible's language continued to occupy Americans' mental spaces.

The tradition of writing in biblical style continued to flourish in the partisan battles of the early republic. Remnants of Anti-Federalism and manifestations of early Jeffersonian Republicanism surfaced soon after the federal government began to operate, and partisans accused the members of the constitutional convention and "[John] Adams their Servant" of conspiring with "the Britannites" to the effect that "all the country round about, even from Dan unto Beersheba, should be subject unto one king, and unto one council." Republicans commonly critiqued Adams's neutrality to the French Revolution (before it deteriorated into a bloodbath) in biblical-style writings, typically depicting Republicans as "Israel," while Federalists were represented as a spectrum of biblical evildoers, from Pharisees to Amalekites. Federalists, by contrast, attacked Republicans for what they interpreted as their anarchic tendencies and Gallic leanings—or, in biblical language, for not being "a goodly people-fearing the lord and submitting to the Rulers placed over them."[26] In the following decades each side continued to endure biblical representations by its political enemies, who saw their rivals as conspiring to subvert the people's will. As relations with Britain worsened, eventually culminating in the War of 1812, a further deluge of biblical stylized texts flooded the printed sphere.

The most impressive text among the many published during the opening decades of the nineteenth century, particularly those related to the War of 1812, was *The History of the Late War* (1819), by Gilbert J. Hunt of New York. The only work comparable to Hunt's history up to that point in its elaboration and richness was Snowden's history (and to some extent Leacock's revolutionary-era *Book of Chronicles*). As in Snowden's case, a contemporary commentator pointed out that "the simplicity of the scriptural style" of Hunt's history, "and the short verses or sentences are calculated to make an impression on the memory more than a regular narrative, told in the usual manner." Probably in a conscious attempt to imitate Snowden's composition and success, Hunt's printers proposed to "consider it a valuable book for schools . . . calculated to give a knowledge of events to youths." The history itself was, again like Snowden's, patriotic and Whiggish in its historical interpretation. Like Snowden's history, as well as numerous earlier works, Hunt's history was nationalistic and humorless, avoiding any attempt at satire or parody. The *History* further made use of the full range of the possibilities that the style of antiquity had demonstrated and developed during many decades by biblicizing American annals. From addressing the "American Sanhedrim" to referring to modern inventions such as cannons as "battering rams" who "cast forth bombs . . . weapons of destruction, which were not known in the days of Jehoshaphat," Hunt rendered the epitome of a biblical American history.[27]

American writers chose to make use of distinctive Elizabethan English for political ends because that language manipulated readers into conjuring up biblical visions only to contrast them with their American past and present. However, we should see the uncanny portrayals of America in biblical language as going beyond authors' immediate intent, namely in the wider context of the young nation's attempts to come to terms with history and historical time. Even before independence, but especially after the creation of the United States, Americans began imagining themselves as reenacting Roman annals and re-creating a Rome-like republic of virtue, as returning to the democratic simplicity of Anglo-Saxon freedom, or, alternatively, as latter-day Israelites led by a Washingtonian Moses to inherit the American Promised Land. These historical discourses underscore the tensions which the American nation and its embryonic nationalism experienced with regard to their past (or lack thereof) and their place in history.[28] These tensions are particularly illustrated through the use of the pseudobiblical style, which compelled Americans to articulate their history and present as if they occurred in a biblical world.

These pseudobiblical texts reflect a distinct historical consciousness, very different from common twenty-first-century historical temporal sensibilities. Tracts like the grand histories in biblical style by Snowden and Hunt, but also numerous other shorter texts, consisted of radical historical statements. By imposing the Bible and its intellectual and cultural landscapes on America, those texts placed the United States in a biblical time frame, describing the new nation and its history as occurring in a distant, revered, and mythic dimension. These texts thus produced a constructive estrangement, rendering the present through biblical forms and structures, which while well known and respected, were linguistically and temporally dissonant. By manipulating time and space, pseudobiblicism proved an effective medium for buttressing notions of chosenness and mission. The countless verses opening with the biblio-temporal statement "And it came to pass" located readers in biblical time, while nomenclature and geography functioned similarly, by turning, for example, Federalists into "Federalites" and New Yorkers into "Manhattanites," and repeatedly sanctifying the expanse of America, describing the United States in Canaanite terms as stretching "from Dan even unto Beersheba." Biblical narratives and modes of action further blended in partisan texts that battled over the legacy of the Revolution. Each party saw the other as sinning Israelites (or gentiles), describing their rivals as "gather[ing] themselves together," wishing for "more honor and reverence showed onto us under a king." This republicanization of the Bible, evinced in repeated biblical representations of America, reorganized Americans' space of experiences, and expanded their horizon of national expectations. By rendering biblical history as immanently relevant to America and constructing their experiences as a reenactment of a biblical script, contemporaries stretched conventional understandings of time and history. Through such temporal modes Americans, representing their nation as led by "George [Washington, who] reigned over all Israel ... execut[ing] judgment and justice among all his people," made sense of understanding the United States as a latter-day biblical society.[29] The rest of the acts of the young United States, to use the parlance of the day, were they not written in the cadences of the King James Version, as a chapter of a biblical history that unfolded regularly in American prints?

If notions of America as second Israel were still tentative at the commencement of the Revolution, by the nineteenth century they were inseparable from the political discourse that would soon spawn Manifest Destiny. Narrating America through a quasi-sacred language deeply associated with ancient Israel conditioned contemporaries to think of an American mission in biblical terms. Americans who saw fit to draw on the most sacred of idioms to describe their past and present perpetuated and intensified the discourse of America as a chosen nation; unsurprisingly, many of the texts written in biblical language referred explicitly to America as "Israel" (and hence of their rivals as helplessly degenerate gentiles). By alluding to the past of God's chosen people through the use of the distinctive language in which that history was originally articulated, Americans attempted not to alter the received facts of that revered history but rather to invoke the authority and meaning which that history exerted and apply it to their present. The use of biblical language was thus not (only) a way to make the Bible relevant to America; it was an effective way to make America relevant to the Bible, to biblicize America.

The fact that the language of the King James Bible was applied abundantly and consistently in texts narrating American accounts and histories, a genre which I have dubbed pseudobiblicism, further demonstrates not merely the extent to which American culture was biblically oriented, but that that biblicism was profoundly focused on the Old Testament. This strong predilection for the Old rather than the New Testament is evident when one surveys extant pseudobiblical texts, a sizable corpus written during more than a century (circa 1740–1850); while each of those texts echoes and resonates with Old Testament narratives and protagonists, it is hard to find even a single reference to Christ, not to mention other New Testament characters or episodes.

The mobilization of the Old Testament for political ends reflects, and may be attributed to, the political nature of the Hebrew Bible, as well as to the inaptness of the New Testament for explicitly political purposes. But Americans' recourse to the Hebrew Scriptures also demonstrates their eagerness to understand themselves as latter-day Israelites. In the process, while never denying the historicity of the original, ancient, and biblical Israel, they subordinated that history, as well as the unique language through which it was conveyed, to their national mission. It is thus fair to say that the robustness of pseudobiblicism—the mobilization of the narratives and literary arsenal of the Authorized Version's Old Testament in public discourse—points to remarkable levels of biblical fluency in the general population (or at least among the vast and ever expanding community of early American newspaper readers); otherwise such language would have been ineffective as a mode of political communication—indeed, unintelligible altogether. The many writers and newspaper editors in the early republic who published the numerous "Chronicles" and "Chapters" knew what Perry Miller reminded us of long ago, namely that the Old Testament was truly omnipresent in early America, and that Old Testament narratives and images had become, in the words of Mark Noll, "the common coinage for the realm."[30] By elaborating the meaning of their national community and its role in history through pseudobiblicism, Americans of the early republic—a Christian people if there ever was one—certainly earned their reputation as a biblical nation.

It would be excessive to list the numerous "Chronicles," "Chapters," and manifold other pieces written in ancient style constantly appearing in newspapers. Many were published in the years and decades following the War of 1812, some comic, others sentimental, some discussing local issues, others questions of national concern, some brief and others long-winded. Those texts kept circulating and were printed and reprinted across the nation. One cannot escape the feeling, however, that after the 1820s, a point in time when "a shift from Old Testament to New Testament dominance" may have been noticeable in the United States, the almost century-old genre of public writing in the style of antiquity had begun to lose its vigor. Certainly impressive texts were still written after that date in antique style, such as the quasi-biblical tracts addressed to the Bank Wars of the 1830s. Even during the 1840s texts like the elaborate *Chapter from the Whig Chronicles* provided an extended Democratic survey of the history of American Federalists-turned-Whigs from the Revolution to Henry Clay, concluding with the biblical form so popular among writers in the genre: "Now the rest of the acts of the Whigs, and the many wicked things which they did, and the sore defeats with which they were discomfited, are they not written in the book of the chronicles of the Whigs of the North Country...?" In the years after 1830, however, pieces written in the style of antiquity become notably sparse and sporadic; after 1850 there were hardly any to be found.[31]

Although changes in aesthetic preferences and cultural tastes are hard to pinpoint, clearly something significant occurred in the relationship between the American people and biblical language after the 1820s. Parallel changes are visible in other cultural realms, such as the decline of republican (and aristocratic) Rome as a model in public discourse, and its replacement by democratic Athens in the Jacksonian era. Significantly, calls to reform the King James Bible's anachronistic language were first heard in America in the same years.[32] As the United States emerged as a modern, commercial, industrial mass democracy during the first decades of the nineteenth century, its earlier genteel and enlightened ethos was quickly fading. Although monocausal explanations hardly serve for transformations in cultural tastes and intellectual sensibilities, it would not be far-fetched to speculate that the slow but steady decline in the pseudobiblical style was due to powerful cultural currents at work in the United States by the early decades of the nineteenth century. Dominant among those forces was the surging democratic populism of the Jacksonian era.

The cultural ethos of the founding era was neoclassical, one that valued formal, refined, and enlightened language and had deep contempt for democracy. Accordingly, eighteenth-century language separated the realms of the refined and the vulgar, the few and the many: the neoclassical and genteel rhetoric implied a social order in which those who ruled were eloquent while those who did not were crude and pitiful. The archaic and arcane language of the biblical style complemented such public tastes by implying a matching ideal of social authority. But once the democratic and liberal forces of the sprawling young nation were unleashed, the move from baroque idioms such as the pseudobiblical style to a more democratic, inclusive, and unpretentious discourse was just a matter of time. Democratic language, defined in the words of the historian Kenneth Cmiel as "plain, unadorned, declarative prose," was averse to the ostentatiously authoritative and aloof biblical style. Indeed, the aggressive, masculine nineteenth-century Jacksonian plain speaking challenged neoclassical sensibilities head-on. The new currents that encouraged informal speech, slang dialect, and familiarity all contributed to a linguistic egalitarianism which the ornate pseudobiblical writing could not accommodate. The genteel sensibilities that the biblical style catered to and elaborated were deemed "polite" and "corrupt" in the age of manly democracy. Among the other transformations in American society during the market revolution and the Jacksonian era, it became much less tolerant toward "aristocratic" manifestations in general, refined modes of expression in particular. The authoritativeness, rationality, balance, and aloofness of the biblical style, characteristics at least partially responsible for its eighteenth-century success, facilitated its eventual fall from grace in an age of antebellum romanticism and popular democracy.[33]

The reformed Protestant heritage, a neoclassical political culture, and a mature culture of print facilitated the rise of this unique mode of representing contemporary American culture. The tradition of writing "in the style of antiquity," the product of an age still suffused with the Bible yet already Enlightened as to the liberal use of that book's language, offers a vantage point for better understanding a lost political, cultural, and intellectual early American world of biblical imagination. The appeal to biblical language helped to make sense of a fast-changing world and of novel American democratic ways. The extensive use of that idiom demonstrates how, by invoking a privileged language, Americans imagined and reclaimed social and political power in a world that experienced the diminishing influence of traditional sources of authority in the decades following the creation of the republic.[34] Although the use of the Bible's language for nonreligious ends would not have been possible before the eighteenth century, when novel attitudes eased restraints for applying Scripture to nonreligious arenas, it would be wrong to see the flourishing of pseudobiblical writing as part of a straightforward process of secularization in America: the story of its use is the story not of diminishing religious sentiment but of a transformation and reconstruction of beliefs and understandings of America's meaning and collective identity.

The usefulness of a refined language such as Elizabethan English diminished once the United States embraced the ethos of popular democracy. It became evident that the formal biblical language belonged more to the eighteenth century than to antebellum America, and more to an age of genteel politics of prudent gentlemen than to the public discourse of democracy and evangelicalism. Only a text in biblical style that adapted to and embodied the deep cultural transformations of the Jacksonian era could thrive in a world of democratic coarseness, of mass revivals, and of relentless industrialization. The tradition of writing in biblical style paved the way for the Book of Mormon by conditioning Americans to reading American texts, and texts about America, in biblical language. Yet the Book of Mormon, an American narrative told in the English of the King James Bible, has thrived long after Americans abandoned the practice of recounting their affairs in biblical language. It has been able to survive and flourish for almost two centuries not because, but in spite of, the literary ecology of the mid-nineteenth century and after.[35] The Book of Mormon became a testament to a widespread cultural practice of writing in biblical English that could not accommodate to the monumental transformations America endured in the first half of the nineteenth century.

Gordon Wood speculated decades ago that if the book of Mormon had been published later than its original appearance in 1830, it would have been inconceivable for Mormonism to take hold, since "a generation or so later it might have been necessary for Smith and his followers to get some university professors to authenticate the characters on the golden plates." Nevertheless,

Smith's timing was providential for yet another reason: the Book of Mormon was published during the final efflorescence of a tradition of pseudobiblical writing in the United States. Published later, the Book of Mormon might not have benefited from Americans' fascination with pseudobiblicism, which gradually lost its appeal in the years after 1830. By the time the effects of this decline were felt, however, the Book of Mormon had gained a momentum of its own, transcending the literary tradition which helped pave the way for that original American scripture.[36] Hence a closer look at the Book of Mormon in light of the popular—and hitherto disregarded—genre of American texts posing as biblical writings will help to contextualize and better understand Joseph Smith's bible in the intellectual culture of the early republic. Understating the Book of Mormon in relation to a well-established pseudobiblical culture might thus shed new light on perennial questions regarding the contentious history of the Mormon bible and thus offer a fresh understanding of the intellectual and cultural, as well as religious, history of the early United States.

When Joseph Smith published the Book of Mormon in 1830, Americans had been producing and consuming faux-biblical texts for close to a century. As we have seen, American colonials, who first merely reissued English pieces, imitating a practice that had originated as a satirical literary genre in the first half of the eighteenth century in Britain, started publishing original pseudobiblical texts in earnest during the Revolution. Thereafter Americans regularly described and were informed of their political realities through texts that featured the full range of the literary conventions of the Authorized King James Version.

In the years leading to the publication of the Book of Mormon, American citizens thus became accustomed to perceiving their recent history in biblical terms, not only in the Bible's distinct language but also in its deep meaning. Pseudobiblical texts habituated contemporaries' historical and biblical sensibilities to understand the Bible and America in similar terms, hence to perceive the United States as a biblical nation. As we shall soon see, the pseudobiblical texts may have helped pave the way to the creation and reception of an American scripture in the cadences and metaphors of the King James Bible. In light of the popular genre of American pseudobiblicism, at least some of the Book of Mormon's accounts—for example, of the Jewish ancestors of the American Indians and their remarkable history in the New World—may seem less extraordinary.[37] The details of the pseudobiblical texts that preceded (and anteceded) the Book of Mormon may have been radically different from the centuries-long history of a family of Jews and their vast progeny in America, as portrayed in the Mormon Bible. But such texts and the Mormon Bible matched and enhanced each other remarkably.

The Book of Mormon, "One of the greatest documents in American cultural history," according to one historian, which, according to another, "occupies a position of major importance in both the religious and intellectual history of the United States," differed, to be sure, in crucial respects from other contemporary texts written in pseudobiblical style. Although its contemporary critics already argued that they could identify in it the fingerprints of nineteenth-century American culture, as a prophetic text it pointedly steered clear of the blunt polemics that characterized many of the political pseudobiblical texts. Moreover, Providence, unlike in those pseudobiblical pieces in which men were the main, if not the sole, historical agents, was omnipresent in the Book of Mormon. Like other contemporary visionary tracts—none of which made use of the Bible's language—the Book of Mormon proclaimed itself a revelatory text intended to tell authentic religious truths, an attempt that even the most ambitious texts written in pseudobiblical style would not make.[38]

Nevertheless, there are good reasons to see the Book of Mormon as intimately connected to the wider genre of pseudobiblicism: the unique combination of the biblical form and style that the Book of Mormon shares with the pseudobiblical texts, as well as their distinctly American content, provide a case for seeing Smith's book as meaningfully affiliated to that American mode of writing. This affiliation is particularly significant once we realize that while few if any other contemporary visionaries claimed the sacred authority of the biblical language, Smith was bold enough to publish his American bible in the sacred idiom.[39] Understanding the Book of Mormon in light of the pseudobiblical tradition may thus shed new light on its origins and conception (or translation, according to Mormon belief), as well as on the context in which it emerged, was received, and proliferated.

While the practice of imitating the biblical style to convey reality appears extraordinary to modern readers, it came naturally to generations of Americans writing and reading pseudobiblical texts, Joseph Smith and his audience included. The numerous texts written in biblical idiom, some of which were, as we have just seen, major and hugely popular literary productions, attest to the vigor of that distinct American tradition. What first strikes the occasional reader of the Book of Mormon is its biblical language, "laced with biblical expressions ... steeped in the words and rhythms of the Authorized Version." Historians of Mormonism are well aware of this, pointing out that Smith "was telling a sacred story, and this demanded a sacred language, which for him meant the English of the King James Bible." Throughout the book the reader hears the intonations of the diction of King James's translators in numerous sentences, such as a random verse from the first chapter of the Mormon canon: "For it came to pass in the commencement of the first year of the reign of Zedekiah, king of Judah ... and in that same year there came many prophets, prophesying unto the people that they must repent, or the great city Jerusalem must be destroyed." If a sympathetic reader may believe that the Book of Mormon "thinks like the Bible," others concluded that it must have seemed to contemporaries "a clumsy parody of the King James Bible. Every verb ended in–*eth*, and every other sentence began, 'And it came to pass.'" Indeed, the "Gold Bible" (thus named after the golden plates upon which it was reportedly originally carved) would have been incomprehensible to contemporaries except in a biblical context, since for them the language it utilized was "the only appropriate language in which to enfold the holy words of Scripture." Like the Bible itself and the imitative pseudobiblical writings, the Book of Mormon was printed as a collection of books, holding Bible-sounding titles such as "The Book of Jacob," or "The Book of Mosiah," and divided into numbered chapters. Like the Bible itself, the Book of Mormon was not composed as verses, but was so arranged only later for convenience and conformity. Many of the pseudobiblical texts were divided into numbered verses, but others were not.[40]

Terryl Givens has noted in an illuminating study that reference to, and interpretation of, specific passages of the Book of Mormon were "surprisingly uncommon" in the early days of the Church. This, according to Givens, is because "the Book of Mormon's place in Mormonism and American religion generally has always been more connected to its status as *signifier* than *signified*, or its role as a sacred sign rather than its function as persuasive theology."[41] The Book's influence thus owed less to what it said than to what it consisted of; it was first and foremost a historical account of events that took place in America written in biblical language. Accordingly, the way in which the Book presents itself, through both its biblical language and its American subject matter, gains further importance: from the opening paragraphs of Nephi I (the first book of the Mormon bible) it is obvious not only that the Book of Mormon is written in the King James Bible's idiom but also that it is an *American* book in the most literal sense, recounting a narrative in which the New World is the promised land upon which its original inhabitants, the descendants of the people of Israel, enacted dramatic and sacred acts. Like many other contemporary texts written in the biblical style, the Book of Mormon makes use of the archaic language to historicize and sanctify American annals, interweaving the Bible and America, America and the Bible.

Without detracting from its innovations and distinctiveness, there is a strong case for viewing the Book of Mormon in light of a larger contemporary textual world, and as part of a long American tradition of comparable texts written in biblical language. While the book's affinities to the original biblical testaments, as well as to early-nineteenth-century prophetic culture, have been well established, its affiliation to the genre of writing in biblical prose still needs to be demonstrated. True, like other writings in that tradition, the Book of Mormon co-opts the American landscape and its (pre)history by incorporating it into a scriptural cosmos. While earlier writings in the style of antiquity tend to hallow the terms in which the United States' history and its present were perceived, the Book of Mormon introduces America's remote past into the biblical canon. The Book of Mormon may be seen as "an extension of the old and new testaments to the Western Hemisphere," but so also may the numerous pseudobiblical texts. Seen in this light, the Book of Mormon thus did not necessarily offer American readers a unique, "wholly fresh, wholly novel, and ... wholly innocent new Scripture."[42] Rather, in light of American pseudobiblicism, the Book of Mormon may be seen as extending prevalent literary conventions to their logical conclusion: like numerous texts in the pseudobiblical style, the Book of Mormon incorporated the Bible into American circumstances through the use of an idiom well known to Americans accustomed to texts written in a language that consecrated America and its history. It was a language through which Americans regularly revealed truths, either scriptural or political.

The generic connection between pseudobiblical writings and the Book of Mormon is further evident in the ways in which authors rendered the alleged origin and source of their texts. The Book of Mormon, like earlier pseudobiblical works, announced itself as a translation of an ancient source. Similarly, "The First Book of Chronicles, Chapter the 5th," a typical pseudobiblical text that was published in South Carolina's *Investigator* a few years before the Book of Mormon, characteristically proclaimed that it was "translated from the original Hebrew, by Rabbi Shaloma Ben Ezra, for the consolation of posterity." However, the Hebrew of the Old Testament was not necessarily what early-nineteenth-century Americans meant as the linguistic source of their pseudobiblical texts. Such writings could refer to themselves, for example, merely as "translated from the original," without naming Hebrew as the specific language of that "original."[43]

Beyond presenting themselves as translated from an ancient language, the pseudobiblical texts also shared with the Book of Mormon the remarkable narratives of the ways in which they had survived for ages and were eventually miraculously discovered. Such a text could fashion itself as "A Fragment of the Prophecy of Tobias," a Hellenized Hebrew name that did not refer to a specific biblical prophet (although the name Tobias, or, in the Hebrew original, Toviah, appears several times in the Bible), or merely as a "fragment [which] was found by the subscriber." The Book of Mormon should thus be seen in the context of contemporary texts written in biblical idiom which presented themselves as ancient, often Hebraic, in origin, mysteriously recovered, and translated from an exotic language for presentation before an American audience.[44]

Some of the recovery stories that pseudobiblical writings told are strikingly similar to the account of the Book of Mormon. The story about the golden plates is well known: buried of yore on rural New York's Mount Cumorah near the Smith family's farm in Palmyra, they waited for ages to be found and translated by Joseph Smith, Jr. Less known is *The Fifteenth Chapter of the Chronicles* (1812), a rather conventional pseudobiblical text published in New York's *Broome County Patriot* years before Smith made public his account of the golden plates in the not too distant Palmyra. *The Fifteenth Chapter of the Chronicles* described a supposedly ancient manuscript whose excavator, "Ben Saidi," appealed to the newspaper's editor to present his extraordinary find to the paper's readers. The choice of Ben Saidi as a pseudonym (or a pseudo-finder's name) clearly alluded to Nathan Ben Saddi, the nom de plume that the English author Robert Dodsley chose for his popular mid-eighteenth-century pseudobiblical *Chronicle of the Kings of England*. However, while the English Ben Saddi had stated a century earlier that he was the *Chronicle*'s author, not mere translator, the early-nineteenth-century American Ben Saidi claimed a different provenance for his biblical text. Ben Saidi's "ancient" manuscript was "found in the hollow of a tree, where it has probably been deposited for ages." He turned to the New York editor: "If you are able to decipher it"—for ancient prophetic texts, Mormon or other, required decoding and translation—"you will oblige me by giving it a place in your paper." Ben Saidi (and Joseph Smith), like other authors of "fragments" and "Ancient Chronicles" which necessitated translation from ancient languages, took part in the contemporary frenetic treasure hunting and digging culture that flourished in the burned-over district. They were fascinated by ancient and puzzling American scriptural texts, written in biblical idiom, hidden for centuries in the western areas of the Empire State, awaiting their early-republic excavators to find and translate them. The line separating political polemics and earnest claims to authenticity, between a pseudobiblical language and a language of prophetic religiosity, was never thinner.[45]

Contemporary texts such as the Book of Mormon and American pseudobiblical writings presented themselves as translations of ancient sources, and fashioned themselves (as pseudoepigraphic texts have done throughout the ages) as mysteriously, if not miraculously, preserved. Nevertheless, the Book of Mormon, while similar to contemporary pseudobiblical texts—and preceded by millennia of pseudoepigraphy and apocrypha—in its narratives of preservation, seems less in line with its congeners in other respects. The Book of Mormon's claim, for example, to have been inscribed on the gold plates in an unknown language that Joseph Smith identified as "Reformed Egyptian" seems particularly idiosyncratic. An Egyptian genealogy for apocryphal texts, as Edwin Firmage points out, "has attracted authors of sapiential, magical, and alchemical works since Greco-Roman times but . . . seems out of place in a work of Christian apologetics."[46]

Nevertheless, even in this regard we may find cultural webs that reveal the deep and yet unnoticed connections among the era's biblical and pseudobiblical imagination, print culture, and the Book of Mormon. Hieroglyphic Bibles, a common and unnoticed genre that circulated in the early American republic, are nodes on such webs. Post-Reformation English Bibles often featured distinctive images in an attempt to clarify obscure and overdetermined sacred phrases and narratives. Such emblematic figures helped form "visible Bibles," which according to the literary historian Lori Anne Ferrell were used as mnemonic devices through visual association. "Curious" hieroglyphic Bibles were an American specimen, issued in multiple editions from the late eighteenth century through the publication of the Book of Mormon and after. The hieroglyphic Bibles took part in this visual-biblical culture by rendering the Old and New Testaments with key words and phrases in the scriptural text replaced by pictorial woodcuts. Self-proclaimed as "hieroglyphic," these Bibles, impressively executed and each containing hundreds of carefully crafted images, while supposedly intended "for the amusement of youth" were actually devices, like some key pseudobiblical texts, "to familiarize tender age" with Scripture. Like "Reformed Egyptian," the ancient language from which Joseph Smith claimed to have translated the Book of Mormon, the widespread use of pictographic symbols to convey biblical narratives manifest early Americans' continuing fascination with the Bible and its relation to ancient forms of presentation. Although Smith never specifically referred to hieroglyphs in the context of Reformed Egyptian, the identification of pictographs with the ancient Egyptian script was universal; so was—and still is, since the Book of Mormon was published—the common understanding that Reformed Egyptian was a hieroglyphic form of writing.[47] Hence the connection of scripture and hieroglyphs, the Bible and ancient Egypt, and the sacred and the pictorial was not unique to Smith but an embedded aspect of contemporary biblical imagination. The Book of Mormon was thus taking the form, and making its impression on, a world attuned to the linguistic and representational sensibilities it evoked. Both the Mormon Bible's language and the original Egyptian writing system supposed by its readership resounded powerfully in the culture of the early American republic.

Attempts to understand the creation of the Book of Mormon have had mixed results over recent decades. Richard Bushman pointed out lately in his magisterial biographical study of the Mormon prophet Joseph Smith that the Book of Mormon has been difficult for "historians and literary critics from outside Mormondom to comprehend." Long ago, Smith's biographer Fawn Brodie suggested that the Book of Mormon "can best be explained, not by Joseph's ignorance nor by his delusions, but by his responsiveness to the provincial opinions of his time." Ever since, scholars, roughly divided into "compositionists," who attribute to Smith the book's creation, or "transcriptionists," who propose that Smith experienced a divine call and merely translated the book into English, have tried to contextualize him and his remarkable book in the intellectual and social history of the early American republic. Consequently, historians have produced a rich literature on the various contexts of the creation of the Book of Mormon, from theories of Smith's acquaintance with contemporary speculation on the Hebrew origins of Indians to structural explanations pertaining to popular culture. Summarizing many of these interpretations, the historian Nathan Hatch concluded that the Book of Mormon was created as "a synthesis which grew out of the Judeo-Christian scriptures, magic and the occult arts, and [Smith's] experience with dreams and visions."[48]

Leaving aside the impressive levels of the sophistication of current understandings of early Mormonism, the "Joseph Smith problem" still seems to generate unease: how could a young man, "reared in a poor Yankee farm family ... [with] less than two years of formal schooling and ... without social standing or institutional backing," come to produce "a second Bible"? Walter McDougall recently argued that "if the book [of Mormon] did emerge unaided from the head of this young, untutored man, he must have soaked up influences both ancient and modern like a sponge, and must have known intuitively how to refine them into ... an extraordinary work of popular imagination." Richard Bushman, a believing Mormon, has pointed out that viewing the Book of Mormon as Joseph Smith's composition (as opposed to revelation) "is at odds with the Joseph Smith of the historical record," not only because Joseph was, according to those who knew him, "an unambitious, uneducated, treasure-seek[er]," but, more important, because he "is not known to have read anything but the bible and perhaps the newspaper."[49] By including American pseudobiblicism in the intellectual inventory of the Second Great Awakening, Scripture and contemporary newspapers might possibly have been content enough to build the literary and imaginative (or religious and divine) framework for an American bible.

Palmyra's inhabitants had access to writings in the style of antiquity during the 1820s, the formative decade in the life of the young Joseph Smith. Most historians have long denied Smith the image of the ignorant rural boy who could not have acquired all the material that he would have needed to write the Book of Mormon. They have been pointing out the reading habits common to the residents of his region, their exposure to newspapers, libraries, and bookstores, the several roads that connected the towns of western New York State with one another and with eastern cities. They have further underscored that the Erie Canal passed a mere block away from Palmyra's main street, connecting the town with the Hudson River as early as 1823, and with Lake Erie by 1825. Those paths enabled eastern newspapers and books to flood the Palmyra-Manchester area. Predictably, we find pseudobiblical writings in Palmyra and its vicinity during those years, including those in a local newspaper into which, according to one of its employees, Smith "once a week ... would stroll into the office of the old Palmyra Register, for his father's paper." We also find an abundance of biblical-style writings in the eastern areas directly on the route of the Erie Canal. By 1828, historians point out, Smith was immersed in biblical language, "whether by personal study of scripture, by listening to sermons, [or] by natural participation in the biblical idioms of family conversation." Clearly Smith's "speech and thought patterns had been profoundly influenced by the common version [the King

James Bible]."⁵⁰ Smith found the vocabulary, idioms, and grammar that he needed to form the style of the Book of Mormon in the King James Version; he could have reinforced that biblicism and learned to apply it to new and American contexts through acquaintance with pseudobiblical writings available in contemporary printings. So if, conceivably or even probably, Joseph Smith was aware of pseudobiblicism, we can only speculate on how writings on America in biblical language would have impressed that young man and influenced his creative mind. Surely it was the Bible that exerted the most influence on Smith. However, pseudobiblicism demonstrates the ease with which writers could lapse into biblical prose when discussing and describing American events. Even without being able to attribute a direct influence of pseudobiblicism on Smith, incorporating the tradition of biblical writing into his, and the early republic's, intellectual cosmos adds a crucial dimension and context for understanding the creation—and reception—of the Book of Mormon.

Non-Mormon scholars tend, as we have seen, to historicize the Book of Mormon. However, faithful Mormons similarly conclude that the Mormon bible is the product of a human being, Joseph Smith, who left his intellectual footprints on his scriptural translation. Hence they too agree that the Book of Mormon's rendition in English represents "the ideas and basic form of the plate text in syntax, vocabulary, and idioms more appropriate to Joseph Smith's language culture than whatever language culture generated the plate text [which Smith translated to English]." Since Mormons can believe that the Book of Mormon is "given in English idiom of the period and locality in which the Prophet lived," they may too appreciate the pertinence of pseudobiblicism to their scripture.[51]

"Let the language of the Book speak for itself," Joseph Smith pleaded an impatient American audience in an apologia for his new Bible.[52] By taking Smith's advice, and juxtaposing the Book of Mormon with the tradition of writing in biblical style, we not only gain new insights into persistent historiographical questions pertaining to the Mormon bible; we also better understand the cultural environment that produced it and in which it thrived. Biblical language defined the Book of Mormon and placed it alongside contemporary pseudobiblical texts, which transported their narratives to America and constantly referred to the same biblical Ur-text for idioms, style, and structure. Detached from the context of the numerous other American writings in biblical style, Smith's scripture is indeed incomprehensible. One wonders how this affiliation influenced the Mormon bible's effectiveness and success: the pseudobiblical language was, after all, essentially political (and often ironic and polemic), making secular use of a sacred language. An association with this at least potentially religiously problematic language could have hampered the Book of Mormon's reception.

However, contemporaries did not deem the pseudobiblical language a form that necessarily degraded the Bible, so nor should we. Pseudobiblicism certainly revolutionized attitudes to the language of the Bible by democratizing the terms of its use. But such use did not necessarily lead to erosion of religious sentiments and sensibilities. Rather, pseudobiblicism incorporated the political into the religious, and may have deepened the hold of pious sensibilities through new epistemic modes in the lives of contemporaries. Such use of the Bible's language was also strongly associated with the quasi-religious undertaking of sanctifying America, depicting it as a chosen nation in the most staid terms. The distinct use of the biblical language, form, and style no longer merely informed early Americans of an ancient history but spawned vivid texts that referred directly to contemporaries' lives. Pseudobiblicism was an ongoing scriptural venture that complemented and fortified notions of national chosenness. By conditioning contemporaries to apply biblical language to American content, and thus to perceive their history and construct their national expectations in scriptural categories, pseudobiblical language may have helped to ameliorate readers' reactions to and digestion of the Mormon Bible.

Since Mormonism drew its followers from other Christian denominations, when Smith published his Book in 1830, potential converts were immersed in the language, narratives, metaphors, and cultural grammar of the King James Bible. But many of them must also have been familiar with the contemporary American narratives and histories presented in that universally revered language. Hence Terryl Givens's remark that Joseph Smith's linguistic and stylistic decisions attest "to a desire to build upon the aura and authority of biblicalism in order to enhance the legitimacy of his work of Christian revisionism" acquires new light.[53] The Book of Mormon's biblical language may not only have catered to audiences' need to hear prophecy in the language that was universally accepted as suitable and even necessary for divine pronouncements; it was also the textual style and mode through which his countrymen had been used to receiving and perceiving historical renditions of America for some fourscore years. Pseudobiblicism then plays an important role in understanding the reception of the Book of Mormon among its early readers, who were operating in a world that sanctioned uses of the

Bible's language that would be culturally impermissible only a few decades later (and had been acceptable for not more than a century before). At the very least, pseudobiblicism points to the extent to which the Bible provided the people of that time with a second language, and reflects their intimacy with that idiom, an intimacy the Book of Mormon surely gained from.

That the Book of Mormon was by far the most successful revelatory text of its age, and as far as we know the only such text presenting itself as the word of God to make use of biblical language, may not have been a coincidence. By the third decade of the nineteenth century Americans were conditioned to perceive and hallow their nation through the medium of Elizabethan English. They might have not found the Mormon Bible as exceptional as a modern reader might think. Its form, style, and aspiration to sanctify America had already been circulating for more than half a century in the republic's printed sphere.

Nevertheless, assessing the assertion that pseudobiblicism had actually participated in and contributed to the reception of the Book of Mormon is a daunting, not to say futile, task. As reasonable as such a hypothesis may be, the evidence is mostly circumstantial: we have few if any direct references to the pseudobiblical language by contemporary consumers of those texts, and no direct ties connecting the Book of Mormon to pseudobiblicism. However, it may be "a dog that did not bark" that demonstrates the remarkable extent to which Americans were accustomed by 1830 through years of consuming pseudobiblicism to absorbing texts about America in biblical language. Indeed, it is astonishing that although the Book of Mormon was among the most criticized, derided, and maligned texts of its age, one is hard pressed to find even a single critical remark about the Book's salient and apparently blasphemous (in the eyes of non-Mormons) use of the language of the Bible. Remarkably, early opponents of the Book of Mormon who did note Smith's use of biblical language, as critical as they might otherwise be, did *not* criticize such use. One commentator, for example, alluding to the Book of Mormon as "full of strange narratives," remarked indifferently that it was written "in the style of the scriptures," and went on halfheartedly to applaud the Book for "bearing on its face the marks of some ingenuity, and familiar acquaintance with the Bible." Lack of concern about the use of the King James Bible's language seemed to have been the norm among its detractors. Noting that the "book is a literary curiosity," another observer noticed that "the style is an affectation of the Scriptural," and went on to criticize not the use of the language in which the Book was written but the mere fact that it was "destitute of the beauties of sublimity." While some critics scoffed the Mormon book as "a ridiculous imitation of the holy scriptures and in many instances, a plagiarism upon their language," others underscored that "every page [bore] the impress of its human authorship."[54] These detractors, evidently aware of the Mormon bible's use of the language Americans were so thoroughly acquainted with through centuries of reading the Authorized Version, were little concerned by the fact that the Book of Mormon used a language that was biblical and traditionally considered sacrosanct. There is little doubt that this silence was due to decades of the incessant production and consumption of American texts written in an idiom that mobilized biblical language to describe American events. The pseudobiblical tradition seemed to have numbed American sensibilities toward the mobilization of the sacred language. By 1830 Americans willingly accepted that that language could describe not only happenings in Canaan of old but also deeds occurring, or having occurred, in the new American Canaan. By acculturating Americans to texts about America written in biblical language, the pseudobiblical tradition thus helped pave the way for the Book of Mormon.

After 1830 the almost century-old genre of public writing in biblical style began to lose its vigor. While pseudobiblical texts were still written for decades after the publication of the Book of Mormon, in the years after 1830 pseudobiblicism became notably sparse and sporadic; after 1850 hardly any such texts are to be found.[55] Pseudobiblicism suggests that we may profit from viewing the Book of Mormon as taking part in that larger biblico-American world that flourished from approximately 1770 to 1830. By doing so we may better understand the literary cosmos in which the Mormon bible was written, while at the same time gaining further insights into what made that American scripture appealing or even intelligible to contemporaries. Americans, who had been reading texts akin in important aspects to Joseph Smith's bible for many years before its publication, were thus conditioned to comprehend texts written in biblical style about America. Hence the genre of pseudobiblicism demonstrates once more, if such a demonstration is needed, how pervasive, indeed omnipresent, the Bible was in the cultural landscape of the young American republic. Americans' intimacy with the Bible is underscored through their habit of effortlessly lapsing into biblical language when discussing their past and present in prolonged and articulated texts. These pseudobiblical texts reveal much about the political and historical assumptions pervading the young American republic. As I have pointed out, however, this relentless pseudobiblical discursive mode also sheds new light on the Book of Mormon, the context in which that American bible was formed, and the cultural ecology in which it was received.

The reformed Protestant heritage, a neoclassical political culture, and a mature culture of print facilitated the rise of a unique pseudobiblical mode of representing contemporary America. By alluding to the Israelite past, to the history of God's chosen people through the use of the language in which that history was articulated, Americans did not challenge the historicity of Scripture. Rather, they invoked its authority, subjugated the meaning which was associated with the history it told, and applied it to their present. The use of biblical language was thus an effective way to merge America and the Bible, hence to pave the way to an original American bible. The tradition of writing in this "truly American spirit" thus offers a vantage point for better understanding a lost political, cultural, and intellectual early American world of biblical imagination, a world to which Joseph Smith and the Book of Mormon belonged. The unmistakable similarities and affinities between the Book of Mormon and the pseudobiblical texts thus provide a significant context for understanding the creation (or translation) and reception of the Book of Mormon, the culture of biblicism in the nineteenth century, and through that the intellectual history of the early American republic.

4
Tribes Lost and Found
Israelites in Nineteenth-Century America

In "about the year 1800" a few "respectable citizens" of Middletown, Vermont, began advertising their belief that they were "descendants of the ancient Jews." These self-proclaimed "modern Israelites," according to a historian of radical religion in New England, constituted a sectarian jumble of "divination, prophecy, and alienation." They adhered to a strict dietary regime—their own interpretation of the Mosaic law—and followed the guidance of divining rods (hence were called "rodsmen" or "rod-men"). Among their fantastic abilities, such as locating hidden treasures, the rods were believed to identify the "many people in America [who] were, unknown to themselves, Jews."[1] These self-styled neo-Israelites founded a church and were urged by the rods to rebuild the Jewish temple—a grandiose project they abandoned even before their church's ultimate collapse.

This esoteric backwoods group, all but forgotten soon after its demise, is significant not only because some of the parents of the future Mormon Church's founders were among its members. In envisioning Israelites in America in 1800, the Vermont Rodsmen indicated how Americans would recurrently weave connections between the United States and ancient Israel after the War of 1812. By the second and third decades of the nineteenth century various Americans in different contexts would transcend the metaphorical and typological exegeses whereby earlier generations merged biblical history and America. They leapt over typology and metaphor to discover actual Israelites, or their biological descendants, walking in their midst. This imparted an immediate sense of the early republic as a "biblical nation," an American Zion.

We have already seen how visions of America as a "second Israel," or readings of specific narratives of covenant, chosenness, and exodus that linked the United States with Israelite history, were standard since the Puritan migration and settlement. While such typological understandings were commonly confined to colonial New England, heightened revolutionary anxieties and a disproportionate influence of a Calvinist political culture on the new nation brought about a broad and spectacular flurry of comparisons between the young United States and biblical Israel after 1776. Such expressions, while not a strictly New England or even Congregationalist trait, were widespread, and, according to a modern scholar, part of a "consistent effort to . . . cast America as the modern Jewish nation." With the evangelical and millennial storm of the Second Great Awakening gathering after the start of the nineteenth century, the War of 1812 begot a potent and revitalized American patriotism. The combustive combination of millenarianism and intense wartime patriotism enabled public speakers to further deepen the links between the early American republic and biblical Israel. John McDonald's *Isaiah's Message to the American Nation: A New Translation of Isaiah, Chapter XVIII* (1814) may have been the most striking example of the power of this mixture. In an extraordinary exegesis of the Hebraic prophet Isaiah's obscure divination regarding a "distant country," McDonald interpreted the prophecy by "comparing it with America." He was in no doubt that Isaiah described "the picture of our own country, painted by our own God," concluding decisively that the "the nation addressed [in Isaiah 18] must be America."[2] While McDonald's *Message to the American Nation* stood out as an unabashedly patriotic and nationalistic reading of the Bible, it manifests a prevalent mindset that habitually linked America to the Bible through typological exegesis. Such understandings of the United States through a biblical lens, whereby the Israelite nation foreshadowed the United States, which in turn fulfilled its biblical type, bore the clear and time-proven marks of Christian typology.

Contemporaries relied on a millennia-long exegetical tradition, namely typology, which was originally developed as an interpretive tool to connect the Old and New Testaments. Now, however, political typologists mobilized this interpretational mode to connect the Old Testament with the American republic. Such appellations were typological in essence, perceiving the relation of an early promise (biblical Israel) and its fulfillment (the United States), in which America was represented not as Israel but as the *second* Israel or God's *new* Israel. Such typological descriptions and ascriptions made clear that the connection between the two Israels was in its essence metaphorical, not ontological or "real"; in this view the two nations may have corresponded through the historical roles they played, but the essence of that correspondence was symbolic, not necessarily one that was tangible or obvious.

A new mode of linking the young United States to the Bible, less conventionally exegetical and not metaphorical (or typological), became discernible as the nineteenth century progressed. Various Americans then transcended typology as they began identifying people in their midst, or fashioning themselves, as actual Israelites or their biological descendants. Seen in this light, the aforementioned Rodsmen were extraordinary only in appearing a decade or two before other Americans began engaging in similar perceptions. The Rodsmen may have been the first nineteenth-century Americans directly to link themselves to biblical Israelites; they were certainly not the last.

Nor, of course, were the Rodsmen the first to imagine Israelites in the New World. Almost from the moment of the encounter between Europeans and New World natives, the former began speculating that they had identified in the people they mistakenly called "Indians" the descendants of nations that once were part of Western history, and then were lost. The discovery of the New World consequently inspired a whole series of questions and debates on the origins, nature, and history of American natives, as Europeans were forced to incorporate the American continents and their dwellers into their cosmologies. A major difficulty stemmed from the fact that the natives, who were not accounted for in any of the hegemonic European canons, namely the Bible and the classics, posed, in the words of Anthony Grafton, "a hard question to scholars who believed that the world had a seamless and coherent history." According to the historian Steven Conn, "the very existence of Native Americans posed fundamental challenges to the way Euro-Americans understood the world." Difficulties pertaining to the identity, history, and indeed humanity of aboriginal Americans would preoccupy Westerners as debating, adapting, and negotiating these and other pertinent questions (not to mention their satisfactory resolution) would go on for more than three centuries.[3]

To locate American natives in their worldview, Europeans classified a wide spectrum of different aboriginal peoples as "Indians," thereby categorizing a "variety of cultures and societies as a single entity for the purposes of description and analysis." Yet even as they played down Indians' social and cultural diversity, even ignored it altogether, Europeans and Euro-Americans had to fall back on their trusted intellectual traditions to make sense of the aborigines' unnerving presence. The tragic history of the Encounter and its disastrous legacy, which is a story of disease, cultural dislocation, and war, should not obscure the fact that some of the early attempts to intellectually incorporate Indians flattered the natives in Europeans' minds. Many commentators constructed Amerindians, for example, in light of the most highly regarded historical positions of the West's culture, namely as classical Greeks and Romans. From the early days of the discovery of the Americas, Europeans commented on the perceived similarities between the classical and Amerindian civilizations. Their physical stature, combativeness, independence, and oratory contributed to the idea that Indians somehow reincarnated, or were actually related to, the revered Mediterranean ancients.[4]

The belief that all human beings were the descendants of Adam and Eve and the seven survivors of the Flood guided most Europeans in their attempt to incorporate Indians into their cosmologies. Hence hypothesizing that Amerindians were outcast Israelites, the remnants of the Lost Ten Tribes, became one of the most, arguably the most, popular of the recurrent attempts to reinsert Indians into world history. The Old Testament told the history of the formation of the Israelite nation out of twelve tribes whose respective progenitors were the twelve sons of the Patriarch Jacob. Under the reign of Rehoboam the united Israelite kingdom of David, Rehoboam's grandfather, split into two rival states, the Kingdom of Judah, comprising the tribes of Judah and Benjamin, and the northern Kingdom of Israel, which consisted of the remaining ten tribes. The Bible narrates the short and contentious simultaneous existence of the two Israelite polities, which ended when Assyria conquered the kingdom of Israel in 722 B.C. and deported its entire population, while leaving intact the southern kingdom of Judah. The ten tribes of Israel, never to be heard of again, were henceforth "lost," becoming in Jewish, and later in Christian, memory the Ten Lost Tribes.[5]

The myth of the Ten Lost Tribes was forged in a world in which contacts between the Near East and Western Europe hardly existed, and was sustained by a long succession of medieval travelers who explored exotic and unknown countries and nations to the south and east of Europe, and reportedly "found" the tribes time and again. A succession of Jewish travelers, from Eldad the Danite in the ninth century A.D. to Benjamin of Tudela in the twelfth and Abraham ben Mordecai Farissol in the fifteenth, kept the interest in the lost Israelite tribes alive throughout the Middle Ages down to the Age of Discovery. Hence it is understandable that speculation about the Jewish origins of the American Indians began immediately upon contact, as sixteenth- and seventeenth-century Europeans, still ardent believers in the revelatory and infallible truth of Scriptures, found it inconceivable that the Indians could not be apprehended through Biblical accounts, and that the

Ten Tribes could not be located upon this earth. If the Indians were indeed remnants of the Lost Tribes, Europeans could solve two most distressing puzzles: the location of the descendants of the tribes would be ascertained, and the identity and history of the indigenous inhabitants of the New World would be revealed.

Spanish explorers and theologians were the first to debate the possibility of the Jewish origin of the Indians, always indicating "that the solution had to involve tracing them back to their biblical roots." These theories received a considerable boost when Antonio de Montezinos, a Portuguese traveler, convinced the Dutch rabbi Menasseh Ben-Israel sometime in the 1640s that the groups he found on his tour of South America might be lost Jews. Ben-Israel responded by producing in England a tract titled *The Hope of Israel* (1650), eventually published in Spanish, Latin, Hebrew, English, and Dutch, elaborating the possible Jewish origins of the American Indians. Despite his caution, according to the historian Richard Popkin, Ben-Israel became "the official spokesman" for the millenarian implications of the Jewish-Indian theory: the reappearance of the Jews, many thereafter believed, signaled the approaching end of days.[6]

In the seventeenth-century British American colonies, the theory of the Indians' Israelite origins attracted men such as Roger Williams, who was acquainted firsthand with native culture. But it was a Norfolk pastor, Thomas Thorowgood (1600–1669), who stressed that the Indians were "of that race." Thorowgood, who was initially skeptical of the Israelite-Indian connection, embarked on a fifteen-year study of Scripture, history, geography, and ethnography to establish whether the Indians were actually of Israelite origins. He published a treatise in the same year as Ben-Israel's book appeared, titled *Jewes in America; or, Probabilities that the Americans are of That Race* (1660). Thorowgood asserted that the American Indians were not native to the New World but had arrived there after the siege of Jerusalem in A.D. 70. The latest drama of English colonization and Puritan settlement was part of a larger providential scheme of the (re)conversion of the Indians. Thus the Israelite-Indian theory in Anglophone circles was "truly launched."[7]

Later British travelers and settlers, famous among whom was William Penn, found it easy to perceive the Indians as lost Hebrews now found. But only on the eve of American Independence did that paradigm receive its most thorough and influential treatment with James Adair's *The History of the American Indians* (1775). Adair, an Irish trader who lived "for forty years" among Indians, as he self-advertised in his book, was motivated by an intellectual impetus starkly different from his religion-driven and millenarian seventeenth-century predecessors. Adair, a child of the Enlightenment, as is evident from every page of the long and exhaustive *History*, and a protoanthropologist by inclination, provided a rational, methodical, and perceptive analysis of Indian culture, language, and practices. If some of his contemporaries were at once aware of the methodological shortcomings and unsubstantiated conclusions of his investigation, they acknowledged, like Thomas Jefferson, his vast knowledge and virtues as a "a man of learning" and a "self-taught Hebraist."[8]

Adair's thorough analysis, his years of experience with Indians, and his systematic observations led him to an unequivocal conclusion: the Indians were "lineally descended from the Israelites." But unlike his precursors Adair seemed almost reluctant to conclude that Indians were descended of biblical Hebrews; he posited this as if persuaded only by his cumulative and incontrovertible evidence, which he tirelessly presented in hundreds of meticulously argued pages. He attempted to prove the Indians' Israelite lineage by closely examining, as the drawn out subtitle of *The History of the American Indians* attests, the "origin, language, manners, religious and civil customs, laws, form of government, punishments, conduct in war and domestic life, their habits, diet, agriculture, manufactures, diseases and method of cure, and other particulars." To complete his encyclopedic endeavor and prove the Israelite-Indian connection Adair divided his book into twenty-three chapters, analyzing a wide variety of parameters and categories of the theory. To take just a few examples, Adair underscored the similarity of the division of Israelites and Indians into tribes, with presiding Judges/chiefs, where "each tribe forms a little community within the nation"; the fact that Indians, like the Israelites of old, held theocratic notions, both believing the deity to be the "immediate head of their state"; their perceived physical likeness to Jews; the fact that Indians "count the Time after the manner of the Jews"; and the "striking resemblances of Indian and Israelite tithes." Perhaps more than anything else, Adair, like Americans in following decades, was impressed by the perceived linguistic similarities between the Hebrew and Indian vernaculars, a point that made his case apparently unassailable: "The Indian Language, and dialects appear to have the very idiom and genius of the Hebrew. Their words and sentences are expressive, concise, emphatical, sonorous, and bold—and often, both in letters and signification, synonymous with the Hebrew language." What particularly struck him was that when the Indians invoked their deity, "the notes together compose their sacred, mysterious name,

Y-O-He-Wah," which seems to be the exact "Hebrew pronunciation of the divine essential name, יהוה, JEHOVA."[9]

As a gentleman-scientist, Adair understood that for his broad thesis to be persuasive he could not depend on a single argument or finding. He warned his readers that the many segments and layers of his reasoning "must not be partially separated." "Let them be distinctly considered," he urged, and "then unite them together, and view their force collectively." Once the masses of data he provided and analyzed were collated and viewed together, Adair was certain that his conclusion was undeniable: the American Indians were, in fact, descendants of the Israelite Lost Tribes.[10]

Adair transformed and shaped the terms of the discourse on the origins of the American Indians for years to come. Only a decade before the publication of *The History of the American Indians*, a commentator could state that the Indians of North America "appear to have a very little idea of God" and "seem to pay some religious homage to the sun and moon"; later, no one could ignore Adair's appealing arguments in chapters such as Their Worship of Jehova (chap. 2), Their Notions of a Theocracy (chap. 3), and Their Belief in the Ministration of Angels (chap. 4), sections that were building blocks in his representation of Indians as the progeny of biblical Israelites.[11] Adair's Enlightened treatise was substantial and erudite enough to spark the imagination of America's intellectual elites and premier political minds. Less than a decade after the publication of Adair's treatises and now in the context of the United States "elevated to glory and honor," Ezra Stiles, president of Yale College, speculated on the biblical origins of the American Indians. In an early-nineteenth-century conversation with the explorer Meriwether Lewis, Thomas Jefferson speculated that lost Israelites could be out roaming the plains of the West (although they agreed that they were more likely wandering Welshmen). The physician and gentleman scientist Benjamin Rush distributed to the Corps of Discovery a questionnaire probing for a possible "affinity between [Indians'] religious Ceremonies & those of the Jews."[12]

By the early years of the nineteenth century, however, Thomas Jefferson and other leading American intellectuals had revealed many of Adair's methodological fallacies. Adair was not an impartial scholar, Jefferson pointed out in a letter to John Adams, but "self-taught" and—even worse—"a trader." Most damagingly in the deist Jefferson's opinion he was "a strong religionist, and of as sound a mind as Don Quixote in whatever did not touch his religious chivalry." This disparaging characterization of Adair as a well-intentioned yet biased and amateurish observer, ingenuously gullible, was most damaging to his "proof" of the Israelite-Indian connection. Adair's preconceived ideas, according to Jefferson, caused him to render unsubstantiated generalizations, for example, "the hundred languages of America, differing fundamentally every one from every other, as much as Greek from Gothic, have yet all one common prototype," namely Hebrew. Although Adair's "book contains a great deal of real instruction on its subject," Jefferson noted, the casual reader was required "to be constantly on his guard against the wonderful obliquities of his theory." The third president of the United States reminded the second, almost four decades after *The History*'s original publication, that Adair was "determined to see what he wished to see in every object."[13] Nevertheless, as with Jefferson's famous miscalculation of the Unitarian direction in which religion in America was headed, his dismissal of Adair's conclusions in no way predicted the nature of the Indian-Israelite theory's future proliferation in the United States. On the contrary, later "strong religionists" would elaborate Adair's theory, and its influence on the reemergence of the discourse of the origins of American Indians after the War of 1812 was enormous. These later partisans brought the theory up to date, however, with the heightened evangelical sentiments of the Second Great Awakening.

Adair proved essential in decades to come for the American discussion of the Israelite origins of Indians. He also emerged as basically different from his antebellum successors: misguided and flawed as it may have been, in the heyday of the European Enlightenment, Adair's book clearly joined in that great European project of reasoned science. In doing so, it left behind the seventeenth-century millenarian impulses of the discourse that followed the publication of Ben-Israel's tract. It also differed fundamentally from the evangelical American patriotism of those who followed his lead in ascribing biblical lineage to Amerindians. While future commentators would return time and again to Adair's rich observations and conclusions, their presumptions diverged sharply from those of the Enlightenment. Rather, Adair's nineteenth-century American followers promoted his arguments and theses in the context of the surging evangelical Christianity of the Second Great Awakening and its particular sensibilities. Adair set the crucial parameters for the ways Americans would intellectually construct Indians throughout the first half of the nineteenth century, but it was left to his followers to set the mode, tone, and implications of that discussion.

Only a handful of early republic authors were responsible for developing and reviving the discussion about the Israelite origins of the Indians in the nineteenth century, but the ensuing debate was in no sense confined to a limited number of intellectuals. The possibility that American Indians were descendants of the biblical Israelites seems to have sparked the imagination of contemporaries and come to occupy a distinguished place in public discourse during a formative period of the American national and religious cultures. Modern historians have noted that speculation about a Hebrew-Indian connection in America belonged to a centuries-old tradition of searching for the Lost Tribes of Israel and returning them to history.[14] Yet the lively discourse on this matter that emerged in the early American republic stands out as a distinctly American chapter in this prolonged discussion. With its particular accents and contexts, this hitherto unfamiliar episode deepens our understanding of various issues in the history of the early United States, from those pertaining to an emerging American nationalism and the role of the Bible in the American national culture to the conflicted attitudes toward American Natives.

The Indians baffled white Americans of the early republic, as they had perplexed Adair's eighteenth-century contemporaries. As a commentator put it as late as in 1829, "It is remarkable that with the opportunities of more than two centuries to become acquainted with the Aborigines of our country, their character and condition should at all times have been so imperfectly understood by us."[15] Not surprisingly, when Elias Boudinot (1741–1821) wrote a book about the Hebrew-Indian connection more than forty years after Adair's *History*, he still relied heavily on the latter's observations and conclusion.

In his treatise *A Star in the West* (1816) Boudinot analyzed the Hebrew ancestry of the American Indians; in the event, the resulting book single-handedly reignited and remained central to a prolonged and remarkable discussion of the Indian theory in the early United States. With the conclusion of the War of 1812 and the opening of new western lands for white settlement, the subsequent renewed and intensified friction with Indians reinserted the Natives into Americans' consciousness. Westward expansion, as the historian Nicholas Guyatt points out, forced white Americans to engage a nonwhite population and to confront questions about their role in history.[16] The remarkable influence of *A Star in the West*, perhaps even its very conception, thus owed nothing to the accidental rediscovery of Adair's dissertation. Boudinot reacted to the now pressing "Indian question" as well as to the murky mix of the American state reasserting itself in the West, the American nationalist sentiment working itself out with the conclusion of what we have come to understand as a "second war of independence" with Britain, and to the intense evangelicalism of the Second Great Awakening, which was already in full swing.

By the time that Boudinot published *A Star in the West* he was already a man of high repute, a New Jersey delegate to the Continental Congress and a former president of that body, a U.S. congressman, the first director of the United States Mint, and a founder and first president of the American Bible Society. He was also a seasoned conservative, frightened after the Revolution of 1800 by the rising popularity of Deism. Boudinot had published two earlier works, *The Age of Revelation* (1801) and *The Second Advent* (1815), which were aimed to counter the secularism and Enlightened skepticism advertised by Thomas Paine's *Age of Reason* and more generally associated with Thomas Jefferson.[17] Hence, by the time the staunch Federalist published his latest tract, Boudinot, like many of his partisans, was disheartened by his party's collapse and the direction in which the republic he had helped create was headed. The glaring providential confidence of *A Star in the West* thus addressed Boudinot's political anxieties by reinserting the United States into the providential plan.

A Star in the West resembled Adair's treatise in many respects, including its argument and conception, deliberately borrowing many of Adair's theses and wordings. Like Adair, Boudinot evinced much sympathy for the Indians, the "unhappy children of misfortune" upon which "society has advanced … like a many-headed monster," and wished to prove them descendants of the Israelites. Yet crucial differences lay behind the superficial similarities of the two works: while Adair engaged in an Enlightened, protoscientific venture, Boudinot was consciously theologically driven, less interested in solving the question of the Indians' identity than thrilled to find in their presence in America elucidation of that country's role in redemptive history. The book's title itself alludes to the Star of the East, which according to the Gospel of Matthew arose to herald Jesus' birth; its subtitle, *A Humble Attempt to Discover the Long Lost Tribes of Israel, Preparatory to their Return to Their Beloved City, Jerusalem*, at once illumined the difference between Adair's and Boudinot's approaches: Boudinot, who had already become convinced of the apocalyptic meaning of the revolution in France two decades before publishing *The Star in the West*, believed that uncovering the true Hebraic identity of the Indians would lead to another kind of unveiling, namely to the apocalypse of the Book of Revelation.[18] The New American Israel would have, according to Boudinot, a leading role in the latter-day apocalypse.

A Star in the West was thus driven not by intellectual curiosity about the origin of indigenous Americans but by an attempt to uncover the fate of the Lost Tribes, which, Boudinot was convinced, "must be some where on our earth, answerable to the north and the west of Jerusalem." He was certain that all signs came from "a serious consideration of all the foregoing circumstances," and pointed out that the Lost Tribes were currently located in "the late discovered continent of America." Then followed a lengthy and "strict enquiry into the following particulars" of the similarities of the Israelites and the Indians along Adair's lines: taking his example, Boudinot found too much similarity to be accidental in the Indians' and Israelites' "language. Their received traditions. Their established customs and habits. Their known religious rites and ceremonies. And lastly, their public worship and religious opinions and prejudices."[19]

Many of Boudinot's arguments and conclusions repeated Adair's, often verbatim. To take two random examples, he asserted, like Adair, that "as the Israelites were divided into tribes, and had a chief over them . . . so the Indian nations are universally divided into tribes, under a sachem or king, chosen by the people from the wisest and bravest among them"; and "they reckon time after the manner of the Hebrews." To conclude the comprehensive tract, after meticulously covering topics ranging across political leadership, theology, linguistics, and nomenclature, Boudinot was poised for a final stroke that would settle the question of Indian origins once and for all. He presented his readers with a hypothetical situation: "Were a people to be found, with demonstrative evidence that their descent was from [the biblical Patriarch] Jacob," how would we expect those lost Israelites to appear after the millennia that passed since their disappearance? It could hardly be expected that "at this time . . . their languages, manners, customs and habits, with their religious rites, should discover greater similarity to those of the ancient Jews and of their divine law . . . than the present nations of American Indians have done."[20]

Boudinot's conclusion was not meant to satisfy any curiosity about the origins of the "people without history." Strikingly, his determination of the Israelite lineage of American Indians was a mere pretext to prove why "God has raised up these United States in these latter days." It was, Boudinot was certain, "for the very purpose of accomplishing his will in bringing his beloved [American] people to their own land," the New Canaan, in which they may, "under God, be called to act a great part in this wonderful and interesting drama." Providential history had wonderfully raised America, God's New

Israel, in the land in which lost biblical Israelites, a people who had forgotten their own history and lost their unique identity, now resided.[21]

Boudinot's treatise transformed the American biblical imagination, in itself reviving the discussion on the possibility of the Indians being of Israelite descent. After a four-decade hiatus following the publication of Adair's treatise in 1775, *A Star in the West* sparked an intense and evangelically accented debate on the Israelite origins of American Indians and thus more broadly on the connection of the United States to the Bible. *A Star in the West*, and the reaction it provoked, reflected the changes that the American intellectual climate had endured since Adair's *History* was published in 1775: no longer a colonial backwater in a world of neoclassical decorum, the young and independent United States was experiencing unprecedented waves of evangelization with a still powerful predilection for the Old Testament, a movement later called the Second Great Awakening. Boudinot's observations reflected a worldview far different from Adair's, one which responded to the revolutionary historical events and changes since Adair had published *The History*. The conceptual transformation wrought by the American Revolution was evident in Boudinot's observations: the Indians were "perfect republicans," who, like the Americans of the early republic (at least as they liked to think about themselves), "admit of no inequality among them." Yet Boudinot's book not only reflected change, but also, more important, revived and altered the understanding of the nexus of Indians, America, and the Bible.[22]

In 1789, some three decades before the publication of *A Star in the West*, a newspaper article titled "A Few Observations on the Western and Indians" asked outright "from whence the Savages, who first peopled America, derived their origin." Characteristically, the answer in the Enlightened intellectual climate of the late eighteenth century was not found in a millennial or national framework. "It appears to me probable," the author wrote, "that the southern Indians were of Carthaginian original [sic]," while "the northern and western Indians, I believe to be of entirely different extraction and descended either from the ten tribes of Israel carried away by Salmanezer into captivity, and planted in the region . . . or descended from those nations with whom they lived." To explain the discrepancy between what seemed the advanced civilization of "southern" Indians, namely those of South and Central America, and the "loss of civilization" by the Indians of North America, "Lucius" invoked the supposedly "wandering position" of the Israelites (hence of the Indians of North America). This account may have differed on some points from Adair's (for example, distinguishing the origins of northern and southern Indians), but it was not yet settled on the Israelite origin of all American aboriginals. As if to highlight this point, the author's discussion of southern ("Carthaginian") Indians was much longer than that of the northern and "Israelite" nations, which the author deemed "sunk" in "low . . . barbarism."[23] Although this speculative piece was published after the creation of the republic and the ratification of the Constitution, it demonstrated neither Boudinot's patriotism (praising, for example, Indians who were not under the United States' jurisdiction) nor the millenarian implication of the Indians' origins (paying more attention to the non-Israelite Amerindians).

Other examples that predated *A Star in the West* demonstrate further how Boudinot's thesis altered the discourse on the Indians' origins. A writer for the *Boston Patriot* speculated in 1810 on the whereabouts of the Ten Lost Tribes, concluding that they inhabited New England. Unlike Boudinot, however, the Bostonian's conclusion was not providential, nor did it connect the Lost Tribes with American Indians. Rather, that comment was a spiteful and anti-Semitic diatribe against moneylenders, a "numerous class and very mysterious people" in Boston who by "Jewing" their compatriots "betray . . . striking marks of resemblance to the children of Israel"; "this recent race of people, distinguished by those striking peculiarities," must have been, the commentator concluded, "the lost Israelites of Israel."[24] Other elaborate works, such as David Tappan's *Lectures on Jewish Antiquities* (1807), did not refer once to the Lost Tribes of Israel, to say nothing of an Indian connection; such silences would be virtually inconceivable in similar works after 1816. Another "dog that did not bark" was John McDonald's aforementioned *Isaiah's Message to the American Nation* (1814), which connected biblical prophecies and the United States and appeared just two years before *A Star in the West*. Although *Isaiah's Message to the American Nation* reflects the heightened providential sensibilities of the War of 1812 years related to the American nation, McDonald's treatise did not so much as mention the Israelite-Indian connection; this too would be hard to conceive only a few years later, when speculation regarding the Israelite origins of the Indians became prevalent with the publication of *A Star in the West*.

Boudinot's restatement—and significant alteration—of the theory of the Israelite origins of the Indians obviously struck a cultural chord: for at least two decades following the publication of *A Star in the West*, Americans hotly debated that possibility. In so doing they transcended the mere question of the Indians' origins (which Adair seemed to have satisfactorily proved), and focused instead on their implications, on the significance of such connections between America and the Bible, and on the significance of such connections for the potential role of the young United States in world history. The discourse initiated by *A Star in the West* was thus about possible links (or the lack thereof) between the United States, a young polity in the New World, and the biblical history of ancient Israel. This nexus of past and present, of an indigenous people and a world unaccounted for in traditional sources of authoritative knowledge, of a nascent American nationalism and the history of ancient Israel, entailed after the publication of *A Star in the West* in 1816 repeated attempts to reinterpret and reconnect the Old Testament and the United States.

Up to the conclusion of the War of 1812, Americans could remain neutral on the possibility of Indians being of Israelite extraction, but with the appearance of *A Star in the West* in 1816 that dramatically changed. The comments elicited by Boudinot's restatement of the Israelite-Indian theory in public discussion attest to the enthusiasm it sparked. A reviewer in the *New York Courier*, for example, commenting on the "ingenious production of Dr. Boudinot's," painted the Indians (that is, the Israelites) as biblical forerunners of the Pilgrim Fathers, fleeing their captivity "to free themselves from an oppressive government and idolatrous neighbors, removed in search of a country where they might enjoy unmolested [the] civil liberty and the religion of their ancestors . . . [until they] arrived finally in America, which they gradually overspread and peopled." From these biblical-era Hebrews, the reviewer concluded, "descended the Indian tribes which were found here on the discovery of this continent by the Europeans."[25] Like Boudinot, his followers and proponents were not content with demonstrating the connection between the American Indians with biblical Hebrews, as Adair had been. They revealed the significance and meaning of a biblical-era migration of Israelites-cum-Indians to the New World, which they could represent, as we have just seen, as a foretelling of the Pilgrim Fathers' ocean crossing. The ties binding Indians and Israelites, the United States and the Bible, were no longer deemed a scientific curiosity; they assumed a new and deeper significance for Americans of the early republic as they contemplated and worked out the meaning of the reassertion of their nationhood after the War of 1812.

A Star in the West awoke a dormant curiosity about Indian origins that reached even beyond America. Soon after the book's publication an English Jew, hearing about "the affinity between the Indians tribes of North America and the tribes of Israel," wished to interview the "six Indian warriors visiting England" who had sailed from Boston to London. As we will see later in this chapter, this was far from the most noteworthy reaction of a Jew to the discourse on the Jewish-Indian theory. Yet most reactions—and the most enthusiastic (and idiosyncratic) of them—came not from Jews but from Protestant commentators. Some of them could at once stand Boudinot's underlying benevolence toward Indians on its head. An author in the *Concord Observer* not only believed that American Indians descended from the Israelites but specifically concluded that they "descended from the tribe of Dan," one of the ten tribes lost in the exile. Taking the Indians' Hebraic lineage as a given, this author was able to discern such minutiae from his comparison of Dan's negative description in Scripture to his own assessment the character of American Natives. The author's main source for the uncomplimentary identification was Genesis 49:17: "Dan shall be a serpent by the way, an adder in the path, that biteth the horse's heels." Did not this description "exactly correspond with the character of the Indians"? It was "well known that they have exhibited more of the crafty cunning of the serpent, in many respects, than any other nation known in history.... And in particular has their serpentine subtlety been manifested, in their modes of warfare. How common has it been for them to display the nature of the adder in the path, by lying in ambush, and shooting the horse or his rider, so that he hath fallen backward?" There were other reasons for the uncanny identification: Indians "like ravenous lions, rushed upon some village in the night season, and having murdered a number of the inhabitants, and burnt their dwellings, they have retreated swiftly to the wilderness," conduct matching Dan's description in Deuteronomy 33:22, as "a lion's whelp: he shall leap from Bashan." Furthermore, the tribe of Dan, allegedly like its American Indian progeny, was "the first which fell away to idolatry, from among the descendants of Israel."[26] This utter distortion of Boudinot's benign attitude to the Indians as Israelites, and of his sympathy and empathy for them in their misery, demonstrates the liberty contemporaries allowed themselves once they began imagining their neighboring American Indians as ancient Israelites.

Boudinot's theory did not, however, enjoy wall-to-wall consensus. Some, like a writer for the *New York Columbian*, criticized the lack of originality in Boudinot's work, as "many other writers," probably meaning Adair, "have suggested and sustained the same opinion." Others censured Boudinot's ideas. A *Rutland Herald* correspondent pointed out that if indeed "the Cherokees have some laws and customs, both civil and religious, resembling the laws and the regulations of the Jews" this by no means proved "that the American Indians are descended from the Jews." Another critic stated that whether Boudinot's hypotheses, "first, that the Indians of North America are descended of the lost Ten Tribes of Israel; or, secondly, that they, with their brethren, will be gathered together in the country of their ancestors," were well founded "must be left for time to shew." That author, who significantly did not participate in Boudinot's millenarian zeal, was "inclined to think . . . that the [biblical] prophecies speak [merely] figuratively" of the Jews gathering in their homeland. He was not persuaded by Boudinot's meticulous argumentation, and concluded that the Indians' being "totally ignorant of their history" while "their former religious rites have been so long . . . forgotten" meant that they could not have been connected to the Lost Tribes. This author could not "find the features of the Jew" in American Indians.[27]

It becomes clear how a millenarian predisposition and the belief in the literal restoration of the Jews to Israel (or rather their presence in the New Israel) were crucial for accepting the idea of Indians as Israelites. These assumptions (or rather presumptions) reinforced each other: viewing the Indians as long-lost Israelites in turn bolstered the belief in a millenarian restoration (as well as in the importance of America in the unfolding of the historical process), and vice versa. In the words of one commentator, "if it be a fact that the native Americans are the tribes of Israel, new evidence is hence furnished of the divinity of our holy scriptures."[28] Omit one of these assumptions, on the other hand, as the case of the aforementioned writer in the *New York Columbian* demonstrates, and the notion of an Israelite-Indian connection or a literal restoration becomes much less convincing.

The reverend Ethan Smith of Poultney, Vermont, was another vocal and important advocate of literal restoration and Indian-Hebraic origins. Smith's *View of the Hebrews* (1823), a long dissertation on the Israelite origin of the Indians and its millenarian significance, became popular in its own right; it was further popularized by Josiah Priest, an uneducated harness maker and successful writer, who announced in the fifth edition of his *American Antiquities and Discoveries in the West* (1833), a book that reproduced extensive verbatim portions of *A View of the Hebrews*, that he had sold twenty-two thousand copies in thirty months, a staggering number for the early republic. Smith's work drew heavily on the writings of Adair and Boudinot, two authors he deemed "great and good men most artlessly uniting in the leading facts [first] stated by Mr. Adair." The pages of *A View of the Hebrews* abound with the now familiar ideas and patterns found in Boudinot's work, from deep perplexity about the disappearance of the tribes of Israel, to the belief that "the Jews are to be restored to Palestine . . . and that the ten tribes of Israel will there be united with them." Ethan Smith even made use of counterfactual logic reminiscent of Boudinot's, and asked his readers to "suppose you find" the "striking" similarities between Indians and Hebrews that he enumerated at length over hundreds of pages. The deep correspondences and similarities between Israelites and "such a people [as Indians], without books or letters, but wholly in a savage state, in a region of the world lately discovered," seemed astonishing. Could you, Smith asked, "hesitate to say you had found the ten tribes of Israel?" Smith could not. He declared his certainty even more forcefully than Boudinot, asserting that the Indians' Hebrew lineage is "more than mere supposition"; Smith firmly believed he had "ascertained [those connections] as facts, with substantial evidence."[29]

Yet Smith's treatise was not a simple restatement of earlier views; he added a significant element to the Hebraic-Indian theory concerning the United States' redemptive role. Referring to the various biblical prophecies pertaining to the restoration of Israel "from far countries, from the west of the going down of the sun . . . their being brought in ships from far, making their way in the sea, their path in the mighty waters," Smith was convinced that the ten tribes would reach the land of Canaan from America. But he also understood the prophecies to imply the "agency by which such a restoration shall be effected." That providential agency would be accomplished by the United States of America, already a half century old confederacy now rapidly spreading westward across the land harboring the Indian remnants of Israel. A restorational vehicle would be "naturally found" among "a great Christian people, providentially planted on the very ground occupied by the outcast tribes of Israel in their long exilement." And who, Smith wondered, "are so happily remote from the bloody scenes of Europe in the last day" as America? He celebrated this redemptive role, "so noble a work" that was assigned "to our nation"; certainly, "no other nation on earth can, from its national character, the excellency of its government, and its local situation, lay so good a claim to this inspired characteristic." Nation and millennium, the United States and biblical prophecies, were intertwined through the belief in the Indians' Israelite origin, the approaching End of Days, and the crucial role of the United States in the theohistorical process.[30]

Praise for *A View of the Hebrews*, which was deemed a "highly interesting work" that would secure "an unusual degree of popularity," was not slow to come. Even readers who had "animadversions" and found it hard to believe that the Indians were of Israelite extraction, speculated that since similarities between the language and traditions of Indians and Hebrews certainly existed, they might have stemmed from aboriginal "heathens" who interacted with migrating Israelites. Critical readers could still agree in the heyday of the Second Great Awakening that "our own country is the land addressed by the prophet Isaiah, as destined to bear a leading part in this restoration." Many who supported Boudinot's and Smith's ideas argued that "unless we place [Indians] in the wilds of America" the Lost Ten Tribes "are not to be found"; "they disappeared from the civilized world, and went somewhere" and "the habitable earth has been, to a very great extent, explored," so America seemed the obvious, if not the inevitable, place in which to locate their remnants.[31]

Other sympathizers, awakened by the debate that started after Smith published *A View of the Hebrews*, had to confront a nagging problem that detractors of the Hebrew Indian theory repeatedly raised, namely how the Indians could lose not only their historical identity but also their acquaintance with mechanical arts and writing that were known to the biblical Hebrews. They speculated lengthily, conjecturing that "finding themselves in a vast wild, filled with the most inviting game, soliciting them to the chase, most [American Israelites] probably fell into a wandering hunting life, and soon became habituated and attached to the employment." This materialist explanation, which went against contemporary beliefs in historical progress, made perfect sense to Christians who believed that the kingdom of Israel (as opposed to the more pious Judea) was punished for its sins of idolatry and thus "became an *out cast*, that no man cared for; were lost from the knowledge of the world."[32] Now, with the millennium approaching and their identity rediscovered, they were about to return to history.

As popular as Ethan Smith's *A View of the Hebrews* may have been in the years after its publication in 1823, it is today obscure and all but forgotten. This cannot be said about another text involving biblical Hebrews in America, published not far from Poultney, seven years after Ethan Smith's. In 1830, after receiving a series of revelations as a teenager, Joseph Smith, Jr., of Palmyra, New York, published the Book of Mormon, a scriptural text that recorded the history of an ancient Israelite race that migrated to America in the sixth century B.C. As we have seen in the preceding chapter, historians within and without Mormondom have long attempted to contextualize Joseph Smith and his writing, and consequently, as a Mormon historian points out, scholars have been increasingly aware of the influence of Joseph Smith's cultural environment on the Book of Mormon.[33] By continuing to contextualize the Book of Mormon in light of the public discussion about the Hebraic origins of the American Indians, we may better understand the potency and dynamism of the culture of Hebraism with respect to the emergence (and early appeal) of the Mormon Bible.

The Book of Mormon joined and captured contemporary American biblicism and its predilection for the Old Testament. Joseph Smith, who was even "more enamored of the Hebrew Bible than most of his Protestant contemporaries," was a product of and mirrored the keen religiosity and biblicism of the Second Great Awakening. It comes as little surprise that the Book of Mormon, whether Smith was its author or merely a scribe of the word of God, manifested Old Testament idioms, phrases, and language, and indeed described America as a New World Zion, "a land which is choice above all other lands" (1 Nephi 2:20). Yet the Book of Mormon, a strikingly original text in many aspects, further demonstrated its originality when it departed from mainstream contemporary understandings of the Israelite origins of the American Indians in two significant respects. Like common speculation about the Hebrew-Indian connection, the Book of Mormon describes its protagonists as biblical-era people who crossed the ocean to America, but that were *not* members of the Lost Tribes; indeed, not all the biblical-era migrants that the Book of Mormon portrayed are Israelites at all. In an 1842 letter from Joseph Smith to John Wentworth, the editor of the *Chicago Democrat*, the Prophet reiterated his view, with which readers of the Book of Mormon were already acquainted, that "America in ancient times has been inhabited by two distinct races of people." The first people, the Jaredites, were not of Hebrew extraction; they were pre-Abrahamic, so they could not be Israelite, and "came [to America] directly from the tower of Babel." The other race, however, "came directly from the city of Jerusalem, about six hundred years before Christ"; that meant that they crossed the ocean more than a century after the ten tribes were exiled and lost to history! Although the people of that second migration to America were not affiliated with the Lost Tribes, they were, according to Smith, "principally Israelites, of the descendants of Joseph. The Jaredites [the pre-Abrahamic earlier migrants] were destroyed about the time when the Israelites came from Jerusalem, who succeeded them" in inheriting the American continent.[34]

The novelty of this narrative of different races and nations of biblical peoples clashing in the New World must have struck contemporaries who were accustomed to associating Indians with the Lost Tribes. The end of the story in the Book of Mormon sounded more familiar, however: "The principal nation of the second [Israelite] race fell in battle towards the close of the fourth century," and Smith's letter revealed what the Book of Mormon only implied: "The remnant are the Indians that now inhabit this country."[35] Thus the Book of Mormon told a narrative that generally conformed to contemporary theories (present-day Indians were descendants of biblical-era Israelite migrants to America), even if its particulars were novel. Further, the Mormon bible, being an ancient text (or, according to its detractors, merely posing as such), could not identify its biblical-era migrants to America as the ancestors of the Native American Indians with whom nineteenth-century citizens of the United States were acquainted. Only a contemporary such as Joseph Smith, the Prophet of the newly formed Mormon Church, could provide such a clarification for his American audience.

So the text of the Book of Mormon did not directly connect its protagonists to contemporary Indians (although Joseph Smith did); but contemporaries did so with ease. As a Mormon scholar points out, "The convergence between the generic 'Lamnite' label of the Book of Mormon and its application to all Native Americans happened so fast and so completely that it is virtually impossible to find a beginning point (other than the Book of Mormon itself)" for such identifications. Early anti-Mormons, such as the newspaper editor Abner Cole, who in his *Palmyra Reflector* printed caricatures of moccasin-wearing Indian Jews, were quick to mock what they understood as the Book of Mormon's synthesis of Israelite history with nineteenth-century realties. Other anti-Mormons, claiming wrongly that their adversaries believed that "the Indians are the lost tribes of Israel," further demonstrated how easily and casually they overcame the actual claims and innovations of the Book of Mormon by confusing the Mormon beliefs (that biblical-era migrants who were *not* the Lost Tribes came to America, without explicitly connecting them to Native Americans) with the Ten Lost Tribes theory prevalent in the first half of the nineteenth century in America.[36]

Claims about the account of American Indians in the Book of Mormon were by no means exclusive to the anti-Mormon camp. The historian Terryl Givens notes that early Mormon missionaries were quick to appeal to what their audiences perceived as familiar, not novel. Joseph Smith's younger brother Samuel and his fellow missionaries tried to lure potential converts by asking whether they wished "to purchase a history of the origin of the Indians," and Smith's scribe Oliver Cowdery described the Book of Mormon as "the history of the aborigines of this country." In an address to an Indian Council, Cowdery further suggested to his native audience that the Book of Mormon was a history "thousands of moons" old, which occurred at a time "when the red men's forefathers dwelt in peace and possessed this whole land." Cowdery wished, no doubt, to arouse his listeners' interest in a book that was the Natives' "history and the things which should befall their children in the latter days." Joseph Smith himself affirmed once more to New York newspaper editor N. C. Saxton that "the Book of Mormon is a sacred record of the forefathers of our western Tribes of Indians.... By it we learn that our western tribes of Indians are descendants from that Joseph that was sold into Egypt, and that the land of America is a promised land unto them, and unto it all the tribes of Israel will come." The Book of Mormon could thereby amend its two departures from the by now nominally canonical view of the Israelite origin of American Indians: only those carefully reading the Book of Mormon—a minority even among Mormons—might trouble to ponder the fact that the biblical people reaching American shores were not the Ten Lost Tribes; everyone else could readily fill the gap between the Indians they knew and the peoples described in the Book of Mormon.[37]

The Book of Mormon was a further and arguably a more significant departure from the other contemporary elaborations and speculations regarding the Jewish Indian hypothesis. Most attempts to connect the biblical Israelites and Indians were indeed *theory*, construed through a deliberate and careful inductive process (or at least one that attempted to pose and argue like a reasoned theory) even when, as in the case of Boudinot and Smith, they assumed that their conclusion was divinely sanctioned. The Book of Mormon, by contrast, was a revelatory *history*, not an exercise in the rational methodology of induction, deduction, and conjecture. The Mormon Bible provided a lengthy and articulate narrative of concrete events, dates, and names, which demanded of its readers a leap of faith, not rational conviction. Yet its remarkable novelties notwithstanding, the Book of Mormon joined in the ongoing American discourse about the Israelite origins of American Indians, a cultural context without which no understanding of the Book of Mormon or of the Indian theory is complete. However, the Book of Mormon developed that discourse beyond its contemporary limits to its logical conclusion: not only were American Indians of Israelite origin, the Mormon Bible asserted, they were, to paraphrase Wolf's famous book title, a people *with* a history. While the Indian-Israelite theory was by 1830 already centuries old, and hotly debated in the United States for more than a decade since its revival, the Book of Mormon remains today the sole testament to a creative discussion of Israelite Indians which was, as we have seen, at least as much a discussion about the United States of America.

American Jews, a small minority in the overwhelmingly Protestant early American republic, had particularly high stakes in the discussion about the origins of the Indians. If the continent's natives proved to be lost Israelites, that would fundamentally affect American Jews' fragile status in an overwhelmingly Christian, increasingly evangelical republic. At least one prominent American Jew, Mordecai Manuel Noah, believed that establishing the Indian-Israelite connection and demonstrating an ancient theological connection between America and the Chosen People might bolster his small religious community's self-esteem and its members' social standing (as well as cure the tragic condition of early-nineteenth-century European Jews). Finding the Lost Tribes in the United States thus proved critical in the grand political scheme that Noah tried to promote from 1820: the presence of Indian Israelites, he hoped, would support a claim for a revived neobiblical Jewish autonomy under the auspices of the American Constitution.

We saw in a previous chapter that Noah, "Tammany Hall Sachem," newspaper publisher, playwright, sheriff, militia major, American ambassador to Tunis, North Africa, and arguably early-nineteenth-century America's most recognized Jew, attempted to establish Ararat, a Hebrew city of refuge on Grand Island, a 17,381-acre isle in the Niagara River a few miles downstream from Buffalo. The Jews of Europe and the Levant would escape to Ararat, Noah planned, from the persecutions they were suffering in their countries of origin. We have also seen that Ararat participated in and contributed to a wider discussion of the Hebrew republic and that biblical polity's relevance to America. Yet Ararat's conception and justification, as well as its promotion plan, were shaped by other contemporary discourses and beliefs too, among them the conviction regarding the Israelite origin of American Indians. For the adherents of the Israelite-Indian connection the presence of lost Israelites in America was deemed a divine omen, and gave M. M. Noah his justification and political motivation to create Ararat as a Jewish autonomy.

At the impressive dedication ceremony that he masterfully organized on September 15, 1825, Noah, Ararat's self-proclaimed "Judge of Israel," promised there to "revive, re-new and reestablish the Government of the Jewish Nation" in America, "under the constitution of the United States." Noah's city of refuge became a nationwide cause célèbre in the weeks and months after the dedication ceremony; events included a pageant, Noah's "Proclamation for the Jews," and an elaborate speech he delivered the following day. Ararat, however, never took off; nothing happened after the grand dedication, and, as I have shown elsewhere, Ararat's ultimate collapse was largely defined by early-nineteenth-century American political culture (and not solely by European Jews' refusal to cooperate in Noah's scheme, as earlier studies suggested).[38]

The very conception of a plan to erect Ararat necessitated, and reflects, the powerful political Hebraism and biblical imagination that pervaded the early American republic's public sphere. Noah's visionary scheme shows how that biblical imagination transformed the United States into the natural place for reenacting a neobiblical political scheme. Further, Ararat demonstrates once more the significance of the idea of the Lost Tribes, and its multiple meanings for various groups as well as its mobilization for different ends. The Israelite-Indian theory was, of course, part of a wider political discussion in which the descendants of Israelites were seen roaming America. In this vein, Noah too forsook typology for ontology: America would not be merely a metaphorical New Israel but a place for a biblical renaissance where the descendants of the Israelites would find a refuge.

As we have already seen, Noah did not have the opportunity to develop the ingenious blend of biblical imagination and the pragmatic measures that pervaded his political scheme into a comprehensive plan. Since Ararat never took off after its spectacular commencement ceremonies, it was destined to remain a vague, rudimentary sketch. Clearly, however, Noah's conviction that the lost Jewish tribes, as he put it, "were the ancestors of the Indians of the American Continent" was fundamental to his conception of a Jewish polity in America.[39] Noah's determined (and as we shall soon see, decades-long) belief that the Indians were the descendants of the Ten Lost Tribes was a crucial building block in Ararat's conception and legitimization.

By 1825, at the height of the debate about the Indians' origin sparked by Boudinot's *A Star in the West*, Noah asserted that the exiled Lost Hebrew Tribes most likely "bent their course in a northwest direction, which brought them within a few leagues of the American Continent and which they finally reached."[40] The presence of Native American Chief Red Jacket at Ararat's dedication was not accidental: it attested to Noah's robust belief in this genealogical theory and its relevance to his scheme's rationale and success. To a large degree, the appeal of the proposed Hebrew City in upstate New York increased tremendously since it bore a millenarian promise to reunite long-lost biblical people, the Indian remnants of the Lost Israelite Tribes, with their newfound Jewish brethren.

Like his Protestant compatriots, Noah saw a striking similarity to biblical Israelites in every feature of the American Natives: "in their worship of one God, in their dialect and language, in their sacrifices, marriages, divorces, burials, fastings, purification, punishments . . . [in their] division of tribes, in their High Priests, and in their wars and in their victories." Significant for the conception of Ararat as a City of Refuge for Jews, the Indians, like the Israelites, had according to Noah "cities of refuge" that were similar to their Jewish counterparts. However, if most Americans of his age understood the presence of Indians Jews in America as a cause for millenarian celebration, which foretold the transfer of the American "Jews" to their land of origin in the Levant and hasten the End of Days, Noah's plans were diametrically the opposite.

In 1825 Noah did not wish to transfer the American Indians whom he identified as the descendants of the Lost Tribes to nineteenth-century Ottoman-ruled Canaan, but to make the Indians "sensible of their origin, to cultivate their minds, soften their condition and finally re-unite them with their brethren the chosen people." The unification of the Jews, "the first of people in the old world," with the American Israelites, the "rightful inheritors of the new," would be a momentous event in world history.[41] Were the Ararat plan to materialize, and the Indian tribes brought together, "civilized, and restored to their long lost brethren, what joy to our people, what glory to our God, how clearly have the prophecies been fulfilled, how certain our dispersion, how miraculous our preservation, how providential our deliverance."[42]

Ararat demonstrates the ease with which the discourse of the Lost Tribes in the early republic could conflate Indians, contemporary Jews, and the idea of America as the chosen land for the chosen American people. Yet despite Noah's millenarian optimism, the Indian and Israelite tribes were not destined to be united. On October 26, 1825, a month and a half after Ararat's dedication, the completion of the Erie Canal, an unprecedented feat of engineering and entrepreneurial vision which connected the Great Lakes to the Hudson River, was marked by a statewide "Grand Celebration." The celebration was supposed to culminate in an impressive flotilla sailing down the new canal from Buffalo to New York City. At the end of the spectacular voyage, New York's Governor De Witt Clinton would ceremonially pour Lake Erie water into New York Harbor to mark the "Wedding of the Waters." Mordecai Noah, presumably still optimistic about his colonization venture, wished to sail in the convoy, navigating a sailboat he named—was it narcissist grandiosity or a pun?—Noah's Ark. Like its biblical namesake, the hull would be "freighted with all manner of animals, and creeping things." This time, however, the ark would also carry Indians—in full costume—symbolically manifesting the reunification of the tribes of Israel in America. The emblematic vessel was planned to "enter the Canal from Lake Erie on the eighteenth" and arrive at New York City with the rest of the celebratory fleet. Reporters found it necessary to reassure readers that the account "in relation to Noah's Ark, was as serious as sober prose could make it." Three days after the flotilla set sail from Albany, the *Boston Patriot* reported that "the Ark is not only completed, but that several animals have already been gathered into it, that many more are in readiness to take refuge therein." The biblical reenactment of the ark harboring representatives of various species of animals and birds (this time, however, *leaving* Ararat for its destination) was supposed to take place—was the reporter writing tongue in cheek?—"when the waters shall cover the dry land." That, however, was not to be. The *Essex Register* confirmed on November 10 that "Noah's Ark, from Ararat, having the bears and Indians, fell behind, and did not arrive in Albany in season to be taken in tow." The *New Hampshire Sentinel* could inform its readers that the mishap occurred when the ark "met with an accident in coming through the locks, which prevented her joining the Canal procession."[43]

Noah's failure to sail his ark in time for the celebratory procession could be read as a symbol of Ararat's meltdown. As a contemporary commented two years after the marvelous dedication of the Hebrew city, "The affair died away." However, Noah never lost hope of ingathering the people of Israel. Ararat's stillbirth could not extinguish Noah's enthusiasm for the Israelite-Indian theory, which he continued to cultivate for years to come. More than a decade after he gave up on founding Ararat, Noah published a lengthy *Discourse on the Evidences of the American Indians being the Descendants of the Lost Tribes of Israel* (1837), in which he laboriously restated the ideas that such advocates as James Adair, Elias Boudinot, and Ethan Smith had expressed before.[44]

In 1845, exactly twenty years after the Ararat debacle, Noah came up with another visionary plan to save the Jews from new persecutions they were suffering in Europe and in Arab lands. This time, however, he forwent the United States as the place for Jewish refuge; now he set his sights on the biblical Canaan, Ottoman Palestine at that time, as a homeland wherein the Jews might exercise political autonomy. This was a remarkable feat of proto-Zionist anticipation more than half a century before that national movement emerged and materialized. Remarkably, with America no longer part of his scheme, Noah did not even mention the American Indians—so important, indeed crucial, in justifying his earlier New World venture; the Indian brethren whom two decades earlier Noah wished to reunite with the rest of the world's Jewry were totally forgotten, abandoned in 1845. For Noah, like his Protestant compatriots who advocated the Indian-Israelite connection, the Israelite Indians were less important, or completely unimportant, in themselves. They were simply instrumental for the construction of an American Zion, for weaving America into the Bible and the Bible into America. In 1825, when Noah still saw America as a place where the problems of the Jews could be solved, he found the Israelite-Indian connection meaningful, seemingly making a strong case for the historical rights of a Jewish autonomy in America. But in retrospect the connection he made seems unfortunate: both Native Americans and Jews would suffer great agony in the coming years before achieving national solutions that would, at least partially, enable them to turn their back on their troubled pasts.

Even after most American nationalists lost interest in the Indian theory as a means to biblicize the United States, Mordecai Noah had remained its champion, persistently trying to weave the New World and its indigenous inhabitants into a biblical narrative. Now, however, he turned his gaze southward, beyond the borders of the United States. Well into the nineteenth century he repeatedly asserted that "the 'ten lost tribes' of Israel were the originators of the cities whose ruins astrew Mexico and Central America." Tellingly, after abandoning Ararat and concluding in 1845, as we have seen, that the Jews should congregate in Palestine and not in the United States, Noah no longer focused on the Indians who inhabited North America; the Lost Tribes still preoccupied him intellectually but ceased to serve his political goals.

Yet Noah's imaginative mind and his continued interest in the fate of the lost tribes caused him to constantly adjust the theory to political developments in ingenious ways. In the early months of 1849 he turned his attention to the newly acquired Pacific territories, as rumors about the discovery of vast amounts of gold in California's ravines the previous summer reached the continent's east coast. California, Noah concluded, was the biblical Ophir, the source of the vast amounts of gold for King Solomon's temple. Characteristically, he provided an argument of "considerable extent," calculating "the length of the voyages of the ships which were sent for the gold, and various other considerations" to prove that "it was California gold that so wonderfully and magnificently enriched the famous temple of antiquity." Since "the ships sent by Solomon and Hiram of Tyre for the Gold and treasures of Ophir, required three years to make the voyage," according to the biblical account, and "as the length of the voyage would seem to correspond very well with the distance of California," Noah concluded that "the ancient Ophir and modern California are one and the same place."[45]

The following year, having had time to further contemplate and digest the astounding news about the riches of California, Noah now concluded that the lost Israelites "resided in California when the ships of Solomon made their three years voyage, and furnished the gold in Ophir for building the temple; they reside there still; the settlers and proprietors of Mexico, Peru; and the whole of America; they have been here centuries before the advent of Christianity and patiently await the promises of redemption." Excited about the splendid news of the newfound western gold, newspapers repeatedly reprinted Noah's attention-grabbing speculations. Although commentators found that Noah's biblically inclined calculations of ancient maritime routes and sailing durations did "not exactly amount to a geometrical demonstration," they still afforded "material for curious speculation," perhaps stimulating even more freebooters to venture across the continent to enrich themselves from the spoils of legendary, and now rediscovered, "Ophir."[46]

The discussion about the Israelite origin of the Indians during the 1820s and 1830s was, as we have seen, pursued nationwide in newspapers and other forms of print. An intriguing concentration of active discussants resided in upstate and western New York, the region that came to be known as the Burned Over District because of repeated waves of evangelizing that swept through it in the early decades of the nineteenth century. Not by chance, many of those who identified Israelites inhabited those "burned over" parts, which harbored the radical fringe of the religious awakening: Ethan Smith, Joseph Smith, Mordecai Noah, Elias Boudinot, among others, operated in the same geographical—and mental—space, in which the early United States seemed to be the stage on which biblical Israelites reappeared to take part in a grand theohistorical drama. Further evidence of the intense religiosity of the area comes from Noah's ardent (and possibly only) followers who also operated in that area; they would also take the American-Israelite connection a step farther.

Regrettably for Noah, his devotees were not the thousands of European Jews he expected to come and seek refuge in America. They were American Christians whose anxious religiosity was sparked by Noah's vision of a neobiblical Hebraic polity. So affected were they by Noah's plan and the surrounding cultural biblicism, they eventually reinvented themselves as American Israelites. Addressing themselves as prophesying Hebrews, these marginal believers operated within an idiosyncratic and eclectic biblical cosmology, yet one that bore the traits of the times.

The scandalous biography of Robert Matthews (1788–1841), the man who became known as the Prophet Matthias, has been skillfully told as a story of "sex and salvation" that epitomized the radical edge of the Second Great Awakening. Nevertheless, understanding Matthias and his followers is worth further perusal in the context of the era's intense biblicism, which may explain why and how this middle-aged New Yorker chose to assume the persona of the "chief High Priest of the Jews of the order of Melchisedeck," or a prophesying Jew; and how and why he was able to form a following of any sort under this peculiar persona in his outlandish attempt of the renewal of a Hebrew patriarchy.[47]

Changing his name from the mundane Matthews to the biblical Matthias, the charismatic leader was able to convert a group of followers into an Old Testament–style mission in which he assumed the role of biblical prophet and began "denouncing a judgment on the Gentiles," a judgment he promised to "execute in this age," passing incomprehensible (but obviously biblical) decrees—for example, that "all the blood from Zehariah till the death of the last witness, is required of this generation, and before this generation passeth away, this judgment shall be executed." Matthias named his follower (and financier) Elijah Pierson "Elijah the Tishbite," after the Israelite original, and his group of followers the Elders of the True Israelite Church. His biblically inspired plans included making "a model of Salomon's Temple"; naming the communal residence Zion Hill, where he presided like a biblical patriarch over his flock; ordering custom silver, decorated with the Lion of Judah; purchasing a lavish wardrobe of emblematic clothes, embroidered with biblical symbolism; and many other gestures that derived from an eclectic and rich biblical cosmology.[48]

Margaret Matthews, Matthias's estranged wife, testified that her husband's assumption of an Old Testament persona was inspired by Mordecai Noah (unbeknownst by him), demonstrating how biblically inspired ideas and notions spread and sprout in the fertile soil of the early republic's Old Testament culture. Margaret spoke out after Matthews's Bible-inspired commune collapsed with his imprisonment for the alleged murder of Pierson ("Elijah"): "His idea of being a Jew, and of making a model of the temple were gathered from Mr. Noah's proclaiming" Ararat as a City of Refuge. Noah's schemes, she continued, "pleased [Matthews] very much. He wanted to go and join Noah in his new city of Ararat, and said Noah could not get along without him. He continued possessed with this idea a long time." Matthews-Matthias in all probability never met Noah. Margaret summed up sarcastically: "Whether Mr. Noah failed for want of my husband I do not say." While delusional (and Christian) individuals made Noah their hero for attempting to resurrect the Bible in America and became "prophesying Hebrews," Noah was never one, as Sean Wilentz and Paul E. Johnson rightly state in their study of Matthews.[49]

Noah's words and plans, which envisioned the revival of a Jewish government on Grand Island led by a Hebrew-American judge, were considered legitimate and normative (even if they ultimately proved insufficiently persuasive and popular to materialize); Matthias was considered deviant and dangerous. However, satisfying as it is to trace the genealogy of his delusional role as a Hebrew prophet to Noah's more mainstream aspirations, these otherwise very different biblical visions shared significant aspects. If Matthias's thoughts and actions can hardly be considered "normal" by any standard, they were, and still are, like Noah's Ararat, at least comprehensible when seen in a larger context of the biblical culture in which Matthias (and Noah) operated; otherwise they could not make, in the words of Wilentz and Johnson, "perfect sense" to his believers.[50] If Matthias's words, deeds, and biblical worldview had been unintelligible to his fellow citizens, they would not have been so inflammatory.

Matthias embodied theological and criminal deviancy for most of his contemporaries, yet his eccentric intellectual universe derived from a shared biblical cosmology that was part and parcel of the lives of Americans of the age of the Second Great Awakening. A self-proclaimed Hebrew prophet such as Matthias absorbed the conceptual language and vocabulary of the biblical culture within which he functioned. That language reflected a culture, as we have seen, that seriously considered its aborigines to be long-lost Israelites, contemplated a political program to revive an Old Testament Hebrew government in its midst, and commonly presented the United States as a "second Israel." In such light Matthias may still seem eccentric in the extreme. But within that context he, as well as the more conventional manifestations of that biblical culture, should also be much more comprehensible.

Matthias operated in tandem with a heavily biblical mode of American nationalism which capitalized on the notion that "real" Israelites in the form of Indians inhabited the United States; however, his self-pronouncement as an Israelite was in no sense an act of participation in a national or collective endeavor. Matthias's True Israelite Church was a sectarian, egotistical, and maniacal project. Nevertheless, the self-proclaimed prophet was driven by the same passion for "ontological Israelism," for identifying the Bible and biblical people in America, that propelled his Protestant, Mormon, and Jewish contemporaries. Earlier generations may have been perfectly content with their identification as the *reincarnation* of Israelites, but nineteenth-century Americans' intense biblicism prepared them for discovering in their midst, or imagining themselves to be, *actual* biblical Israelites.

A southern expression of similar sensibility also emerged on the margins of American society, manifesting itself in the figure of Billy Simons, an "ascetic Negro Jew" (the only recorded instance of a black Jew in the whole Old South) who proclaimed himself a "Rechabite" in antebellum Charleston. "Uncle Billy" was a familiar figure in the streets of the slaveholding city, a slave who carried and delivered local newspapers for many years. Surprisingly, the city's Jews admitted him to their congregation, Kahal Kodesh Beth Elohim, regardless of a proscription in its constitution against people of color. His Charlestonian coreligionists noted and appreciated Billy's "exemplary devotion," which he exhibited every Yom Kippur, as he was "wrapt in thought," contemplating deeply and atoning for hours. Consequently, the managers of the Hazel Street synagogue "very commendably honored the old man with one of the most respectable front seats" in their house of worship.[51]

Billy, probably born free in Africa around 1780, related to Jews and gentiles alike that his father frequently told him of their descent from the Rechabites, a group he believed "still exist[ed] as a separate tribe in Africa." The Rechabites from whom Billy claimed his ancestry were a biblical clan, the progeny of Jehonadab (or Jonadab), the son of Rechab. In following God's commandment to live ascetically, to avoid wine, and "not to build houses" but to dwell "in tents all your days," as told in Jeremiah 35, the Lord promised that the Rechabites would "not be cut off . . . [but] stand before Me for ever."[52] Billy's father, and no doubt Billy himself, were thus said never to have tasted "any wine or other spirituous liquors," following the customs of the Rechabites of old.

There is no evidence of Africans or African-Americans other than Billy Simons identifying themselves as Rechabites, a clan that has not been known to exist for millennia. Hence, that he had probably been brought to America by Jewish masters, as he often pointed out, may well explain Simons's assumption of a biblical identity. Whether Charleston Jews and gentiles believed in Simons's ancient ancestry as a Rechabite is unknown; that they tolerated his testimony surely affirms, as Ralph Melnick pointed out more than three decades ago, his unique social approval despite his status as an enslaved black.[53] More important for our purpose, it further demonstrates how far contemporaries' imaginations willingly incorporated biblical history into their own American present—and how receptive, or at the very least nonresistant, audiences were to such Hebraic-American accounts. A biblical ancestry presented an enslaved black with a rare opportunity to increase significantly his social (and self-)esteem while titillating the imaginations of his free white and Jewish contemporaries, even while they themselves were a minority in an overwhelmingly Protestant South.

By the middle of the nineteenth century Americans' interest in the possibility that North American Indians were of Israelite origin was faint. The fall from grace of the Hebrew-Indian theory was undoubtedly part of wider cultural processes, including the abatement of the radicalism of the Second Great Awakening as the century progressed, as well as the rise of the New Testament and the simultaneous decline of the Old Testament in American culture; this was a significant process, which I discuss in the final chapter. The virtual disappearance of Indians from most of the settled areas of the United States, and hence from Americans' consciousness, after successive removals, must also have contributed to their marginalization as potential harbingers of the apocalypse. In later years American commentators would occasionally speculate on the Hebraic origins of Indians, but by midcentury interest no longer centered exclusively on Indians residing in the United States or even in North America: newspapers characteristically reported about the Mexican Aztecs as the Hebrews' possible descendants. The Israelite-Indian theory ran out of steam in the United States, but even when it was evoked, it no longer contributed to the discussion on the country's Hebraic origins. In a larger sense, this theory no longer took part in the discourse of American nationalism.[54]

The ideas regarding the American Ten Lost Tribes would continue to echo in the late nineteenth century in the so-called "British-Israelism theory." This theory posited that the Angles and Saxons, the tribes that invaded the British Isles during the fifth century, were the descendants of the lost tribes of Israel. By the 1890s this notion of the Israelite origins of the English people found expression in the United States in the founding of the Society of the Ten Tribes.[55] Once again, Americans—now imagining themselves an Anglo-Saxon "race"—connected themselves directly to a biblical Israelite lineage (if a circuitous one). In the same years black Americans such as William Saunders Crowdy (1847–1908) also started to identify themselves as descended from the Ten Lost Tribes, a belief that culminated in the founding of the Church of God and Saints of Christ in 1896. This early Black Hebrew Israelitism proved a formidable mode of thought, and continued to develop throughout the twentieth century as members of black congregations identified themselves as descendants of biblical Israelites. One such person was Albert B. Cleage, Jr. (1911–2000), who founded the Shrine of the Black Madonna Church in the Midwest and preached his beliefs, among them that the Israelites were a black-skinned people who sojourned in Africa (Egypt) and were led by Moses, "a revolutionary black man, a Zealot." Blacks, according to Cleage and the other Black Hebrew Israelites, were literally—not metaphorically or typologically—the Chosen People. While black Methodists and Baptists, as the historian Stephen Prothero points out, drew analogies and typologized African-Americans and Israelites, Black Hebrews literally identified themselves *as* the people of Israel.[56] The identification of Israelites in America, which during the early nineteenth century turned into a tool of a burgeoning nationalism, had come, with Cleage and his black *separatist* nationalism, full circle.

The mid-nineteenth-century explorer John Lloyd Stephens observed that Americans "have ascribed the honour of peopling America" to an assortment of races and nations "under the broad range allowed by a descent from the sons of Noah, the Jews, the Canaanites, the Phoenicians, the Carthaginians, the Greeks, the Scythians in ancient times; the Chinese, the Swedes, the Norwegians, the Welsh, and the Spaniards in modern." Lloyd's tongue-in-cheek attitude aside, the Israelite theory of the identity of the Indians was arguably the most popular among its alternatives well into the nineteenth century. As a contemporary acknowledged, "that the Indians are descendents of the Jews" was "generally entertained among the learned."[57] At its height during the first decades of the nineteenth century, particularly after the publication of *A Star in the West* in 1816, the Israelite-Indian theory participated in a wider discussion of an emerging American nationalism, as it helped situate the United States as a redemptive force in history. Americans from Elias Boudinot to Joseph Smith, from Mordecai Noah to the prophet Matthias, linked the American continent with the sprawling political confederacy that inhabited increasingly large parts of that landmass and the Old Testament. This linking of geography, politics, and history—or, rather, of North America, the United States, and the Bible—provides a deeper understanding of the role of the Old Testament in shaping the national culture, and of the intellectual environment in which notions such as the "American mission," "manifest destiny," and the "second Israel" emerged, evolved, and matured.

The dividends of connecting biblical Israel and America through a unified historical narrative, one in which ancient Israelites migrated and inhabited what would become the United States, were of a potentially millenarian magnitude: the presence in America of the Lost Tribes (or other biblical-era Israelites) seemed to that theory's proponents to demonstrate the United States' role as a world-redeeming force. However, the stakes of such assertions were extremely high as well: as opposed to metaphorical or typological connections which were ahistorical, ontology—the actual presence of Israelites in America, which was set forth as a historical fact—was potentially subject to logic and reason, not to faith and exegesis: a "theory," in short, which could be refuted. This might explain why, as the nineteenth century wore on and more verifiable information accumulated, it became in Steven Conn's words, "increasingly clear that Indians were descended neither from a lost tribe of Israel nor from any colony of displaced Etruscans." The failure of canonical Western texts, namely Scripture or the classics, satisfactorily to make sense of questions pertaining to Native Americans, coupled with the advance of Higher Criticism and Darwinian natural science, indeed might have "shaped the transition from a sacred world view to a secular one."[58]

Nevertheless, even if such a movement toward modernism did take place in America, it was not a linear or smooth transition. If anything, during the first half of the nineteenth century science and history were subjected to the dictates of religion and nationalism. For at least three decades during the first half of the nineteenth century, the Israelite-Indian theory flourished, and was an important element in shaping the United States' intellectual discourse, its national identity, and its imagined history. Traditional understanding of America as a Second Israel encountered an alternative mode of powerfully, if fleetingly, connecting America and the Bible. By the era of the Civil War advocates of the view of the United States as the Second Israel reverted once more to typology, proclaiming assertions such as "just as the Jewish Church was a type of the Christian Church," there was "no doubt that the Hebrew theocracy was a prototype of the United States."[59] Yet for a while the New Israel was more than a mere metaphor, as early republican biblical ontology transcended typology and Israelites roamed America.

5
Evangelicalism, Slavery, and the Decline of an Old Testament Nation

The idea that the young United States was a latter-day Israel was so pervasive in the revolutionary era that even the least orthodox Christians of the American founding generation, such as Thomas Jefferson and Benjamin Franklin, could communicate that notion through their allegorical suggestions for the nation's Great Seal.[1] Fourscore years later a much more pious—if by no means conventional—Christian such as Abraham Lincoln would add a most significant qualifier, "almost," before designating Americans as "God's chosen people." Lincoln's limitation on America's chosenness was telling. While Americans would never stop expressing and modifying the notion that Providence had a special relationship with the United States, a bond consciously derived from ancient Israelite history, by the second half of the nineteenth century the Old Testament's influence on the American political imagination had dramatically diminished. As that century progressed it became clear that public language was losing its earlier characteristic explicit and robust biblicism; the repeated and unabashed references to, and articulation of, the image of America as the New Israel and the accompanying identification with the biblical Israelites of old waned as years went by, never to regain their former vitality. As fundamental as those biblical notions were to the emerging national culture during the first half-century of the republic's existence, by the era of the Civil War their earlier popularity and sway were evidently spent.

These significant changes in American modes of national identification and representation were bound up with larger historical processes, particularly the Second Great Awakening. As the nineteenth century advanced, multitudes of Americans were swept by recurrent evangelical revivals and became more attuned to Christ and his redeeming mission; their newfound evangelicalism placed Jesus, hence the New Testament, at the center of their theological yearning. This revamped emphasis on Jesus would transform the economy of American biblicism and political imagination. Paradoxically, the golden age of the Hebrew Bible in American public life ended not with secularization but when it was overshadowed by a New Testament–centered evangelical religiosity.[2] This terminated the pervasive, literal, immediate, and frequently uninhibited portrayals of America as a biblical Israelite nation. In this chapter I explore the dramatic rise in the prominence of Jesus and the New Testament in the new evangelical landscape of nineteenth-century American religion and their assumption of the Old Testament's leading role in the political discourse. Through that century, politically conscious Americans of all camps came to recognize that the New Testament was as relevant as the Old, or even more so, to the most critical issue of contemporary political debates, namely slavery. The new historical consciousness that arose as a result of the repeated comparisons between biblical and American slaveries would further render the American Israel as an anachronistic image for exactly those who were its most ardent proponents.

During the colonial period beliefs regarding the national election of God's New Israel were virtually confined to New England, where even after the dénouement of the Puritan theocracy, Calvinism and the accompanying predilection for the Old Testament prevailed. The historian of religion Sydney Ahlstrom may have exaggerated in claiming that "Puritanism provided the moral and religious background of fully 85 percent of the people who declared their independence in 1776"; yet for various reasons Reformed Protestantism certainly exerted a disproportionate influence in revolutionary British North America. Historians of American religion have subsequently concluded that Americans, in line with Reformed Protestantism, were heavily inclined to the Hebraic rather than the Greek parts of the Scripture, as was the norm particularly in the Calvinist tradition, in which Jesus was a subordinate figure. This was apparent in the realm of conviction, exegesis, and even ritual, evinced in New Englanders' singing "nothing but a cappella versions of the Old Testament Psalms" in their worship. In such a Hebraic atmosphere, Christ remained an abstract notion, and until the late eighteenth century the cultural heirs of the Puritans remained by and large "a Godfearing rather than Jesus-loving people."[3]

We should not confuse an emphasis on the First Person with the eradication of the Second. While subordinate, Christ (seldom called proverbially Jesus before the nineteenth century) was crucial to the Puritan scheme of salvation, in which the Son became incarnate as the God-man and accomplished his earthly mission through his traditional three "offices" in Calvinist doctrine: as prophet, priest, and king. Union with Christ was a pivotal moment in the order of salvation, and thus disputes over the exact nature of that union facilitated heated theological debates, which surfaced in Massachusetts Bay as early as in 1636 during the antinomian controversy. Perhaps it would be useful to describe Reformed attitudes as expressed in a tacit division of divine labor, in which the "Lord" (the Father) was the chief protector (and prosecutor) and Christ offered salvation to God's elect. Such attitudes were not, however, exclusively Puritan, as virtually all Christians on the North American continent in the seventeenth century understood Jesus as the divine Son of God, sole redeemer of humankind. The great American revivalists of the eighteenth century continued to emphasize the theme of Christological consolation in their preaching (indeed, the great theologian Jonathan Edwards wrote and preached about Christ throughout his lifetime). Early abolitionists such as the New Divinity theologian Samuel Hopkins could transcend earlier antislavery reliance on the Old Testament (evident in Samuel Sewall's *The Selling of Joseph* [1700]) and emphasize Jesus—and the New Testament—in revolutionary-era attacks on slavery.[4]

Nevertheless, before 1800 Christianity in America, which was overwhelmingly Protestant, was not a Jesus faith. American evangelicalism, a tradition whose "every second word" was to become Jesus, is so closely identified with the Son of God that it is hard to imagine Protestantism in the United States without Christ revered as the Alpha and Omega of the faith. Perry Miller observed that the Puritans went "as far as mortals could go in removing intermediaries between God and man," to the extent that they even minimized "the role of the Savior in their glorification of the sovereignty of the father." More recently a historian of Jesus' role in America has argued that in Puritan theology Christ—the *kristos* or Second Person and Son of God—played a relatively minor role, while Jesus, the human and soothing face of the Messiah, had almost none. In light of what we have just seen such statements may be in need of qualification; but there is no escape from the fact that Calvinist cosmology, which revolved around the infinite gap between God and fallen humanity, left little room for a humanly divine or a divinely human being.

Late-eighteenth-century Americans' religious culture carried over many of the Puritans' Calvinist sensibilities, and perpetuated this inclination in particular. According to a historian of Jesus' role in American culture, many found that "the Hebrew Scriptures, centered on the chosen people and the

Providence of God, [were] more pertinent" to revolution, state building, and constitution making than the pacifist and martyr Christ. Americans of the early republic thus clearly preferred the deeply nationalist and territorial Old Testament for elaborating their political theologies, or the religious justification and legitimization for their political projects. Christ may have mediated between God and the souls of politically literate Americans, but the Son of God was surprisingly absent from late-eighteenth-century political forms of expression in that most political of eras. Once again, Americans as far from a Puritan outlook as Benjamin Franklin and Thomas Jefferson reflected such tendencies, as they demoted Jesus from his divine role to that of a moral philosopher in an Enlightened attempt to "disentangle the 'mythical' from the 'real' Jesus."[5]

The Old Testament's predominance in the early United States undoubtedly owes a debt to the Hebrew Bible's preoccupation with territoriality and nationhood, hence its easy adaptation as a guide for earthly politics, particularly for a country involved in a nation-building project. Furthermore, the New Testament is easily interpreted as shunning an earthly Promised Land as expounded in the Old Testament, perhaps because Christianity's founders, headed by Jesus and Paul, did not expect there to *be* any land for much longer. When Jesus told Pilate, "My kingdom is not of this world" (John 18:36), and when he refused Satan's offer of endless earthly power (Luke 4:5–8), he denounced what Augustine would later call the Earthly City and embraced the promise of the City of God: power and politics, dominion and control are deemed in the New Testament carnal and satanic, directly opposed to the perfection and eternity which would characterize the End of Days. As Conor Cruise O'Brien has observed, the contrast between the Old and New Testaments in this matter could hardly be more stark: if in the Old Testament, God offered land to Abraham and Abraham accepted it, in the New Testament, Satan is the one to offer political power to Jesus, an offer which Jesus of course refuses. Mark Lilla comments that while "the New Testament expresses moral principles and anthropological assumptions that might contribute to political theory, it does not articulate a clear, coherent picture of the good Christian political order."[6] The Old Testament, on the other hand, provides the model of the Mosaic constitution (and the Davidic kingship) but is also more generally immersed in questions involving political power and its uses and misuses. Such themes, which recur throughout the history of the Israelite (and early American) nation, seem to have disappeared from the New Testament.

The American Revolution thus created a republic, but also an imagined community, a people that would understand its purpose and find its significance in decades to come through a powerful biblical cosmology. The New Testament would never disappear from the intellectual horizon of early Americans. Nevertheless, the emerging political culture demonstrated a clear disposition to the Old Testament and to the portrayal and interpretation of the United States as a New Israel. Such an exegetical temper may have stemmed from Congregational (therefore deeply Calvinist) roots, but it was rapidly acquiring a strong national appeal, which steadily increased and was to peak *after* the revolutionary period. Contemporaries confirmed this observation. Harriet Beecher Stowe, for example, averred that early Americans "spoke of Zion and Jerusalem, of the God of Israel, the God of Jacob, as much as if my grandfather had been a veritable Jew; and except for the closing phrase, 'for the sake of thy Son, our Saviour,' might all have been uttered in Palestine by a well-trained Jew in the time of [King] David." Similarly, Henry Adams wrote in the opening pages of *The Education* that to be born to an elite family in the Boston of his childhood was similar to being "born in Jerusalem under the shadow of the Temple and circumcised in the Synagogue by his uncle the high priest, under the name of Israel Cohen." Herman Melville, always a cogent observer of the country's zeitgeist, concluded that America was "the Israel of our time."[7]

These great writers knew from experiencing early America intimately not only that their compatriots were biblically oriented but that their culture was profoundly committed to the Old Testament. That American biblicism still manifested the characteristics of the religiosity of colonial British North America, where "the Old Testament trumped the New, and Jesus the son cowered in the shadow of God the Father."[8] For twenty-first-century readers, acquainted with the potent evangelicalism of American Christianity, the relegation of the New Testament and the elevation of the Old are hard to imagine. Still, early-republic biblicism was infatuated with the history of the Israelite nation and its perceived relevance to the United States; it left little room for a countering Christology.

Such a proclivity for the Old Testament rather than the New manifested itself already during the Revolution, a time when, as the historian Richard Wightman Fox has concluded, patriots "rarely invoked Jesus himself in support for their cause." Another historian observed that American patriots mustered the Old Testament liberally, but only pacifists or loyalist ministers referred to the New Testament.[9] To early Americans the protagonists and the essence of the Old Testament seemed utterly political and relevant, and the examples of the New Testament and of Christ were deemed apolitical, if not antipolitical.

A sizable corpus, such as the pseudobiblical texts, written over a period of more than a century and equating the United States to a biblical nation, further manifests the insignificance of the New Testament to the American political cosmology in the republic's early decades: numerous pseudobiblical texts assumed the voice of the Old Testament to narrate American political plots, without their authors' showing the slightest interest in the New Testament. Every text depicting America in biblical language resonates with Old Testament narratives, themes, and protagonists, as well as the distinct textual formulations of the Hebrew Bible; a single reference to New Testament characters or episodes is hard to find—even to Christ himself! In these articulations of their nation as a New and Second Israel and the Americans as a chosen people, citizens of the early United States virtually ignored the Christian Bible and chose to focus on their Hebraic image.[10]

Americans so perpetuated the seventeenth- and eighteenth-century Reformed tradition of emphasis on the Old Testament that Mark Noll concluded that "well into the national period, the public Bible of the United States was for all intents the Old Testament." This situation would eventually change—and dramatically at that, as the "almost sensually masochistic" Calvinist language about God, one that centered more on God's power than on his love, became by the antebellum era an eccentric rarity.[11] This is not to say that the Old Testament suddenly or conclusively lost its power and allure by the time of the Civil War. It certainly did not, and it maintained a distinct presence in the national culture of the United States for decades and centuries to come, as Americans continued to address, compare, and juxtapose their polity to that of the ancient Israelites. Nevertheless, as the New Testament's presence steadily rose in the political discourse particularly and in American culture generally, the role of the Old Testament in antebellum America became ever more subdued and subtle compared with its place in the nation's early years.

Even examples that seemingly prove the robustness of political Hebraism in the era of the Civil War paradoxically underscore the incremental weakening of the Old Testament in American culture: Mark Noll has observed that out of a sampling of 77 eulogizing sermons preached after Abraham Lincoln's assassination in 1865, 45 (58 percent) used Old Testament texts, while

24 (31 percent) turned to the New Testament. However, this supposed sign of post–Civil War Old Testament vitality looks different once we note that on the occasion of another president's death more than six decades earlier, only 7 (6 percent) of the 120 texts that eulogized George Washington came from the New Testament, and of these, 4 referred to Old Testament persons cited in the New Testament.[12] So while Noll rightly emphasizes the still significant presence of the Old Testament in the Lincoln eulogies, a comparison of the biblical sources used to commemorate the two towering presidents attests to a substantial change: from the virtual absence in descriptions of Washington, the New Testament is well represented in Lincoln's portrayals. As the nineteenth century progressed a tectonic change, which as we shall now see was much more decisive than the above numbers might suggest, was agitating the relationship between the American people and their Bible. This shift in the political use of the Bible involved refocusing on the Christian Gospel and reassessing the relevance of the Hebrew Bible to the United States and its unfolding history.

Cultural change involves numerous causes and effects, and is always laden with factors, parameters, and diverging motivations and varying contexts. So it might be futile to attempt to pinpoint the exact timing of the shift from the predilection for the Old Testament to a preference for the New in the history of the United States. But clearly, something significant occurred in the relationship between the American people and the Old Testament as the nineteenth century advanced. Assessments such as that of Philip Barlow, the historian of Mormonism, that "a shift from Old Testament to New Testament dominance" could be sensed in the United States sometime around 1820, are provocative and suggestive, if hard to evaluate. Certainly, 1820 is a reasonable time for such a change (Perry Miller similarly pointed to "1800 or 1820" as a milestone year in attempts to periodize the heyday of American Old Testamentism); yet equally plausibly such a transformation in American intellectual and cultural history can be dated decades later. A good moment to locate the watershed date might well be 1830, after which "the tide was turning."[13] All in all, sometime around that year the shift occurred, and with it the long and tortuous diminution of the role of the Hebrew Bible as a prime source for America's political vocabulary. That process, however, did not take the form of an abrupt alienation but was more of a long and genial drifting apart. With the fading of the Old Testament in the nation's imagination, Americans would witness the reinvigorated presence of the New Testament in the political sphere.

The early-nineteenth-century emergence of the United States as a sprawling commercial and industrial polity, a cluster of processes collectively known as "the market revolution," and swift changes in politics and political culture in the form of democratization and empowerment, provided the backdrop to the transition from the Old Testament to the New. More immediately related to the shift was the movement that later commentators dubbed the Second Great Awakening, "a massive outpouring of evangelical religious enthusiasm" between the Revolution and the Civil War, particularly from 1800 to 1840. The Awakening was more a long-term process than a series of distinct events, which brought about a decisive turn to more manifestly evangelical forms of religious expression in the United States. The most vital proxies of that monumental change were the Methodists and Baptists who perfected such vehicles as the itinerary preacher circuit system and the mass camp meeting to evangelize unprecedented numbers of Americans during the opening decades of the nineteenth century.[14]

The Methodist message ran particularly deep. Methodists, who were to become the most active agents promoting Jesus as the key figure in the Godhead, emphasized the merciful deity of Christ, evident in the sermonizing of itinerant preachers that manifested a clear preference for the New Testament (as far as we can tell: the vast majority of those sermons were preached *ex tempore* and were never recorded). The first American Methodist Bishops, Thomas Coke and Francis Asbury, reminded their preachers, who acted as the shock troops of the evangelical conversion of the expanding nation, that God's grace must never slip from view and that "there must be nothing now held forth to the view of the penitent but ... the mercy which is ready to embrace him on every side."[15] The source and provider of that mercy would be not the Father but his merciful Son, who was powerfully lodged at the center of the yearning of a rapidly growing number of believers.

This prolonged Awakening eventually made American society much more religious than it had been during the revolutionary era, as it transformed the shape and tone of American Christianity. A long-term process more than a distinct event, this epoch-making expansion of evangelical Protestant Christianity consisted of a double transformation: a dramatic rise in the number of religious adherents, even faster than the rapid growth of the general population; and a reversal in their denominational affiliation. All churches did well in absolute numbers in that period, but the Congregationalists and Episcopalians, which had dominated the colonial era and were the largest eighteenth-century churches, were by 1860 dwarfed by the evangelical churches, which by then formed the huge majority (at least 85 percent) of American congregations.[16] By midcentury evangelical Christianity had taken over the American religious landscape.

A deep theological transformation accompanied the institutional changes in American Protestantism. Americans, who by the late eighteenth century started to discover that traditional Christianity did not satisfy them spiritually, "began looking elsewhere," according to Gordon Wood, "for solace and meaning." They found it in droves in evangelical creeds, whereby believers acknowledged their sin before God, looked upon Jesus Christ (crucified—dead—resurrected) as God's means of redemption, and saw their faith in him as Savior as a way to reconcile with God. Evangelical sensibility was recognized through its renewed emphasis on the Bible as the ultimate religious authority, on conversion as the means to relate to God, and on Christ's redemption as the heart of true religion. By the era of the Civil War evangelicalism with these tenets had become, in Mark Noll's words, "the unofficially established religion in a nation that had forsworn religious establishment."[17]

Historians of religion have noted that by the 1840s, with evangelicalism in full swing, "preaching and worship increasingly centered on the figure of Christ."[18] The earlier understanding of a frowning, omnipotent, and unalterable God (a traditional Calvinist view readily distilled from the Hebrew Bible) may have well suited the patriarchal ideal of the eighteenth-century family. But once old hierarchies began to collapse in the wake of the Revolution and new ideals arose related to Victorian notions of domestication and the mother as the center of the household, Americans found a loving and compassionate Christ much more congenial than an angry God holding sinners over the pit of hell. As awakened Americans increasingly emphasized Jesus' humanity over his divinity, they also became uneasy with the doctrine of predestination, which seemed to offend divine mercy. By the second third of the nineteenth century a new American religiosity, centered no longer on a wrathful father but on the loving son, had emerged: Jesus' martyrdom and his death on the cross were now believed to be not merely for a select band of Puritan saints but for humanity in its entirety. This universal call was embraced by evangelical Christians who would no longer wait passively for conversion, sainthood, and salvation, as earlier generations of Reformed Protestants had done.

The rising Arminian denominations, especially Methodists and Baptists, freed ordinary Americans from the stern predestinarianism of the Reformed churches and offered them the opportunity to seize control of their own spiritual destiny. The evangelicals embraced Jesus' universal call to all Christians, and virtually jettisoned the earlier harsh Calvinist fatalism. Free-willed decision making was not a foreign concept to growing numbers of nineteenth-century Americans, living in a society that was swiftly democratizing and thus increasingly empowering its constituents, particularly, but not exclusively, white male citizens. Numerous American Methodists and Baptists now believed that they could define for themselves their eternal fate: they could *choose* to continue to sin, or *decide* to accept Christ's calling. As in the democratized political sphere, individuals (not subjects!) were now free to accept or reject the salvation that Jesus so graciously offered.

By redefining Christian theology and religious practice, the Great Awakening of the early nineteenth century helped contemporaries to recalibrate their faith to catch up with and suit the rapid democratization of American politics: the free, republican-like choice to be saved was now universal, open to all.[19] The older determinism was replaced by a people who by now felt at ease in conversing in the language of political empowerment and democracy. As the political decision-making capability of the citizens of a democratic republic was transposed to the realm of the spiritual (and vice versa), millions were converted to the notion that they could make the most fateful decision to join (or not to join) Christ to save their own souls. This major theological transformation, which was particularly visible through the hierarchy-shattering praxis of the mass revival, adjusted the by now lagging beliefs in predestination and damnation to the emerging and powerful American democratic political culture.

The remarkable rise of evangelicalism at a time when American religion was still an overwhelmingly Protestant affair meant that millions of evangelicals now positioned Jesus at the center of their piety. Americans were becoming fixated on a Jesus who was more of an intimate friend than an aloof deity, and experienced what future generations would articulate as "accepting Jesus as one's savior," the formula that has become a virtual American Protestant mantra. For more and more Americans, Jesus became a spiritual "person" whom they wished to obey, follow, or even converse with; by mid-nineteenth century only a tiny population of Jews, Indians, and freethinkers would not subscribe to this Jesus-centered "cultural program."[20]

Early in the century, writings elaborating the relation of republicanism to religion still typically dwelled at length on Old Testament themes such as Exodus, the rules of the Israelite Judges, and the Mosaic constitution. Tracts and published sermons, such as Elias Smith's *The Loving Kindness of God Displayed in the Triumph of Republicanism in America* (1809), characteristically still focused solely on Hebraic themes when applying biblical political wisdom to the United States; authors found it unnecessary to refer to Jesus or even to the New Testament in any meaningful way. A few decades later, with Jesus' rise as the leading spiritual force in the realm and as a central figure in the political discourse, such practice would become extremely rare. With the publication of tracts such as *Republican Christianity; Or, True Liberty, as Exhibited in the Life, Precepts, and Early Disciples of the Great Redeemer* (1849), the previous absence of Jesus from the republic's political life was already a distant memory.[21] While the titles of such theopolitical tracts remained quite similar over time (such as *Republican Christianity*), their content noticeably changed from a strong emphasis on the Old Testament to New Testament–centered political theses.

Enoch Pond's "Republican Tendencies of the Bible" (1848) demonstrates this development well. Published earlier, a treatise such as Pond's would have no doubt expounded lengthily on the Old Testament. But writing at midcentury, Pond dedicated only three paragraphs to the Old Testament, remarking offhandedly that he did not wish "to go into a critical examination of the political institutions of Moses." It seemed sufficient for Pond to comment that the Mosaic constitution was "pervaded by the spirit of freedom, *so far as the circumstances of the people and age would allow*." This backhanded compliment to the Israelites of the age of the Hebrew republic reflected the winds of change, as Pond went on to an extensive examination of the political freedom that characterized, in his view, the New Testament.[22] By 1848 the "Bible" in the title of Pond's political discourse, which early in the century would have meant the Old Testament, now referred exclusively to the New.

Henry Ward Beecher, the "minister Plenipotentiary" of mid-nineteenth-century America, found "the very genius of Christianity" not in its dogmas, rites, or institutions but in the person of Jesus. Beecher could indeed still "gather a great deal from the Old Testament." Yet he remained "conscious that the fruit of the Bible is Christ. The rest to me is just what leaves are on an apple-tree. When I see the apple I know that there must have been a tree to bear that fruit; but after that I think of the fruit, and nothing else." Accordingly, historians have concluded that the real revolution in nineteenth-century American religion was not the rise of Arminianism or the novelty of the mass revival, but the renewed recognition of Jesus as "the main religious story in the first century of U.S. history." Naturally, this reawakening also meant a return of the stress on the New Testament. The restorationist Alexander Campbell, cofounder of Disciples of Christ, could proclaim, "we only aim at substituting the New Testament in lieu of every creed in existence whether Mahometan, Pagan, Jewish or Presbyterian." He explained that "we neither advocate Calvinism, Deism, or Sectarianism, Arianism, Socianism, Trinitarianism, Unitarianism, Deism, or Sectarianism, but New Testamentism." This ardent "New Testamentism" followed the "Jesus Christism" that asserted itself as a major cultural force in nineteenth-century America.[23]

The expanding evangelical churches' emphasis on Christ and the New Testament meant that the Old Testament inevitably became less prominent in evangelical Christians' cosmology. This erosion in the Old Testament's stature in American culture did not reflect a process of secularization, seen as an unambiguous transformation from a pious to a skeptical society. More nuanced processes implying change in religious attitudes and preferences were taking place; the view of a republican political religion focused on the Old Testament made way for a more liberal and individualistic salvation-centered democracy centered on the appeal to Christ. The new roles of Christ and the New Testament, accompanied by the diminishing stature of the Old Testament in American political culture, certainly do *not* constitute the story of diminishing religious sentiment; they manifest, rather, a significant, if mostly unfamiliar, transformation and reconstruction of beliefs and biblical sensibilities.

Cultural change often defies straightforward quantification, and the decline in the centrality of the Old Testament in the political discourse is no exception.[24] Nonetheless, the vivid biblical imagination that defined much of the early political culture of the United States was obviously waning as the nineteenth century progressed. The whole range of phenomena that this study has been tracing, from the confident renditions of America as a Second Israel to the depictions of American Indians as descendants of the Lost Ten Tribes, and from understanding the American confederacy through the lens of the Mosaic constitution to the sanctification of the United States through pseudobiblical texts, become rarer and less flamboyant after the 1830s. Literature is a particularly telling medium through which the prolonged moment of the shift of balance between the Old Testament and New may be discerned. Timothy Dwight's aforementioned *The Conquest of Canaan* (1785) and works such as Hannah More's late-eighteenth-century biblical dramas—based on such Old Testament characters as Moses, David, Daniel, and Hezekiah, but with no New Testament figures—captured and manifested the early republic's aroused Hebraic sensibilities and the importance of the Old Testament in contemporaries' consciousness. The two biggest bestsellers of the second half of the nineteenth century would also be based on biblical motifs; however, these massively popular works of fiction did not take their cue from the Old Testament but were Christ-centered: both Harriet Beecher Stowe's *Uncle Tom's Cabin* (1854), with two Christlike figures, Tom and Little Eva (to be further explored later in this chapter), and Lew Wallace's *Ben Hur: A Tale of the Christ* (1880), reflect Americans' insatiable thirst for Christ after the century's opening decades. Furthermore, throughout it, the number of Catholics in the United States steeply rose; by century's end one in every five Americans was a Catholic.[25] Catholicism, which traditionally preferred the New Testament to the Old, made the national inclination unlikely to reverse.

By the middle of the nineteenth century the United States was considerably more religious and Christian than the young republic it had been a few decades earlier. The waves of evangelical revivals responsible for this new Jesus-centered religiosity were inevitably related to the marginalization of the Old Testament in American culture. As Perry Miller stated, it was the evangelical "revolution in Protestant piety, with its communal shouting to the Lord for a mass salvation, that gradually shifted attention away from the Old Testament."[26] Nevertheless, the Second Great Awakening does not in itself provide a causal or complete or sufficient explanation for the demotion of the Old Testament in what earlier historians would have called "the American mind." We need to look beyond the rise of evangelical Christianity and the subsequent new and revamped role of Jesus in American culture for a full account of that change.

To be sure, the powerful evangelical orientation that emerged in the wake of the Second Great Awakening provides the context and intellectual circumstances for the deposition of the Old Testament in the political imagination. While the impulses that the Second Great Awakening generated certainly (and mostly unwittingly) helped marginalize the Old Testament, for a complete understanding of its dethroning, as well as its replacement by the New Testament, we need to look into the actual dynamics of contemporary political debates. Specifically, we should pay close attention to the various ways in which American partisans utilized the Bible in the most significant and bitterest political questions in antebellum America, namely slavery. The ways in which the Bible participated in the struggle over the institution's legitimacy and morality shed further light on the reasons for and the nature of this major, albeit gradual, cultural shift to the New Testament from the Old in the American political imagination.

The debate over slavery in America would count among its victims the Union itself, finally torn apart by the quarrel in 1861, and the Old Testament. In part collateral damage—none of the participants in the debate wished to damage the Hebrew Bible—and in part a reflection of independently existing processes, the decline of the Old Testament was firmly bound to the prolonged and consuming discussions about the Bible and slavery and slavery in the Bible. That debate was part of a larger discourse about the legality and morality of southern slavery, that, as the historian Molly Oshatz points out, participated in an extraordinarily rapid process through which a marginal eighteenth-century view that slavery was sinful had become by the Civil War "for vast numbers of northern Protestants an obvious statement of moral fact."[27]

Oshatz's point is excellent, but only in retrospect does that process seem rapid and indeed inevitable; by the 1830s both supporters and opponents of slavery had already deliberated human bondage in theological terms for centuries, while American slavery expanded numerically and geographically. Like their predecessors, nineteenth-century Americans were sure that the Bible was "clear as a bell" in its attitude toward slavery; they could not agree, to say the least, on what Scripture's position actually was. The question became increasingly pressing after 1830, as worsening sectional tensions and the escalating tone and stakes of the debate over slavery drove all sides to entrench their views in opposition to their ideological rivals. For more than thirty years Americans deliberated slavery and Scripture in bitter exchanges that did not abate until the physical demise of the Confederacy in 1865.[28]

The contours of this antebellum debate were plotted early on and had not significantly changed by the early 1850s, by which time the lines of the argument were firmly set. The dispute became less innovative as earlier works were reprinted and, in the words of the historian Michael O'Brien, "a canon developed." The question would be settled only on the battlefield. Those opposed to slavery, mostly northerners, generally argued that biblical "slaves" were actually better described as servants, not chattel; that the Mosaic laws forbade Israelites to enslave their coreligionists; that the enslavement of the heathens was rare and heathen slaves were commonly converted to Judaism; and that the spirit of the teachings and beliefs of Christ and the Apostles was clearly opposed to any form of human bondage. Advocates of slavery, on the other hand, pointed to Noah's curse, which seemed to sanction slavery—

moreover, slavery racially based. They adduced the meticulous regulation of slavery in various biblical books; they enumerated many biblical protagonists, first and foremost the patriarchs, who held slaves; and pointed out that even those who did not hold slaves, namely Jesus and his disciples, never spoke clearly—or even implicitly—against that universal social institution.[29]

Historians tend to agree that the proslavery advocates developed a sounder scriptural argument in the debate on slavery and the Bible.[30] Nevertheless, whoever the victor in that significant theological debate might be, it brought the New Testament to the forefront in a political debate as never before. It also made the Old Testament seem, perhaps for the first time, less relevant, even wholly irrelevant in the most urgent of political questions before the United States. What follows is not intended as a comprehensive survey of the biblical debate on slavery, a task that would necessitate an endeavor much beyond the present scope. In the remainder of this chapter I will demonstrate how the general thrust of both the anti- and proslavery arguments worked, in different ways, to elevate the New Testament and relegate the Old Testament in the political discourse, significantly contributing to the decline of the Old Testament biblicism that I have explored.

Contemporary Americans recognized that "to an extent wholly unknown in other lands," in the United States even the most important "questions of right and wrong, and its decisions" were put to the test of the Bible, a practice "recognized at the South as well as at the North." Accordingly, historians have long been interested in the religious and theological dimensions of the debate over slavery, producing impressive and nuanced studies on its biblical aspects. Referring randomly to sources from the Old and the New Testaments, they implicitly acknowledge the obvious fact that antebellum Americans derived arguments for and against slavery from both. In these analyses American historians have yet to divide "Scripture" into its Old and New elements, certainly not in the context of the question of slavery, although such indiscriminate treatment makes sense: for Christian believers the Bible was a scriptural whole composed of two divine testaments connected through typological logic and tradition. Nevertheless, many of the extensive polemic commentaries on either side justify separate treatment of the uses of the Old and New Testaments in the bitter debate, if only because contemporaries themselves often devoted separate chapters and sections to the distinct attitudes of the Hebrew and Greek Bibles to slavery.[31] Most important, by making this distinction we shall better understand significant issues and cultural dynamics that otherwise remain undetected. Once the roles of the Old and

New Testaments are differentiated and examined separately, a new understanding of the antebellum political and biblical imagination, hence of the era's cultural and intellectual history, will emerge.

The underlying premise of both sides of the debate was the division and periodization of sacred history. The Virginia Baptist pastor Thornton Stringfellow first published a methodical proslavery essay in 1841 in a Richmond newspaper and nine years later in pamphlet form; his work, which was widely hailed as "vastly the best" religious defense of slavery, demonstrated this shared outlook: the first epoch was "the portion of time stretching from Noah, until the law was given to Abraham's posterity . . . [in] Mount Sinai," an era dubbed "the patriarchal age." The second was "from giving the [Mosaic] law until the coming of Christ," known as the Mosaic or legal dispensation. While these two periods were largely covered by the Hebrew Bible, the era "from the coming of Christ to the end of time" was called the Gospel dispensation.[32] (The Gospel dispensation, which signaled a sharp break in history, carried an especially heavy moral weight: it opened an entirely new chapter in the relations of God and man through the life and death of Jesus Christ, which continued with the teachings of the Apostles and the creation of the Christian Church.) Both sides in the biblical debate over slavery acknowledged the relevance of these eras to the question they were pursuing. They also understood these distinct historical eras as proving their diverging attitudes to slavery.

The New Testament gained fresh political importance after 1830, when Jesus Christ was increasingly politicized in the slavery debate, each side endowing him with its own social identity: Jesus (and consequently the Apostles) could be portrayed as anything from ardently opposed to slavery to unquestioningly welcoming slaveholders—hence slavery—into the early Christian Church. For the first time in the history of the republic, Christ, in addition to his role as ethical teacher or holy redeemer, assumed the mantle of a partisan in a major political battle. Emphasizing his divinity and perfect and pure humanity enabled the antislavery camp to show Jesus as an angry critic of any person who sinned by tolerating enslavement; supporters of slavery or proponents of political compromise could portray their Jesus a supporter of hierarchical order and social conformity. These polar views of Jesus also reflected the positions on the New Testament as a whole, as the teachings of the Apostles were similarly mobilized for each camp's cause.

This politicization of Christ, which coincided with the antebellum rise of Christ-centered evangelicalism, underscores the New Testament's new role in the American public arena. After decades in which Jesus and the Apostles had little to say to American audiences in the way of politics, suddenly the New Testament was thrust into the political fray and played a central role in this most important of contemporary debates. The New Testament—considerably less prominent than the Old Testament in earlier national political discussions during the Revolution, deliberations over the Constitution, and later national debates—was now ensconced at the political center in a way hardly imaginable only a few years before. The debate on slavery thus simultaneously elevated the importance of Jesus and the New Testament (and for different reasons, as we shall see, furthered the loss of the Old Testament's status in the political discourse). The biblical debate on the most political of antebellum issues was therefore crucial for the process that the religious historian Stephen Prothero has described as the shifting of the "Scriptural center of gravity" of the United States from the Old to the New Testaments.[33]

When the debate over slavery intensified in the 1830s, biblical defenses of the institution in America were anything but new. They had been erected intermittently in the United States since the 1770s in response to attacks by Quakers and Anglican evangelicals. Proslavery, however, "enjoyed a new beginning with the radicalization of antislavery" following the appearance of William Lloyd Garrison's newspaper *The Liberator* and the Nat Turner rebellion in 1831. Ministers, according to the historian Michael O'Brien, were "consistently the most energetic proponents of slavery," preaching to a proslavery camp that, as Eugene Genovese and Elizabeth Fox-Genovese remind us, supported it because they genuinely believed that the Bible sanctioned the Peculiar Institution, and that it could rely on Scripture to validate and substantiate its cause. Apologists for slavery, who helped to legitimate the expansive evangelicalism once suspect for its radical tendencies, resorted time and again to the Bible for vindication in a discourse that was cumulative in which thinker referred to thinker, and repeatedly turned to the numerous instances in which slavery was implicitly or explicitly discussed and regulated in various places, for example, Genesis 9:25–27 and 14:14–15, Deuteronomy 20:10–11, or Leviticus 24:44–54. The Old Testament's sanctioning of slavery seemed obvious to slavery advocates. "Of the great antiquity of slavery no one can doubt," stated the eminent biblical scholar Moses Stuart. As proof he presented "the curse that Noah lay on the progeny of Ham, that Canaan his son should be 'a servant of servants unto his brethren.'" Noah's curse seemed to many to sanction a *racially* based slavery, as Ham was believed—without scriptural grounds—to be the progenitor of black Africans. In the words of the abolitionist Theodore Weld, the curse of Noah may indeed have been the "*vade mecum* of slaveholders, [which they] never venture abroad without." It was definitely not, however, the only Old Testament justification for slavery.[34]

Contemporaries who held proslavery attitudes gladly pointed out that "the patriarchs, whose piety is held up in the Bible for our admiration, were masters of slaves." The "natural descendants" of the patriarchs Abraham, Isaac, and Jacob—the Israelites—were also "holders of slaves [whom] God took ... into special relation." According to this line of argument, the Israelites' government established by the laws of Moses "expressly incorporated a [godly] permission to buy and hold slaves. These institutes not only recognize slavery as lawful, but contain very minute directions." Much of the argument for slavery drawn from the Old Testament was based on divine permission to hold "heathen" slaves, who were presumably outside God's covenant. The historian Charles Irons argues that when black men and women joined southern evangelical churches "in numbers that far surpassed white evangelicals' expectations," white evangelicals realized "the irrelevance of the Old Testament model of slavery" to the situation in the American South. Even if such an assertion might be overstated, the developments that Irons convincingly describes suggest that the master class had to search for new ways to understand and justify slave ownership.[35]

Slavery advocates relied more on the New Testament than on the Old in their attempt to justify the Peculiar Institution. A limited quantitative study of proslavery argumentation by the historian Larry Tise suggests that they used the New Testament at least as much as the Old to justify antebellum American slavery. In absolute terms the sheer volume of the references to the New Testament in proslavery argumentation was a novelty in political rhetoric. This prolific use of the New Testament for the proslavery cause was particularly impressive since, as the historian Mason I. Lowance notes, "many of the Old Testament texts clearly show, in graphic detail, how slavery was practiced by God's chosen people, the Hebrews." Still, proslavery polemical works, some of them hundreds of pages long, dedicated more space, occasionally much more space, to the New Testament than to the Old.[36] Contemporaries did not abandon the Old Testament in their attempt to justify and defend American slavery; yet the extensive use by slavery advocates of the New Testament, a Scripture that until recently had by no means been at the center of the political fray, was in itself innovative and forward-looking.

The renewed interest in the New Testament is also evident in slavery apologists' emphasis on its alleged greater importance than the Old Testament: "None can reason from the case of the Jews," argued the eminent biblical scholar Moses Stuart, since the Old Testament narrated the history of a "favored, [and] secluded nation." "The case of men, who lived after the coming of Him," however, was a valid example. Christ's divine moral example, perfect and loftier than anything the world had seen before or after his short life, underlay what arguably was the commonest, the firmest, and the most convincing argument in the biblical proslavery arsenal: if slavery was such an obnoxious sin, its advocates repeatedly asked, why did neither Jesus nor the Apostles, who lived in societies in which slavery was ubiquitous, never condemn the institution? As "A Southern Farmer" put it, "there is not a precept in the writings of the Saviour and his Apostles which denounces the morality of the institution of slavery. . . . On the contrary, we find the moral right to own slaves, justified by the act of the Saviour and his apostles receiving slave-owners in the church and greeting them as brethren in the faith." Although slaveholders seemed vindicated through the precedent of slavery in both the Old Testament and the New (slavery, "established in the days of Moses . . . [was] justified by the act of the Saviour and his apostles"), much greater importance was attributed to the New Testament's example: "Why was the compassionate Redemer [*sic*] silent on a subject so momentous?" proponents of slavery, north and south, repeatedly asked. Even resolute opponents of slavery such as James Freeman Clarke conceded "the fact, which always remains a fact, that Jesus and his Apostles did not attempt violently to overthrow and uproot this institution, did not denounce all slaveholders, and that while we have catalogues of sins which are to be repented and forsaken, slaveholding is not among them."[37] Slavery advocates could thus confidently conclude that Christ must have tolerated it because it was, in biblical times as well as their own, a moral and lawful institution.

Supporters of slavery found in the New Testament vindication for their position. "At the time of the advent of Jesus Christ," proclaimed a contemporary article that gave "great satisfaction to the friends of slavery in the South," slavery in its "worst forms prevailed over the whole world. The Saviour found it around him in Judea; the Apostles met with it in Asia, Greece, and Italy." How did Christ and the early Christians react to the pervasive slavery? Not by denouncing it "as necessarily and universally sinful," slavery advocates pointed out; "the subject [was] hardly alluded to by Christ in any of his personal instructions. The Apostles refer[red] to it, not to pronounce upon it as a question of morals, but to prescribe the relative duties of masters and slaves." Southerners were convinced that, in the words of the Virginian John Thompson Brown, while Jesus "came into the world to reprove sin . . . he rebuked not slavery." The conclusion seemed obvious: that slavery was "not a moral evil, is evident from the fact, that it is nowhere condemned by the Redeemer, or his apostles, in the New Testament." The argument from "the conduct of Christ and his immediate followers" seemed to slavery advocates "decisive."[38]

Introspective (and northern) Christians such as Moses Stuart who grappled with Christ's attitude to slavery could consequently describe Jesus as a realist who acknowledged that sin and social hierarchies were elements inseparable from the human condition. Christ thus purposely and carefully avoided "meddling with those matters which belonged to the civil power. Slavery was one of these." If slavery was indeed a dire condition, Stuart was certain that Christ felt that it "might be made a very tolerable condition, nay, even a blessing to such as were shiftless and helpless, in case of kind and gentle mastership."[39] So even northerners like Stuart, who considered slavery a scourge and who implored his slaveholding compatriots to treat their slaves humanely, could reconcile Christ, and therefore the American republic, with slavery.

Proslavery Americans commonly interpreted the New Testament as favoring social stability and clear social hierarchies. They enjoined "obedience upon the slave as an obligation due to a present rightful authority," as Wilbur Fiske, president of Wesleyan University, pointed out. This northern reverend argued that social rigidity was favored in the New Testament, which taught that "the freeman was to remain free, and the slave, unless emancipation should offer, was to remain a slave." As opposed to what may have been superficially and mistakenly assumed, the New Testament, according to this view, was "not silent as to slavery; it recognises the relation, and commands slaves to obey their masters." Thornton Stringfellow believed that all Christian churches in the New Testament were "recognized as compounded of masters and servants; and that they [were] instructed by Jesus Christ how to discharge their relative duties," and that the words of Jesus Christ added "to the obligation of the servant to render service with good will to his master."[40]

One of the key scriptural texts in this respect was the Epistle to Philemon, a canonized letter written by Paul in his prison cell to a church member, asking forgiveness on behalf of his "separated," probably runaway, slave Onemius. Slavery advocates repeatedly referred to that Pauline epistle, which proved, if nothing else, that slavery existed at "the time when the apostle Paul sent a runaway slave home to his master, Philemon, and wrote a Christian and paternal letter to this slaveholder." On the eve of the Civil War, John Richter Jones remarked that the biblical justification of slavery in Philemon was so "clear and conclusive [that] . . . it is one of the curiosities of ecclesiastical literature that our clerical [abolitionist] friends could pronounce slavery 'utterly irreconcilable with the spirit and principle of the Gospel of Christ.'" Philemon seemed to prove more than the mere existence of slavery: it demonstrated to numerous Christians who supported the perpetuation of slavery in the United States that Paul, "as the Great Head of the church has recognized the relation of master and slave." Even southerners such as Bishop George Pierce, who criticized their region for failing to reform its slave system, could confidently assert that "the Southern people, with all their faults—vices if you please—have never corrupted the gospel of Christ."[41]

Many Bible readers, among them southerners, felt that slavery was evil. They were also convinced that the Bible must support that feeling, and they cited it extensively to demonstrate that chattel slavery was sinful and against the word of God. Even more than the proslavery position, the biblical arguments hurled by antislavery supporters at their opponents in an intersectional dialogue damaged the traditional primacy of the Old Testament, and reinforced the rising tide of New Testamentism in American political culture.[42]

Like slavery advocates, the antislavery camp generally favored the New Testament as a moral compass; they too appealed incessantly to Jesus to make their case. This preference for the New Testament was evident in the radical wing of the abolitionist movement: William Lloyd Garrison (1805–1879), an abolitionist leader and among the founders of the Anti-Slavery Society, claimed to dislike the Hebrew Scriptures for recording "exterminating wars . . . expressly commanded by Jehova."[43] Garrison founded his biblical case against slavery not on the Old Testament but on the figure of Jesus, pointing out that the early Christians and the martyred Christ were not uniformly "venerated and honored" in the years after his death; but like American abolitionists they had been castigated as "pestilent and seditious fellows" in their own time. Jesus' symbolic importance in abolitionist rhetoric was further demonstrated on the iconic masthead of Garrison's newspaper *The Liberator*, which carried a striking image of "Jesus, the Liberator," under the text *I come to break the bonds of the oppressor*. Even a violent abolitionist such as John Brown, described lately as "an Old Testament Christian" who was inspired by such fierce biblical figures as the judges Gideon and Samson, reverted to the teachings of the New Testament when justifying his raid on Harpers Ferry: "The New Testament . . . teaches . . . that all things whatsoever I would that men should do to me, I should do even so to them. It teaches . . . to 'remember them that are in bonds, as bound with them.'"[44]

Abolitionists, too, thereby imparted to the New Testament a political role that it had lacked in earlier decades. "Abolitionists take their stand upon the New Testament doctrine of the natural equity of man," asserted Jonathan Blanchard, the future president of Wheaton College; "the one-bloodism of human kind," an idea set out in Acts 17:26, attested to a shared origin of mankind. Blanchard appealed to American-Christian patriotism by bundling together the edicts of Jesus Christ and Thomas Jefferson, the two who authored and elucidated "those great principles of human rights, drawn from the New Testament, and announced in the American Declaration of Independence, declaring that all men have natural and inalienable rights to person, property, and the pursuit of happiness."[45]

Yet convinced emancipationists were not unconditionally committed to the Bible when they asserted that "if the religion of Christ allows us to take such a license from such precepts as these, the New Testament would be the greatest curse that was ever inflicted on our race."[46] However, even abolitionists with a less controversial all-or-nothing stance would face, as Mark Noll has pointed out, a double burden: even moderates had to demonstrate that proslavery biblical arguments were in the wrong, a formidable exegetical task in itself; in view of the general reverence and deference toward the Bible, they had to make sure that their own arguments did not appear to assault scriptural authority. Antislavery biblical exegetes thus walked a tightrope when advancing their most widely used propositions: first, the Hebraic bondage described in the Bible was categorically and inherently different from the slavery practiced in the American South, hence the South's Peculiar Institution could not be sanctioned by biblical example; second, even if slavery had existed in biblical times, Scripture's spirit, if not its exact word, was hostile to it. Both these popular lines of argument further weakened the Old Testament's traditional cultural standing.

As the historian Molly Oshatz points out, moderate antislavery proponents needed to demonstrate a theory of moral progress that would invalidate the applicability and acceptability in modern society of biblical practices such as slavery; in order to do so their primary strategy was to "privilege certain New Testament texts over those biblical passages that referred directly to slavery and to interpret the entire text in the light of these privileged passages." The Mosaic code of laws, which seemed to affirm a certain form of slavery—if not the slavery that was practiced in the American South—had to be brushed aside as merely preparatory, and inadequate to the nineteenth-century United States.[47]

Hence antislavery activists who appealed to the Bible to argue against southern slavery found their inspiration, and possibly their strongest argument, in Christ's example. Colonial opponents of slavery had already expressed the belief that "the Spirit of Christ" was incompatible with depriving one's "fellow creatures of the sweetness of freedom"; they had consequently established a tradition of understanding the teachings of Jesus in particular, and the New Testament more generally, as incompatible with slavery. Nineteenth-century abolitionists elaborated this idea of incompatibility, arguing that the spirit of Christianity as revealed through the New Testament self-evidently refuted slavery. Treatises such as Joseph Thompson's *Teachings of the New Testament on Slavery* (1856) explored that argument, and it became common to appeal, as the New York minister George Cheever did, to the inconsistency between slavery and "the benevolence commanded" by the New Testament. Even if the New Testament left no explicit instruction forbidding slavery, it "prohibited it in a manner far more emphatic than could have been done by any [direct] precept"; Christ and the Apostles dealt with the sin of slavery, according to Francis Wayland (1796–1865), the Baptist president of Brown University, not directly but by "promulgating such truths . . . as should render the slavery of a human being a manifest moral absurdity." As Albert Barnes put it, "the spirit of the New Testament is against slavery, and the principles of the New Testament, if fairly applied, would abolish it."[48] Seldom would such views be attributed categorically and in general terms to the Old Testament, a corpus that minutely detailed and regulated bondage and coercive relations between humans (whether "slaves" or not) in a pre-Christian world which, evangelical Christians believed, was still ignorant of the grace and love of Jesus.

The Methodist Nathan Bangs (1778–1862) argued that the relevant question was not whether Jesus had ever explicitly condemned slave ownership, as slavery proponents never ceased to point out, but whether Jesus could plausibly be imagined as owning a slave himself. His own human comportment, antislavery supporters argued, not his recorded verbal commands, should have become the ultimate standard for Christian living. Opponents of slavery agreed that "the institution of slavery [was] contrary to the Christian religion, and inconsistent with its spirit," and that "the Saviour and his apostles inculcated such views of man as amount to a prohibition of slavery." Obviously, slavery's opponents held, Jesus and his early followers "gave such views of man, that . . . no one would make or retain a slave." It followed that the principles of the New Testament "must of necessity abolish slavery . . . just in so far as slavery is . . . in variance with . . . elementary truths."[49]

Beyond this common appeal to the New Testament's "spirit," namely that slavery was "condemned by the general tenor and scope of the New Testament," abolitionists cited Jesus Christ's actual words.[50] Henry Ward Beecher was most emphatic in his Plymouth Church sermon (1861) as he referred to Christ, who "came to open the prison to them that are bound." Quoting Jesus' words in Luke 4:18, Beecher preached that it was the New Testament, the same text

> on which men justify shutting them and locking [slaves]. "To proclaim liberty to the captives"; and that is the text out of which men spin cords to bind men, women, and children. "To set at liberty them that are bruised"; and that is the Book from out of which they argue, with amazing ingenuity, all the infernal meshes and snares by which to keep men in bondage.[51]

Albert Barnes (1798–1870) argued at length that slavery as such did not exist in the time of Christ, so neither he nor the Apostles could have come in contact with the institution; slavery advocates were thus wrong to conclude that Jesus implicitly approved it, as one could not expect Jesus to denounce an institute he never witnessed. Yet even to abolitionists who conceded that Jesus did not explicitly denounce servitude, it seemed obvious that at the very least he would have condemned "such a monstrous system as that of American slavery."[52]

Abolitionists repeatedly resorted to the phrases "bleeding humanity" and "meek and lowly Jesus," derived from Matthew 11:29, in reference to the enslaved Africans, thereby likening them to the crucified Christ. So frequent were these phrases that they became the virtual mottoes of the antislavery movement. The abolitionist Angelina Grimke characteristically appealed to "the meek, the lowly, and compassionate Savior," who could be envisaged as "a slaveholder" no more than as "a warrior." Even Frederick Douglass, who attacked southern Christians' "slaveholding religion," made sure to proclaim his own devotion to "the meek and lowly Jesus." But not Jesus alone was deemed sensitive to the pain of the humble: the New Testament as a whole taught and embodied "patience, meekness, fidelity and charity," according to Francis Wayland.[53]

Those against slavery also took other approaches to confront the problem of the New Testament and slavery. Professor Tayler Lewis, for example, attacked the proslavery position based on the Old Testament's alleged sanction of enslavement of the heathen. Through Jesus' acceptance of salvation for all, Lewis argued, emerged the doctrine of Christian universalism, as opposed to the restrictiveness and insularity of ancient Judaism. Such universalism made it necessary to recognize that "theologically, ecclesiastically, Christianly, there are no heathen." Since blacks in America were all at least nominally Christians, there was no longer any "heathen" whom it was acceptable to enslave.[54]

Nevertheless, the appeal to Jesus' person was the most effective weapon in the arsenal of the antislavery movement. The unprecedented success of Harriet Beecher Stowe's *Uncle Tom's Cabin* manifested Jesus' ability to effectively express antislavery ideas and sentiments. That immensely successful Victorian novel appealed to the powerful evangelical sensibilities of the time by rendering two Christlike characters: the horrendously maltreated and meek Tom and the tubercular and ill-fated Little Eva. If Eva was "not only an imitator of Christ . . . [but] an image of Christ," Tom in his saintly perfection of character and the brutal horror of his death was Christ himself. In this most influential of American books, Stowe offered the two Christs, the female and black, as sacrificial lambs in the cause of antislavery.[55] A meek and lowly Jesus who was crucified for the sake of a bleeding humanity, and not an Old Testament figure, had become the personification of the antislavery movement.

The emphasis on Jesus' and the New Testament's crucial role in the antislavery cause does not mean that activists stopped invoking the Old Testament for their attacks on the Peculiar Institution; like their proslavery adversaries, they often presented their case and argumentation through the Old Testament as they set out to demonstrate that the Hebrew Scripture too proved them in the right.[56] Yet in doing so, the antislavery activists underscored the sharp differences between biblical Israel and the United States. Contrary to the general thrust of the political use of the Old Testament in earlier decades, slavery opponents called attention to how *different* the First and

Second Israels were; inadvertently, they helped to dismantle the formerly prevalent view of the biblical American nation.

Even in a society in which Scripture was still a highly authoritative source of truth, Israelite slavery, which antislavery activists did not even acknowledge as "slavery" at all, as we shall soon see, could still prove very little—or so abolitionists thought. They assailed the proslavery mode of argumentation from history, pointing out that other malignant, impious, and unacceptable social practices—repeatedly giving the examples of polygamy and "arbitrary" divorce—also existed among the Israelites, as even the most ardent slaveholder had to admit. No one (except perhaps the marginalized and maligned Mormons) would suggest, however, that polygamy's mere practice among the Israelites in biblical times sanctioned, not to say sanctified, those practices.[57]

Yet antislavery activists sought to prove that slavery did not even exist in biblical times; that what appeared to be "slavery" in the Old Testament was actually completely different from the social condition prevailing in the American south. Lewis of New York characteristically pointed out that the Old Testament discussed "distant ages," and in applying it to contemporary America one had to take account of "the vastly changed condition of the world," as well as the "differing circumstances" in ancient Israel and the modern United States. One salient difference was that regardless of the obscure curse of Noah, abolitionists found no proof that the master-servant relations described in the Bible were racially defined. Albert Barnes, in his comprehensive and hair-splitting *An Inquiry into the Scriptural Views of Slavery* (1846) argued that slaveholders and their apologists were mistaken in feeling that the example of slavery in the Old Testament justified their practice. To prove their point it was "indispensable [for slaveholders] to show that the slavery which existed then was essentially the same as that which it is proposed to vindicate by it."[58] Antislavery activists believed passionately that their ideological rivals failed to do so.

Most abolitionists understood the biblical practice of bondage as a mild form of indentured servitude, resembling wage labor more than modern slavery. Biblical servitude was limited and defined by the freedom granted to Israelite servants in the Jubilee year, according to the antislavery position, so Hebrews' servants, who by law were to be freed every fifty years, could not have sunk into perpetual chattel slavery. Abolitionists often engaged in intricate philological and exegetical examinations to underscore the deep differences between Hebrew bondage and American slavery. A crucial question hinged on how to translate the Hebrew *eved*: was "slave," "bondman," or "servant" the appropriate translation? Old Testament "bondmen" (as well as New Testament "servants") were not slaves at all, the New York Congregationalist George Cheever characteristically concluded such a discussion.[59]

Protracted treatises such as Theodore Weld's *The Bible against Slavery* (1837) were dedicated to proving that the slave system practiced in the South could not by any means be considered similar to biblical bondage. A conceptual analysis of Old Testament slavery demonstrated the contrast: Weld argued, for example, that biblical masters were not their servants' "owners," that biblical servitude was voluntary, and that servants were paid wages and were expressly distinguished from property. *The Bible against Slavery* also incorporated historical analysis, examining such specific examples as the condition of the Gibeonites, an enslaved Canaanite people. This case demonstrated that even the miserable situation of that gentile people was different from that of American slaves: the Gibeonites' servitude, unlike American blacks', Weld asserted, was of their free will; no less important, unlike slaves in the South, they were able to preserve their society's communal framework, and they never lived with or near their masters or acted as "domestics."[60]

Weld's attempt to differentiate Old Testament from southern servitude underscores how abolitionists enumerated what seemed to be substantial differences between the ancient and modern biblical forms of servitude in their attempt to prove that biblical bondage could not justify American slavery. Old Testament protective measures (such as forcing masters to manumit abused slaves "even to the breaking of a tooth") and laws such as the one forbidding the Hebrews from delivering up "a slave who had escaped from his master, but [they] were [even] commanded to allow him to dwell in the place which he chose," were conjured to highlight the leniency of Hebraic servitude as against the harshness of American slavery. No wonder that abolitionists concluded that patriarchal-age and Mosaic slavery stood "in strong contrast" to the American system: Israel's example could in no way justify America's, and actually proved how wrong the slaveholder's position was. The brutalities of slave trafficking and of the characteristics of "social death" attributed by modern scholars to southern slavery were lacking in the mild master-servant relationship of "the Hebrews," whom American abolitionists passionately concluded "were not a nation of slaveholders." In keeping with the fantasies of Americans of the era of the founding who disapproved of slavery and hoped it would collapse under its own weight and fade away, slavery in biblical Israel seemed to have "finally ceased to be known in the nation."[61]

In sum, the abolitionists held that Old Testament slavery (if slavery it was) was a benign, lenient, temporary, and emancipatory social practice, one that differed completely from the atrocious, hereditary, and racial institution practiced in the American South.[62] Albert Barnes argued,

> In the Hebrew commonwealth scenes could never occur such as are constantly taking place in the United States, where families are separated for ever by sales at public auction, or where, at the pleasure of the master, a husband and father may be removed to a distant part of the land, to see his wife and children no more. It is only necessary to read the description of such scenes as frequently occur in the Southern states of this Union, to be forcibly impressed with the humanity of the Mosaic law, and to see the strong contrast between servitude under that law and slavery in our own country.[63]

Abolitionists further claimed that proponents of slavery did not take into account the specific historical and theological contexts and circumstances under which slavery was mandated and prevailed in Israel. Daniel Coker summarized: "The Israelites were not sent by a divine mandate, to nations three hundred miles distant, who were neither doing, nor meditating any thing against them, and to whom they had no right whatever, in order to captivate them by fraud or force." Americans, in short, could not infer permission to enslave blacks from the Israelite mandate to hold slaves. The Jewish law, through which southerners wished to substantiate their social system, "was made exclusively for that [Hebrew] people and can be pleaded in justification by no other people whatever." Even when antislavery supporters conceded that slavery did exist in the Old Testament ("the Hebrews," some could admit, "held slaves from the time of the conquest of Canaan, and . . . Abraham and the patriarchs had held them many centuries before"; or "Moses enacted laws with special reference to that relation"), the point was that biblical slavery *did not* sanction American slavery; instead, they argued, if and only if all southern slaveholders were Hebrews, and only if they could locate Canaanites to enslave, could the Bible provide a warrant for slavery.[64] Since the divine permission to the Hebrews to enslave was historically specific, and Americans were obviously not Hebrews and blacks were not Canaanites, southerners had no biblical justification to enslave African-Americans.

Abolitionists' recurrent attempts to historicize biblical slavery in order to demonstrate how unlike its American counterpart it was underscored the stark contrast between the American and Israelite societies. A few decades earlier Americans had been diligently constructing elaborate representations of their nation as the American Israel, referring to what contemporaries saw as striking similarities between the two nations. Consequently, Americans could relate to the belief that "the people of the United States come nearer to a parallel with Ancient Israel, than any other nation." With the debate over slavery intensifying, however, opponents of slavery found themselves working hard at *differentiating* the two nations. Even southern preachers, such as "the hard nosed" James M. Pendleton, dared to exclaim that "there are points of material dissimilarity between that [Israelite] system and our system of slavery." These attempts to render Hebrew slavery *sui generis* amounted to what may be termed "Hebraic exceptionalism": while the Israelites may have received an explicit divine grant to take slaves among the heathen when they conquered Canaan, that grant was "peculiar" and "anomalous." It was an approval given "to one people, and to one people only, the Hebrews."[65]

Americans who held antislavery sentiments concentrated mostly in the North, which in the decades following the Revolution was the region most invested in understandings of America as the Second Israel. After 1830, however, it was northerners who repeatedly expressed the belief that what the Children of Israel did millennia ago in Canaan did not authorize "American citizens here at home to destroy, or to enslave, or to hold in slavery, the people of another continent." Such effective historicization of Israelite slavery, describing their grant to hold slaves as historically specific and one which could "be of force at no other time, and to no other people," considerably weakened and subverted attempts to understand America as a New Israel. The debate over slavery "forced antislavery moderates to utilize the idea of moral progress" that unfolded gradually through time, thus intensifying an awareness of history and historical change; it introduced both sides of the debate to a historical consciousness through which it was becoming increasingly problematic to view themselves in terms of a New Israel.[66]

Perry Miller was thus only partially correct in pointing out that Americans, or rather antislavery Americans, gave up their reliance on the Hebrew Bible because they "no longer [stood] up to the violence in the Old Testament," which earlier generations had taken in their stride.[67] It was more their struggle to come to terms with that biblical violence—by presenting it as a lesser evil than that encountered in their America—that coerced them to present biblical Israel and the United States as categorically dissimilar. The repeated attempts to differentiate American slavery from that of biblical Israel, which constituted a central line of reasoning in the antislavery argument, should be understood in the more general trajectory of the contemporary parting ways with the Old Testament. The evangelical emphasis on the New Testament—in both the North and the South—compounded by the attempts to differentiate America from ancient Israel, transformed the biblical and political imagination by the eve of the Civil War. With the political tensions between the North and the South mounting, the vivid early-nineteenth-century renditions of the American New Israel were becoming subdued, mellow, and less frequent.

Reference to the Hebrews' own enslavement in Egypt provided a striking counterpoint to the extensive discussion about whether and in what form slavery existed in biblical times, and the implications of Israelites and early Christians keeping slaves (or not). As shown in earlier chapters, by the antebellum period the story of the Exodus had a formidable history in America, having provided seventeenth-century Puritans and later American revolutionaries with a founding myth and usable history: both the Puritans and revolutionary patriots understood their deeds as flights from their respective houses of British, "Egyptian," bondage. These Exodian precedents, which were central in the postrevolutionary construction of the image of the Second Israel, surfaced once more in antislavery accounts; now, however, their emphasis was not on the Exodus as a narrative of liberation but on the Israelite enslavement in Egypt as an example of the most brutal of biblical slaveries. Yet severe as antislavery spokesmen described it, they depicted Egyptian slavery as less harsh—indeed as lenient, compared with American slavery. Some abolitionists pointed out that Israelites, unlike blacks in America, were not dispersed among their captors but were allowed to form their separate and autonomous community; they also noted the Israelites' relatively high standard of living.[68] Such comparisons were in line with the standard antislavery argument that biblical bondage—even as practiced in Egypt—and American slavery were essentially different institutions.

However, some slavery opponents believed that the Egyptian example was relevant to the American case. Albert Barnes asserted that "strong points of resemblance" between Egyptian and American slavery were "so remarkable" that they could not "fail to strike every one who reads the account in Exodus" of Israel's slavery. Being a foreign race, "as the African race is with us," the Israelites "had no share in the government; they had no appointments under the crown; were eligible to no office; had no participation in making or administrating laws. They were dissimilar in religion, in language, in customs, in employment ... [or] in manners ... they were a race introduced from abroad, and kept throughout, and on principle distinct." Barnes's vehement attack on Egyptian, and American, slavery must have struck contemporaries, much as it strikes modern readers, not for elaborating the Egyptian example but for applying it in reverse: if the black American slaves played the role of the Israelites, which was the role that Americans traditionally assumed when co-opting the story of the Exodus, then the horrifying implication was that white Americans had become enslaving Egyptians.[69]

In light of the long and rich tradition of Americans identifying as Israelites enslaved in an Egyptian house of bondage, this reversal should not be taken lightly. Yet Barnes elaborated his insight, finding a "striking resemblance in regard to the numbers held in bondage in Egypt, and those [blacks] now in servitude in this country." Such arithmetic, which was a mainstay of the typological renditions of America as the New Israel, must have struck Americans when applied in reverse to represent them as Egyptians enslaving a black Israel. Now, while still making use of a familiar typological reading of a biblical narrative that Americans had long since adopted, Americans became the sinful evildoers; no less significant was that they were the side that was ultimately punished by God. Here was a striking reversal of revolutionary-era biblical logic: while "the calamities brought upon the Egyptians for holding a foreign people in bondage, and for the measures to which they resorted to perpetuate that bondage, were an expression of the views which God entertained," this time the "Egyptians" were not a British Pharaoh and his Redcoat host. Like so many revolutionary sermons in the past, this one concluded that "the deliverance of the Hebrews from Egyptian bondage ... brought out an oppressed people by His own hand." But now blacks were oppressed Hebrews striving for freedom, and white and politically privileged Americans were tyrannical and oppressing Egyptians.[70]

Such inversions and striking portrayals of Americans as oppressing Egyptians clearly demonstrate how much the question of slavery could disturb Americans' traditional reliance on the Old Testament as a source for identification as the New Israel. This topsy-turvy typology that rendered white Americans as Egyptian taskmasters, and blacks as liberty-seeking Israelites, further spotlights the one group that did *not* take the privileged American majority's lead in preferring the New Testament to the Old: black Americans, enslaved and free, would remain committed to the Hebrew Bible throughout the antebellum period and beyond. For many years after the heyday of comparable white identifications, African-Americans continued to construct their communal identity in Old Testament terms as a New Israel.

The historian Stephen Prothero states that while antebellum white Americans were "crafting a form of Christianity rooted almost entirely in the New Testament," this redefining of American Christianity made a much lesser impact on the black spiritual community. African-Americans continued to hold the Old Testament and its narratives in special regard; in particular, the story of the Exodus became "the most influential of all biblical narratives among American slaves, who came to see divine worship as unfettered service to the God who had liberated Hebrew slaves." Focusing throughout the antebellum years on the story of the liberation of the Children of Israel from Egyptian slavery, this black biblical culture had a strong "Old Testament bias" and was "Hebraic to the bone." The historian Eddie Glaude has written, "The analogy with the Jews of the Old Testament occupied the religious and political imagination of antebellum blacks . . . [who] collapsed the [biblical] past with the present." Praying for deliverance from slavery, African-Americans interpreted their experience "in light of Exodus themes, claiming for themselves God's promise to deliver His chosen people from captivity, and finding in their midst a series of Moses figures."[71]

The Exodus in particular, according to Mark Noll, provided black Americans with "the framework for a social hope, for communal aspirations, in which the power of God would break in pieces the fetters of slavery and the bonds of sin together." Contemporaries, white and black, already realized the special meaning that enslaved blacks ascribed to the story of Exodus. A white Union soldier commented that "there is no part of the Bible with which they are so familiar as the story of the deliverance of the children of Israel"; an enslaved Polly explained to her mistress that when she heard of God's "delivering his people from bondage I know it means the poor Africans."[72] Through the lens of their American Exodus, blacks' longing for freedom and flight from slavery took the form of concentrating on a biblical Promised Land, a yearning for a Canaan of freedom. The metaphors of bondage, Exodus, liberation, and nationhood provided a full account of African-American slavery and eventual deliverance.

"Our cruel oppressors and murderers . . . treat us more cruel [*sic*] as Pharaoh did the Children of Israel," lamented the black abolitionist David Walker (1785–1830) in his famous *Appeal to the Coloured Citizens of the World* (1829), a pamphlet strewn with references to Exodus. "How cunning [American] slave-holders think they are!!!" Walker censured his white compatriots, "how much like the king of Egypt who, after he saw plainly that God was determined to bring out his people, in spite of him and his, as powerful as they were." So prevalent and powerful was the Exodus trope that by the mid-1840s it had "sedimented as the predominate political language of African Americans." Frederick Douglass (himself seen by contemporaries as a Moses-like figure) said that any "keen observer might have detected in our repeated singing of 'O Canaan, sweet Canaan / I am bound for the land of Canaan,' something more than a trope of reaching heaven. We meant to reach the North, and the North was our Canaan."[73]

Exodus thus gave slaves hope of imminent deliverance from their bondage, but also proved that slavery was against God's will. The consequent identification with the Children of Israel was expressed and consolidated in slave spirituals that drew inspiration from the biblical story. An example is "The Ship of Zion," which placed Jesus at the helm of "de good ole ship o' Zion" in an exodus toward Canaan:

> King Jesus is de captain, captain, captain,
> And she's makin' for de Promised Land.[74]

"The Ship of Zion" manifests African-Americans' distinct antebellum religiosity, which was based on a biblicism that went beyond traditional typology by fusing and merging, not merely connecting and relating, the Old and New Testaments. Eugene Genovese indicates that in blacks' renditions "Moses had become Jesus, and Jesus, Moses; and with their union the two aspects of the slaves' religious quest—collective deliverance as a people and redemption from their terrible personal sufferings—had become one." Slaves and their free and marginalized brothers conflated the two figures of Moses and Jesus, producing a unified liberator who promised individual redemption from sin and a collective, national deliverance from slavery. This Mosaic Jesus functioned both as a savior from sin and a deliverer from slavery, becoming the harbinger of the saving grace of the New Testament as well as Old Testament–inspired escape, justice, and vindication. By appealing to Jesus their "king," African-Americans kept up with the evangelicalism of the time; yet their form of evangelical Protestantism did not duplicate contemporary white Christianity. They maintained their commitment to the Old Testament and their identity as a Chosen People by creating the Mosaic Jesus of their dreams, a figure that was "first and foremost as a Hebraic hero."[75] With the gradual weakening of white Americans' commitment to a political worldview in which the Old Testament played a central role, African-Americans held fast and maintained an Old Testament cosmology. Although the Old Testament would continue to influence the United States' national culture in intricate ways, after the Civil War, the American Zion would become first and foremost a black Zion.

Conclusion
Beyond Old Testamentism:
The New Israel after the Civil War

The Georgian newspaper the *Macon Daily Telegraph and Confederate* published a "New Revelation" in the bleak fall of 1864, when the doom of the Confederate States of America seemed to draw closer by the day. The revelation, a pamphlet of twelve pages, was an extraordinary piece of American Old Testamentism that recast the central narratives of the Hebrew Bible as chronicles about America: North America, "the birthplace of mankind," was sanctified, or rather Canaanized, and became the geographical center of the biblical drama: "the river that went out to water the garden of Eden . . . was the Mississippi-Pison, the river compassing the land of Havilah, the Arkansas; Gihon, the river lining the boundary of Ethiopia, is the Ohio. Hidekel, the Missouri, and Euphrates, the Upper Mississippi." The New Revelation wholly conflated the biblical and American landscapes, with "the Hebrew Canaan [identified as] the United States, Mexico and Central America." "Joshua," the Revelation's author, could even identify "the site of the present city of New York" as the place where Noah built his ark and made preparation for his voyage. Another crucial moment in the Amero-biblical drama that the revelation narrated took place five thousand years after the deluge, when "a weather-beaten vessel is seen, laden with the first Virginia colony." When it lands, the sons of Abel (the Europeans, according to Joshua's account) face the sons of Cain (the Indians) as they "swap beads for whisky."

The original thirteen colonies in North America, the revelation continued, "were none other than a regeneration of the twelve tribes of Israel," neatly corresponding to their biblical counterparts: North Carolina was Gad, South Carolina was Simeon, Dan was New York, Manasseh was Virginia, and so on, each colony "named after the corresponding territory in Israel." At that point Joshua extended the liberty he took with interpreting the original narrative and described "the terrible conflict between Monarchy and Republicanism," which apparently matched the American sectional conflict between the Union and the Confederacy. The discord ends with "the Jews' return to Palestine with a free Government, the negroes to Africa, and a republican form of government extends from the western border of British America, half way round the globe," throughout Europe. Only the progeny of Cain, incapable of any government, "dwell in the lands of his brothers." These, the newspaper's editor commented, must have been "the niggers and Yankees."[1]

The Revelation is remarkable in its imaginative ingenuity, but also in capturing the whole spectrum of the Old Testamentism that I have mapped out in *American Zion*: the political interpretation of the Jewish republic, the rendition of American history as an event in biblical chronology, the biblical origin of the Indians, and the rest of Old Testamentism—all appear in some manner in the Revelation. Beyond these particular strands, the piece manifests the fascination with biblical authenticity that characterized much of American Old Testamentism: the conflation of North America with the biblical Canaan and the United States with Israel (the New Revelation significantly avoids the typological adjectives "second" or "new") is complete and unconditional. It is revealing to read the piece, particularly its utopian ending, while keeping in mind the abject condition of the Confederacy in its final months and the existential anxieties contemporaries confronted during that testing time; the Old Testament biblicism, as we have seen throughout this study, could not only express chauvinistic self-assuredness but also attempt to ameliorate national diffidence and tragedy.

This idiosyncratic rendition was striking, however, only because it appeared some three decades after the peaking of the political theology I have called Old Testamentism. Had the New Revelation been published in the 1820s in the western parts of New York, for example, and not in war-ravished Georgia, it would have been but one of many such manifestations of raw biblical sensibilities and would have easily blended with other biblical accounts of American history. Nevertheless, as we saw in the previous chapter, things changed after the first third of the century, which might explain why the New Revelation failed to resonate with the larger society in the closing months of the Civil War: the newspaper's editor admitted that he published the piece only because he felt that his weary "readers are willing to forego for a time the hackneyed theme of war, for something entirely new." Even wartime escapism had its limits, however, as the editor published the Revelation only "in a nut shell" as "a brief synopsis," and concluded that the piece was a "grand farce."

The New Revelation demonstrates, however, that while the Old Testamentism that I have explored may have receded in the decades leading up to the Civil War, it did not vanish. The heightened religiosity and millenarianism that scholars associate with the war years indeed stemmed the decline in the disposition to make use of Old Testament metaphors and images. Even in wartime slaveholding Delaware advocates of the Union could still describe their "government [as] the modern Israel of God, in its national capacity," while southerners and their sympathizers in the North would see Abraham Lincoln as an American Rehoboam who split the Union, and Jefferson Davis as a Jeroboam leading a justified secession. In the same vein, northerners equated the southern secession to biblical rebellions, notably to Absalom's disastrous revolt against his father, David, while southerners drew comfort in seeing themselves as the outnumbered kingdom of Judah led by Abijah and Asa, fighting the mightier and errant kingdom of Israel. More generally speaking, the older forms and structures of the references to the United States and the Second Israel resurfaced remarkably during the years of struggle, apparently in order to ensure Americans that God had not abandoned them.[2]

Though substantial, this wartime biblical resurgence was limited in scale and never reached the intensity of the first third of the nineteenth century. Furthermore, that revival was temporary, with the disillusioning experience of the war and its unprecedented carnage completing Old Testamentism's downfall when the hostilities were over; the Old Testament would never regain its former stature or exercise the dominance it possessed in the politics of the nation. Tellingly, when Americans heard of "new Israels" late in the nineteenth century, these were often not American but "Hebrew sects" forming outside the United States.[3]

We have seen that before the Civil War many Americans across denominational lines blended their sense of being a New Israel and God's chosen people with their evolving national consciousness, hence, according to a recent account, "endowing the nation-state with a quasi-religious identity." This theonationalism had enormous consequences, as contemporaries could justify public policy and ideology (such as westward expansion) in religious terms. Seeing the United States as a New Israel chosen for a special calling, however, did more than merely justify national creeds ex post facto; it also firmly suggested that the United States, like Israel of old, was at the center of history, leading national politicians such as John Quincy Adams to declare that "the Declaration of Independence was a leading event in the progress of the gospel dispensation."[4]

However, after the Civil War, discussions on the American nation, its history, and its future responded to the decline of the Old Testament in American culture: the political and national language, which in the past had commonly referred to the United States in terms of Israel, transformed after the war into one that was more abstract, and often less historically committed. Even with the amount of printed material increasing exponentially with every passing year, after the war it becomes harder to find the once so common appeals to "our Israel," the "Second Israel," or "New Israel" (at least as those phrases referred to the American nation and not to various, often religious, communities and congregations within it). Characteristically, a popular tract such as Josiah Strong's *Our Country* (1885), which repeatedly addressed America as an "elect nation" and its citizens as "chosen people," abstained from referring to the United States directly as an Israel; a decade later Senator Albert J. Beveridge, in a speech that captured America's imperial and self-confident turn-of-the-century zeitgeist, similarly addressed Americans as the "Chosen people" and "Chosen nation" who were to "lead the regeneration of the world," without directly referring to biblical Israel.[5]

A comparable shift was noticeable in the rise of the Holy Land in the American popular imagination. Before the Civil War the focus of American "geopiety" was on the sacralization of North America through understanding the country as a New Canaan and a Promised Land, by employing measures such as the unique and widespread imposition of biblical names on American towns. After the war, however, the former and rather mild interest in the actual biblical lands rose on an unprecedented scale. The newfound interest in the lands of the Bible was clearly evident by the late nineteenth century as tourists, colonists, pilgrims, explorers, and scholars, "more Americans than ever before," rushed to see Ottoman-ruled Palestine. That interest was nourished by a stream of reports of American travelers participating in what one scholar described as a "Holy Land mania"; hundreds of popular monographs and periodical articles about the Holy Land, "a huge storehouse of thoughts and descriptions," became available to American readers, testifying to a deep-seated yet novel interest in the Holy Land. This postbellum attraction to the land of the Bible, to which excellent scholarly studies have been dedicated, reveals a hitherto unnoticed shift from the construction of an American Canaan to a deep interest in the actual Holy Land.[6] Once again, a keen interest in the Bible and biblical history paradoxically weakened a former biblicism, displacing in this instance the effort to sacralize (or Canaanize) the United States. The majority of the Americans who believed that they were God's New Israel probably never interacted with, or even saw, real-life Jews, who were relatively few before the closing decades of the nineteenth century, and mostly clustered in commercial centers in an overwhelmingly agricultural country. Yet that the American Hebraic imagination developed in the absence of Jews was in no sense unique: for millennia Christians have conjured "the Jew" as a figure of thought for their particular needs (typically to serve as an ultimate Other), often with little regard to actual Jews.[7] Hence, when thousands of Jews began arriving in North America after 1880, God's New Israel had mostly ceased to conceive itself in such terms.

The Old Testamentism of the revolutionary and antebellum eras that was characterized by recurrent and explicit attempts to construct the United States as a Second Israel had changed by the late nineteenth century into post–Civil War discussions on "mission" and "holy cause" in the name of "the banner of liberty." Nevertheless, the Bible still prevailed as America's most popular book, and to this day American patriotism draws on familiar biblical themes. In the meanwhile, generations of immigrants continued to articulate their experience as a liberating Exodus and their newfound country in terms of a Promised Land. "Exodus" and "promised land," among other figures of speech, still represent, as the eminent historian Harry Stout reminds us, "staple metaphors in American speech and letters that express America's messianic 'mission' to be a 'redeemer nation.'"[8]

The fingerprints of the Old Testament were—still are—particularly evident in the language of chosenness, itself, of course, a Hebraic concept. What has widely become known as the American "mission," the idea that the United States is endowed with an errand to promote liberty, was formed closely related to the belief that the United States was the Israel of its time. Hence more generally in "American exceptionalism" there existed the pervasive and enduring idea that the United States had a designated role in world history and that it did not obey "normal" historical rules. Nevertheless, after the Civil War most intellectual and political advocates of what we have come to call American exceptionalism would not refer directly to the Old Testament to explain the United States' character and role in history. Still, it is hard to conceive of such an exceptionalism emerging as powerfully as it has without the persistent identifications of the United States as biblical Israel during the first decades of the republic's existence. The construction of the United States as a biblical Israel justified, fortified, and perpetuated the self-confidence, dynamism, and assertiveness that characterize much of American culture and history that played out long after that political theology faded. Here too, Old Testamentism helped fashion what would become fundamental tenets of the nation's culture.[9]

As we saw in the final chapter, the marginalization of biblical Israel in the political discourse was surely no indication of decline in American religiosity (or providentialism). To the contrary, scholars are still searching for explanations how "Western Civilization seems to have divided in two: to the east a godless Europe, to the west a God-fearing America." Some persuasively argue that the disestablishment of churches in America, or the fact that religion was (and still is) based on choice rather than state fiat, allows open competition among multiple sects and denominations, hence best explains religion's proliferation in the United States. Since in religion, as in other areas of human endeavor, monopolies are inefficient, advocates of this open-market hypothesis believe that it is "the best explanation for the strange death of religion in Europe and its enduring vigor in the United States."[10]

Yet beyond the question of its thriving in America, the unique blend of religion and politics also requires an explanation. American Old Testament biblicism suggests that the origin and shape of the nation's modern theopolitics (as well as the paradox of a disestablished religion that infiltrates so effectively into political language) is not rooted solely in disestablishment and evangelicalism, two salient characteristics of modern American Christianity. Indeed, the once potent image of the Second Israel, and the corollary examination of the biblical history of the Israelites in light of the United States' novel political system and budding nationalism, helped structure the rhetorical modes that we associate with modern American politics.

Twentieth-century sensibilities such as the belief in a Judeo-Christian tradition that deeply resonated in post–World War II America—and only in America—demonstrate the continuing and enduring effects of the Old Testament on the American imagination. So does the American public's consistent backing of the State of Israel (far beyond the constituency of evangelical Christian Zionists), which politically translates into a robust and bipartisan support that defies the arithmetic of appeals to Jewish voters (or donors). Yet how might one appraise this lasting impact of the Old Testament, especially since it became much harder to identify the biblical fingerprints on American politics after the late nineteenth century? One way would be to hypothesize counterfactually how different American history or culture would have been without it. Take, for example, the American "discernibly religious mode of public argument... that bequeathed a style of public discourse," which according to Mark Noll "continues to exert great influence"; one may speculate that without the grounding in years of contemplating the United States in terms of Israel this mode of public rhetoric would not have matured and fully developed, resulting in a much tamer version of the characteristic American osmosis of religion and politics. For example, various attempts to reform American society by such undertakings as the twentieth-century civil rights movement would probably have been far less effective without enlisting the Old Testament. Leaders from Martin Luther King, Jr., whose powerful allusions to Exodus and his own image as a Moses leading his people to a Canaan of freedom, to Bill Clinton, in his appeal to a "New Covenant" with America, testify to the enduring ways in which the Old Testament provides the American political culture with one of its most lasting and distinct characteristics.[11]

It is not my intention to imply monocausality in explaining the rise of either American exceptionalism or the shaping of the nation's political rhetoric, or even to suggest that Old Testamentism was more important than other factors in the construction of a national consciousness. Still, it seems safe to assume that a powerful outlook like that of the Old Testament biblicism in the United States' first half-century helped set major cultural processes on a course that would define much of the nation's later history. The articulation of the United States as a Second Israel set the stage for the nation's distinct confluence of Christianity and modernity, helping to ensure that the two would never be in confrontation as they were (and still are) in Europe. While seldom referred to any longer as a Second Israel, the United States was created in the shadow of the biblical Israelite nation. It should not surprise us that so many of its citizens still ardently believe that God regards their nation with special favor.

Notes

INTRODUCTION

Epigraphs: Abiel Abbot, *Traits of Resemblance in the People of the United States of America to Ancient Israel* (Haverhill, MA, 1799), 6; Teachings of the Prophet Joseph Smith, Section Six 1843–44, 362.

1. Mark A. Noll, *God and Race in American Politics* (Princeton: Princeton University Press, 2010), 24–25. For explorations of the concept of chosenness and modern nationalism see Anthony D. Smith, *Chosen Peoples: Sacred Sources of National Identity* (Oxford: Oxford University Press, 2003); Adrian Hastings, *The Construction of Nationhood: Ethnicity, Religion, and Nationalism* (Cambridge: Cambridge University Press, 1977); William R. Hutchison and Hartmut Lehmann, eds., *Many Are Chosen: Divine Election and Western Nationalism* (Minneapolis: Fortress, 1994). Quotations in: "Integer," *New York Gazette*, Mar. 10, 1777, and "A True Patriot," *New Jersey Gazette*, Mar. 31, 1779. For an essay on the belief that America has been elected by God for a special destiny, see Conrad Cherry's introduction to the popular reader *God's New Israel: Religious Interpretations of American Destiny*, ed. Conrad Cherry (Chapel Hill: University of North Carolina Press, 1998), 1–21.

2. Perry Miller, "The Garden of Eden and the Deacon's Meadow," *American Heritage* 7:1 (December 1955), http://www.americanheritage.com/content/garden-eden-and-deacon%E2%80%99s-meadow [viewed 1/23/2012]. For a recent account of American chosenness see Todd Gitlin and Liel Leibovitz, *The Chosen Peoples: America, Israel, and the Ordeal of Divine Election* (New York: Simon and Schuster, 2010); for Hebraic influences in America see Shalom Goldman's illuminating *God's Sacred Tongue: Hebrew and the American Imagination* (Chapel Hill: University of North Carolina Press, 2003). See also the entertaining and insightful popular history of the cultural role of the prophet-lawgiver Moses in American history: Bruce Feiler, *America's Prophet: Moses and the American Story* (New York: William Morrow, 2009).

3. John Pocock is the key figure in revealing the deep antimodern strains in late eighteenth-century American political culture. See especially J. G. A. Pocock, *The Machiavellian Moment: Florentine Political Thought and the Atlantic Republican Tradition* (Princeton: Princeton University Press, 1975), 506–532. For a thoughtful discussion on American understandings of modernity that equates modernity with "a stage of history characterized by national state formation, industrialization, and the rise of new ideas of reason, human agency,

and historical progress," but mostly concerned with its implications for American identity after World War II, see Dorothy Ross, "American Modernities, Past and Present," *American Historical Review* 116:3 (June 2011), 702–714. The classical statement about the significance of the absence of feudalism in America is Louis Hartz's *The Liberal Tradition in America* (New York: Mariner, 1991), 3–34 and passim. New studies in American intellectual and cultural history further complicate understandings of American optimism and self-assuredness; see, for example, Maurizio Valsania, *The Limits of Optimism: Thomas Jefferson's Dualistic Enlightenment* (Charlottesville: University of Virginia Press, 2011).

4. Theodore Bozeman, *To Live Ancient Lives: The Primitivist Dimension in Puritanism* (Chapel Hill: University of North Carolina Press, 2011).

5. Adam Sutcliffe, *Judaism and Enlightenment* (Cambridge: Cambridge University Press, 2003); Eric Nelson, *The Hebrew Republic: Jewish Sources and the Transformation of European Political Thought* (Cambridge: Harvard University Press, 2010). Guy Stroumsa remarked recently that biblical Israel functioned for early modern European scholars as "a Gordian knot of sorts, whose understanding would solve, at once, the main problems of ancient history, Christian theology, and European politics"; Guy Stroumsa, *A New Science: The Discovery of Religion in the Age of Reason* (Cambridge: Harvard University Press, 2010), 39. Gordon Schochet, "Hebraic Roots, Calvinist Plantings, American Branches," *Hebraic Political Studies* 4:2 (2009), 99–103, quotation on 101. The classical study of early modern political biblicism is Christopher Hill, *The English Bible and the Seventeenth-Century Revolution* (London: Penguin, 1995).

6. The historian of religion Sydney Ahlstrom claimed that "Puritanism provided the moral and religious background of fully 85 percent of the people who declared their independence in 1776"; Sydney Ahlstrom, *A Religious History of the American People* (New Haven: Yale University Press, 1972), 124. See also William R. Hutchinson, *Religious Pluralism in America: The Contentious History of a Founding Ideal* (New Haven: Yale University Press, 2004), 20–21; and Daniel Elazar, *Covenant and Constitutionalism: The Covenant Tradition in Politics* (Piscataway, NJ: Transaction, 1997), 68. For the sermon as a cultural vehicle in the development of New England's culture see Harry Stout, *The New England Soul: Preaching and Religious Culture in Colonial New England* (New York: Oxford University Press, 1988). For chosenness and Exodus in the context of the Puritans see Avihu Zakai, *Exile and Kingdom: History and Apocalypse in the Puritan Migration to America* (New York: Cambridge University Press, 2002). For the politico-theological context see Glenn A. Moots, *Politics Reformed: The Anglo-American Legacy of Covenant Theology* (Columbia: University of Missouri Press, 2010), and Glenn A. Moots, "Response: The Complications and Contributions of Early American Hebraism," *Hebraic Political Studies* 4:2 (2009), 157–168. Jorge Canizares-Esguerra explores the Atlantic context of chosenness in an important study that crosses the boundary between Catholicism and Protestantism. Canizares-Esguerra points out that the Puritans and their successors were not alone in understanding and justifying colonization as an act "foreordained by God, prefigured in the trials of the Israelites in Canaan." According to this novel interpretation, English Calvinist and Spanish Catholic settlers were Atlantic "cultural twins," each group equally "interested in developing typological readings of colonization." Jorge Canizares-Esguerra, *Puritan Conquistadors: Iberianizing the Atlantic, 1550–1700* (Stanford: Stanford University Press, 2006), 14, 72, 83.

7. For political Hebraic studies see Gordon Schoschet, Fania Oz-Salzberger, and Meirav Jones, eds., *Political Hebraism: Judaic Sources in Early Modern Political Thought* (Jerusalem: Shalem, 2008); Michael Walzer et al., eds., *The Jewish Political Tradition*, 2 vols. (New Haven: Yale University Press, 2000); for a non-Anglo example see Miriam Bodian, "The Biblical 'Jewish Republic' and the Dutch 'New Israel' in Seventeenth-Century Dutch Thought," *Hebraic Political Studies* 1:2 (2006), 186–202. Fania Oz-Salzberger points out that "Political Hebraism flourished in European thought for about a century and a half, roughly between Bodin and Locke"; Oz-Salzberger, "The Political Thought of John Locke and the Significance of Political Hebraism," *Hebraic Political Studies* 1:5 (2006), 568–592, quotation on 569. For the enormous influence of New England on the cultural and intellectual development of the United States see Peter Dobkin Hall, *The Organization of American Culture, 1700–1900: Private Institutions, Elites, and the Origins of American Nationality* (New York: New York University Press, 1984). See also George McKenna, *The Puritan Origins of American Patriotism* (New Haven: Yale University Press, 2009). New England Puritanism had particular influence on the development of what Sacvan Bercovitch had described as the "American Self" in *The Puritan Origins of the American Self* (New Haven: Yale University Press, 1975). Quotations in Mark A. Noll, "The Image of the United States as a Biblical Nation, 1776–1865," in *The Bible in America: Essays in Cultural History*, ed. Nathan O. Hatch and Mark A. Noll (New York: Oxford University Press, 1982), 39–58: 39, 45. Americans were unique not only in the extent to which they employed the Old Testament for political ends but also in doing so more than a century after such use had run its course in Europe. American biblicism was thus "exceptional" both in its intensity and its lasting effects, as well as in blooming so late.

8. Ruth Bloch, *Visionary Republic: Millennial Themes in American Thought, 1756–1800* (New York: Cambridge University Press, 1988); Nicholas Guyatt, *Providence and the Invention of the United States* (New York: Cambridge University Press, 2007); Nathan O. Hatch, *The Sacred Cause of Liberty: Republican Thought and the Millennium in Revolutionary New England* (New Haven: Yale University Press, 1977). For the notion of redeemer nation see particularly Ernest Lee Tuveson, *Redeemer Nation: The Idea of America's Millennial Role* (Chicago: University of Chicago Press, 1968).

9. Paul C. Gutjahr, *An American Bible: A History of the Good Book in the United States, 1777–1880* (Stanford: Stanford University Press, 1999), 1, 32–33; Philip L. Barlow, *Mormons and the Bible: The Place of the Latter-Day Saints in American Religion* (New York: Oxford University Press, 1991), 5.

10. On the New England clergy's extension of covenant promise to "America" see Sacvan Bercovitch, "How the Puritans Won the American Revolution," *Massachusetts Review* 17 (1976), 597–630; Thomas Jefferson, *First Inaugural Address*, Mar. 4, 1801; Thomas Jefferson, *Second Inaugural Address*, Mar. 4, 1805. For the Christian-republican synthesis see Mark A. Noll, *America's God: From Jonathan Edwards to Abraham Lincoln* (New York: Oxford University Press, 2002), 9 and passim.

11. The notable exception was the Jewish Mordecai Noah, further discussed in chapters two and four. For the Bible as "culture" see Jonathan Sheehan, *The Enlightenment Bible: Translation, Scholarship, Culture* (Princeton: Princeton University Press, 2005). While the 1780s and the Federal Constitution may have been "godless," such specific moments of secular sentiment (if indeed they were such) did not necessarily affect Old Testament biblicism; in this

context see Eric Slauter's chapter on the "godless constitution" in *The Constitution as a Work of Art: The Cultural Origins of the Constitution* (Chicago: University of Chicago Press, 2009).

12. The classical work on Exodus in the American context is Michael Walzer's *Exodus and Revolution* (New York: Basic, 1986). William B. Wedgwood, *Reconstruction of the Government of the United States of America: A Democratic Empire Advocated, and Imperial Constitution Proposed* (New York, 1861), 10.

13. Wedgwood, *Reconstruction of the Government of the United States of America*, 10. For similar revolutionary-era enumeration of the Israelite tribes as thirteen instead of the traditional twelve and intentional confusion of the biblical and contemporary nomenclature of "state" with "tribe," see chapter 2.

14. John C. Calhoun, "Speech on the Force Bill" [1833], in *John C. Calhoun: Selected Writing and Speeches*, ed. H. Lee Cheek, Jr. (Washington, DC: Regnery, 2003), 444.

15. "A Striking Parallel," *Poulson's American Daily Advertiser*, Jan. 13, 1813; David Lee Child, *The Taking of Naboth's Vineyard; or, History of the Texas Conspiracy* (New York, 1845). For Ahab in the context of *Moby-Dick* see Ilana Pardes, *Melville's Bibles* (Berkeley: University of California Press, 2008), 98–122.

16. For Lincoln as Rehoboam see "Jeroboam and Jeff. Davis," *New York Herald*, Jan. 31, 1861.

17. For biblical nomenclature see Moshe Davis, *America and the Holy Land* (Westport, CT: Praeger, 1995), 133–162.

18. Ezra Stiles, *The United States Elevated to Glory and Honor* (New Haven, 1783), 7, 5, 37.

19. Nicholas Street, *The American States Acting Over the Part of the Children of Israel in the Wilderness and Thereby Impeding their Entrance into Canaan's Rest* (1777), in Cherry, *God's New Israel*, 67–69. Wedgwood, *Reconstruction of the Government of the United States of America*, 10.

20. Street, *The American States Acting Over the Part of the Children of Israel*, 69.

21. For the rise of the example of democratic Athens in lieu of Rome see Carl J. Richard, *The Golden Age of the Classics in America: Greece, Rome, and the Antebellum United States* (Cambridge: Harvard University Press, 2009), 41–82. Quotation from George S. Phillips, *The American Republic and Human Liberty Foreshadowed in Scripture* (Cincinnati, 1864), 23–24.

22. Donald Lutz, "The Relative Influence of European Writers on Late Eighteenth-Century American Political Thought," *American Political Science Review* 78 (1984), 189–197: 192.

23. Carolyn Eastman studies the intersection of oratory and printed material as "the means by which [elite and nonelite Americans] learned to conceive themselves as members of a public and eventually to identify as national citizens"; Carolyn Eastman, *A Nation of Speechifiers: Making an American Public after the Revolution* (Chicago: University of Chicago Press, 2009), 5.

24. For the Bible as an influence on American public discourse, particularly on republican deliberation, see Sandra Gustafson, *Imagining Deliberative Democracy in the Early American Republic* (Chicago: University of Chicago Press, 2011), 86–96.

25. Hannah More, *Sacred Dramas, Chiefly Intended for Young Persons: The Subjects Taken from the Bible* (Philadelphia, 1787), iii.

26. For a masterful discussion of Renaissance and early modern republicanism see Pocock, *The Machiavellian Moment*.

27. Alan Heimert, *Religion and the American Mind* (Cambridge: Harvard University Press, 1966), 11, 12. I focus on the biblical political "language" as a discrete and lasting intellectual universe through which Americans construed their collective predicament. My use and conceptualization of "language" is indebted to John Pocock's definition and usage of that term. For a theoretical exposition of political languages, see "Introduction: The State of the Art," in Pocock, *Virtue, Commerce, and History* (Cambridge: Cambridge University Press, 1985), 1–36; and Pocock, *Politics, Language, and Time: Essays on Political Thought and History* (Chicago: University of Chicago Press, 1989).

1. "THE JEWISH CINCINNATUS"

1. "The Ingratitude of the Hebrew Republic toward the Family of Gideon," *Jenk's Portland Gazette*, Nov. 19, 1804. For Washington as an American Cincinnatus, and more generally on the Cincinnatian model in American politics, see Eran Shalev, *Rome Reborn on Western Shores: Historical Imagination and the Creation of the American Republic* (Charlottesville: University of Virginia Press, 2009), 217–240, and Garry Wills, *Cincinnatus: George Washington and the Enlightenment* (New York: Doubleday, 1984).

2. On major additions to our understanding of the classics in the early United States see Carl J. Richard, *The Golden Age of the Classics in America: Greece, Rome, and the Antebellum United States* (Cambridge: Harvard University Press, 2009); Caroline Winterer, *The Mirror of Antiquity: American Women and the Classical Tradition, 1750–1900* (Ithaca, NY: Cornell University Press, 2007); Caroline Winterer, *The Culture of Classicism: Ancient Greece and Rome in American Intellectual Life, 1780–1910* (Baltimore: Johns Hopkins University Press, 2004); Carl J. Richard, *The Founders and the Classics: Greece, Rome, and the American Enlightenment* (Cambridge: Harvard University Press, 1995).

3. By referring to "civic humanism" instead of "classical republicanism," John Pocock and others underscore the importance of early modernity in the reformation of that language. Here, however, the terms are treated interchangeably.

4. For an up-to-date review of that voluminous debate see Alan Gibson, *Understanding the Founding: The Critical Questions* (Lawrence: University Press of Kansas, 2010), 134–168.

5. On the relative widespread appeal of the classics see Shalev, *Rome Reborn on Western Shores*, 10–14. Quotation in Gibson, *Understanding the Founding*, 142. For the roots and long trajectory of American permissiveness see Jack P. Greene, *Pursuits of Happiness: The Social Development of Early Modern British Colonies and the Formation of American Culture* (Chapel Hill: University of North Carolina Press, 1988).

6. Mark A. Noll, "The Image of the United States as a Biblical Nation, 1776–1865," in *The Bible in America: Essays in Cultural History*, ed. Nathan O. Hatch and Mark A. Noll (New York: Oxford University Press, 1982), 45. Paul Gutjahr, *An American Bible: A History of the Good Book in the United States, 1777–1880* (Palo Alto: Stanford University Press, 2002), 2. See also Lori Anne Ferrell, *The Bible and the People* (New Haven: Yale University Press, 2008), 95–126, 192–220. For civic texts in the early republic see François Furstenberg, *In the Name of the Father: Washington's Legacy, Slavery, and the Making of a Nation* (New York: Penguin, 2007),

34–46. For the Bible in the rhetoric of the Founders see Daniel L. Dreisbach, "The Bible in the Political Rhetoric of the American Founding," *Politics and Religion* 4 (2011), 401–427.

7. "Cranmer's Preface to the Great Bible," in *Documents of the English Reformation*, ed. Gerald Bray (Cambridge: James Clarke, 2004), 239; Gutjahr, *American Bible*, 119.

8. Gustafson, *Imagining Deliberative Democracy in the Early American Republic*, 87. Quotation in Dorothy Ross, *The Origins of American Social Science* (New York: Cambridge University Press, 1992), 23. Edmund S. Morgan, "The Puritan Ethic and the American Revolution," *William and Mary Quarterly*, 3d. ser., 24:1 (1967), 3–43. Nathan O. Hatch, *The Sacred Cause of Liberty: Republican Thought and the Millennium in Revolutionary New England* (New Haven: Yale University Press, 1977). Ruth Bloch, *Visionary Republic: Millennial Themes in American Thought, 1756–1800* (New York: Cambridge University Press, 1988). Mark A. Noll, "The American Revolution and Protestant Evangelism," *Journal of Interdisciplinary History* 23:3 (1993), 615–638. For some of the important studies discussing the convergence of political and religious discourses in early America see Patricia U. Bonomi, *Under the Cope of Heaven: Religion, Society, and Politics in Colonial America* (New York: Oxford University Press, 2003); James T. Kloppenberg, "The Virtues of Liberalism: Christianity, Republicanism, and Ethics in Early American Political Discourse," in *The Virtues of Liberalism* (New York: Oxford University Press, 2000), 21–37; Jon Butler, *Awash in a Sea of Faith: Christianizing the American People* (Cambridge: Harvard University Press, 1992); Nathan O. Hatch, *The Democratization of American Christianity* (New Haven: Yale University Press, 1989).

9. The classic book on Exodus as a political model is Michael Walzer's, *Exodus and Revolution* (New York: Basic, 1986). For a recent popular history focused on America see Bruce Feiler, *America's Prophet: Moses and the American Story* (New York: William Morrow, 2009). For the Puritans and Exodus see Avihu Zakai, *Exile and Kingdom: History and Apocalypse in the Puritan Migration to America* (New York: Cambridge University Press, 2002). See also Michael Hoberman, *New Israel / New England: Jews and Puritans in Early America* (Amherst: University of Massachusetts Press, 2011).

10. Gad Hitchcock, *A Sermon Preached at Plymouth* (Boston, 1774), 20. Street, *The American States Acting Over the Part of the Children of Israel in the Wilderness, and thereby Impeding Their Entrance into Canaan's Rest* (New Haven, 1777), 3, 9.

11. Harry S. Stout, "Rhetoric and Reality in the Early Republic: The Case of the Federalist Clergy," in *Religion and American Politics: From the Colonial Period to the 1980s*, ed. Mark A. Noll (New York: Oxford University Press, 1990), 62–76: 70. See also Sacvan Bercovitch, "How the Puritans Won the American Revolution," *Massachusetts Review* 17 (1976), 597–630. "From the Pennsylvania Packet," *Continental Journal*, July 18, 1776.

12. Similarly, Quentin Skinner differentiates between early modern republicanism that could potentially tolerate monarchism and an exclusionary, "neo-Roman" republicanism that was adamantly antimonarchical. Skinner, *Liberty before Liberalism* (Cambridge: Cambridge University Press, 1998).

13. The three classic statements on American republicanism, and thus on the dangers of corruption, are Bernard Bailyn, *The Ideological Origins of the American Revolution* (Cambridge: Belknap Press of Harvard University Press, 1967), 55–60 and passim; Gordon Wood, *The Creation of the American Republic, 1776–1787* (Chapel Hill: University of North Carolina Press, 1969); J. G. A. Pocock, *The Machiavellian Moment: Florentine Political Thought and the Atlantic Republican Tradition* (Princeton: Princeton University Press, 1975). For general dis-

cussions on political corruption see Christopher J. Berry, *The Idea of Luxury: A Conceptual and Historical Investigation* (Cambridge: Cambridge University Press, 1994), and John Sekora, *Luxury: The Concept in Western Thought from Eden to Smollett* (Baltimore: Johns Hopkins University Press, 1977).

14. John Murrin, "Religion and Politics in America from the First Settlements to the Civil War," in *Religion and American Politics: From the Colonial Period to the Present*, 2nd ed., ed. Mark A. Noll and Luke E. Harlow (New York: Oxford University Press, 2007), 23–46: 35. See also Thomas S. Kidd, *God of Liberty: A Religious History of the American Revolution* (New York: Basic, 2010), 7–8.

15. J. G. A. Pocock, *Barbarism and Religion*, vol. 3, *The First Decline and Fall* (Cambridge: Cambridge University Press, 2005).

16. For understandings of decline in the revolutionary south see Eran Shalev, "Jefferson's Classical Silence, 1774–1776: Historical Consciousness and Roman History in the Revolutionary South," in *Thomas Jefferson, the Classical World, and Early America*, ed. Peter S. Onuf and Nicholas P. Cole (Charlottesville: University of Virginia Press, 2011), 219–247.

17. Antoine De Baecque, *The Body Politic: Corporeal Metaphor in Revolutionary France, 1770–1800*, trans. Charlotte Madell (Palo Alto: Stanford University Press, 1997). For eighteenth-century biopolitical metaphors, see Drew McCoy, *The Elusive Republic: Political Economy in Jeffersonian America* (Chapel Hill: University of North Carolina Press, 1996), 33. Joseph Huntington, *A Discourse Adapted to the Present Day, on the Health and Happiness, or Misery and Ruin, of the Body Politic, in Similitude to that of the Natural Body* (Hartford, 1781), 8.

18. Huntington, *A Discourse Adapted to the Present Day*, 9–10.

19. David Jones, *Defensive War in a Just Cause Sinless* (Philadelphia, 1775), 3–4. The Israelites were also deemed virtuous during other eras of their history. William Gordon, for example, believed that "the Jewish state flourished amazingly under the reign of [king] Solomon, whose court was the resort of the wise and noble.... His subjects enjoyed not only plenty, but security: Judah and Israel dwelt safely, every man under his vine and under his fig tree, from Dan even to Beersheba"; Gordon, "The Separation of the Jewish Tribes, after the Death of Solomon . . . a Sermon, delivered on July 4th, 1777," in *The Patriot Preachers of the American Revolution*, ed. Frank Moore (New York, 1862), 161. Samuel Langdon, *Government Corrupted by Vice* (Boston, 1775), 12.

20. Langdon, *Government Corrupted by Vice*, 12. Huntington, *A Discourse Adapted to the Present Day*, 20. Gordon, "The Separation of the Jewish Tribes," 161–164.

21. Jones, *Defensive War in a Just Cause Sinless*, 3, 4. Peter Powers, *Tyranny and Toryism Exposed: Being the Substance of Two Sermons, Preached at Newbury, Lord's Day, September 10th, 1780* (Westminster, VT, 1780), 5–6. John Murray, *Nehemiah; or, the Struggle for Liberty Never in Vain, When Managed with Virtue and Perseverance* (Newbury, MA, 1779), 11.

22. Langdon, *Government Corrupted by Vice*, 13.

23. Huntington, *A Discourse Adapted to the Present Day*, 10.

24. Ibid., 18. For civic humanist history see Philip S. Hicks, *Neoclassical History and English Culture: From Clarendon to Hume* (New York: Macmillan, 1996).

25. Langdon, *Government Corrupted by Vice*, 12–13, 14.

26. Oliver Noble, *Some Strictures upon the Sacred Story Recorded in the Book of Esther* (Newbury-Port, MA, 1775), 7.

27. Noble, *Some Strictures upon the Sacred Story Recorded in the Book of Esther*, 8.

28. For a different political tradition that emphasizes opposition to the crown and not to corrupt ministers see Jack P. Greene, "Political Mimesis: A Consideration of the Historical and Cultural Roots of Legislative Behavior in the British Colonies in the Eighteenth Century," *American Historical Review* 75:2 (1969), 337–360.

29. Brendan McConville, *The King's Three Faces: The Rise and Fall of Royal America, 1688–1776* (Chapel Hill: University of North Carolina Press, 2006).

30. *Boston Gazette*, Nov. 24, 1766.

31. Bailyn, *The Ideological Origins*, 127.

32. James Murray, *Sermons to the Ministers of State: By the Author of Sermons to the Asses* (Philadelphia, 1783), 49.

33. Thomas Reese, "The Character of Haman" in *The American Preacher*, 4 vols., ed. David Austin (Elizabethtown, NJ, 1791–1793), 2:324. Haman's rise and fall also seemed to vindicate in the age of classical republicanism a "pregnant example of the instability of secular things," evidence for a republican time scheme. Ibid.; *New York Journal*, Sep. 1774. For the Burgoyne reference see "Burgoyne's Proclamation" in *Songs and Ballads of the American Revolution*, ed. Frank Moore (New York, 1855), 173. *Sermons to the Ministers of State*, 52.

34. Reese, "The Character of Haman," 2:325.

35. Ibid., 2:331. *Sermons to the Ministers of State*, 52.

36. *Boston Gazette*, Nov. 4, 1765. *Sermons to the Ministers of State*, 52–53, 49.

37. "Amicus Republica," *Freeman Journal*, Aug. 3, 1776. "The Parody Parodized" (1768), in Moore, *Songs and Ballads of the American Revolution*, 45.

38. Bailyn, *The Ideological Origins*, 55–60. *Sermons to the Ministers of State*, 52. Reese, "The Character of Haman," 329, 331. Noble, *Some Strictures upon the Sacred Story Recorded in the Book of Esther*, 5–6, 11. *New York Journal*, Sep. 1, 1774.

39. Reese, "The Character of Haman," 330, 331. Noble, *Some Strictures upon the Sacred Story Recorded in the Book of Esther*, 5.

40. Alan Heimert, *Religion and the American Mind: From the Great Awakening to the Revolution* (Cambridge: Harvard University Press, 1966), 333. In the context of the Puritan Revolution, Stephan Marshall preached to the House of Commons the famous sermon *Meroz Cursed* (London, 1641). Hill, *The English Bible*, 88–89.

41. Jonathan Parsons quoted in Heimert, *Religion and the American Mind*, 333 (see also 334). Jonathan Edwards, *The Distinguishing Marks of a Work of the Spirit of God . . . A Discourse* (Boston, 1741), 88. Gilbert Tennent, *The Necessity of Holding Fast the Truth Represented in Three Sermons on Rev. III* (New Brunswick, NJ, 1743), 64. George Whitfield, *Some Remarks Upon a Late Charge Against Enthusiasm* (Boston, 1745), 19–20.

42. Samuel Davies, *Religion and Patriotism the Constituents of a Good Soldier, A Sermon preached to Captain Overton's Independent Company of Volunteers, raised in Hanover County, Virginia* (Philadelphia, 1755), 14. Samuel Davies, *The Curse of Cowardice. A Sermon Preached to the Militia of Hanover County, in Virginia, at a General Muster, May 8, 1758* (Boston, 1759), 21–22. Samuel Finley, *The Curse of Meroz; or, The Danger of Neutrality, in the Cause of God, and Our Country* (Philadelphia, 1757), 23.

43. Heimert, *Religion and the American Mind*, 334. Joseph Bellamy to Israel Putnam's army preparing to march on Boston, quoted ibid., 348.

44. Philo-Patria, *New York Gazette*, Aug. 20, 1770. Nathaniel Whitaker, "An Antidote Against Toryism, or the Curse of Meroz" (1777), in Moore, *The Patriot Preachers*, 186–231: 191.

Nathaniel Whitaker, *The Reward of Toryism. A Discourse on Judges V. 23* (Newbury-Port, MA, 1783), 7, 9.

45. Philo-Patria, *New York Gazette*, Aug. 20, 1770.

46. Ibid. George Washington to John Augustin Washington, Mar. 31, 1776, in *George Washington: Writings*, ed. John H. Rhodehamel (New York: Library of America, 1997), 222.

47. Philo-Patria, *New York Gazette*, Aug. 20, 1770. "Hampden's friendly Address to the Freemen," *Providence Gazette*, Oct. 9, 1774.

48. Whitaker, "An Antidote Against Toryism," 202. Whitaker, *The Reward of Toryism*, 9.

49. Finley, *The Curse of Meroz*, 28.

50. At least nine editions of the works of Josephus were printed before 1800, and fifteen by 1820.

51. "From the South Carolina Gazette," *Pennsylvania Packet and the General Advertiser*, Aug. 3, 1782. Powers, *Tyranny and Toryism Exposed*, 4.

52. Powers, *Tyranny and Toryism Exposed*, 3.

53. Ibid., 3, 4, 7; Aunorepene, "From the South Carolina Gazette," *Pennsylvania Packet*, Aug. 3, 1782. Sallust, *The Jugurthine War and the Conspiracy of Catiline*, trans. S. A. Handford (London: Penguin, 1964), 73.

54. Philalethes, *New York Journal*, Apr. 6, 1775. Hitchcock, *A Sermon Preached at Plymouth*, 20. For an Old Testament–based defense of monarchy see "To the People of Pennsylvania," *Virginia Gazette* (Dixon and Hunter), Mar. 4, 1776. A Moderate Whig, *Defensive Arms Vindicated, and the Lawfulness of the American War Made Manifest* (n.p., 1783), 7.

55. *Boston Gazette*, Nov. 4, 1765. A Moderate Whig, *Defensive Arms Vindicated*, 43. *New York Journal*, Sep. 1, 1774. Powers, *Tyranny and Toryism Exposed*, 5.

56. Powers, *Tyranny and Toryism Exposed*, 4–5. A Moderate Whig, *Defensive Arms Vindicated*, 31. For Washington as Judas Maccabeus see "Extract from a Sermon on the Death of General Washington, Preached at Burlington, New Jersey," *Providence Journal, and Town and Country Advertiser*, Jan. 22, 1800.

57. Philo-Patria, *New York Gazette*. Whitaker, "An Antidote against Toryism," 204–205. Mary Truth, *Massachusetts Spy*, Oct. 1, 1772. In similar fashion but drawing his republicanism not from the Bible but from the history of classical Rome, the South Carolina judge Henry Drayton wished that when America needed a savior, an American "Brutus [would] not be wanting." John Drayton, *Memoirs of the American Revolution, From its Commencement to the year 1776, Inclusive; As Relating to the State of South Carolina and Occasionally Referring to the States of North Carolina and Georgia*, 2 vols. (Charleston, SC, 1821), 2:386.

58. A Moderate Whig, *Defensive Arms Vindicated*, 37.

59. Nathan Perl-Rosenthal, "'The Divine Right of Republics': Hebraic Republicanism and the Debate over Kingless Government in Revolutionary America," *William and Mary Quarterly* 66:3 (2009), 535–564.

60. Algernon Sidney, *Discourses Concerning Government*, 2 vols. (Edinburgh, 1750), 2:144. Thomas Paine, *Common Sense* (Los Angeles: IndoEuropean Publishing, 2010), 10.

61. John Murray, *Jerubbaal; or, Tyranny's Grove Destroyed, and the Altar of Liberty Finished. A Discourse on America's Duty and Danger* (Newbury Port, MA, 1783), 13. George Washington, "Acceptance of Appointment as General and Commander in Chief," June 16, 1775, in *The Writings of George Washington from the Original Manuscript Sources*, 39 vols., ed. John Clemens Fitzpatrick (Washington, DC: U.S. Government Printing Office), 3:292–293.

62. Murray, *Jerubbaal*, 20–21.

63. Washington, "Acceptance of Appointment as General and Commander in Chief." Murray may have also been addressing the Continental Army's soldiers' disgruntlement regarding the lack of payment after the long hardships of war. Murray, *Jerubbaal*, 21.

64. Murray, *Jerubbaal*, 11, 43. Lyman Beecher observed that Israelite judges "answered, in some degree, to the dictators, who, in circumstances of great national peril, were placed in power by the Romans. Such were Gideon, Jephtah, and many others"; Lyman Beecher, "The Republican Elements of the Old Testament," in *Lectures on Political Atheism and Kindred Subjects* (Boston, 1852), 182.

65. Murray, *Jerubbaal*, 38–39, 47.

66. "The Ingratitude of the Hebrew Republic Toward the Family of Gideon," *Jenk's Portland Gazette*, Nov. 19, 1804. See also "For the Washington Whig," *Washington Whig*, Sep. 20, 1828. For a postrevolutionary southern recounting of Gideon see "Of Monarchy and Hereditary Succession," *South Carolina State Gazette and Timothy's Daily Advertiser*, Nov. 4, 1794.

67. "Jephtha's Daughter," *Spooner's Vermont Journal*, June 11, 1810.

2. "THE UNITED TRIBES, OR STATES OF ISRAEL"

1. Enoch C. Wines, *Commentaries on the Laws of the Ancient Hebrews* (New York, 1855), 637–638.

2. Ibid., 633–634.

3. For Reformation-era uses of the Bible as a political text, see L. W. Gough, *The Social Contract: A Critical Study of Its Development* (Oxford: Clarendon, 1957), and John Kincaid and Daniel J. Elazar, eds., *The Covenant Connection: From Federal Theology to Modern Federalism* (Lanham, MD: Lexington, 2000). Wines's contemporaries who developed similar notions were J. M. Matthews, *The Bible and Civil Government, in a Course of Lectures* (New York: Carter and Brothers, 1850), and George S. Phillips, *The American Republic and Human Liberty Foreshadowed in Scripture* (Cincinnati, 1864). Fania Oz-Salzberger, "The Political Thought of John Locke and the Significance of Political Hebraism," *Hebraic Political Studies* 1:5 (2006), 568–592.

4. Quotation in Daniel J. Elazar, "Deuteronomy as Israel's Ancient Constitution: Some Preliminary Reflections," *Jewish Political Studies Review* 4:1 (1992), http://jcpa.org/dje/articles2/deut-const.htm [viewed 5/22/2012]. Harry S. Stout, *The New England Soul: Preaching and Religious Culture in Colonial New England* (New York: Oxford University Press, 1986), 4. As Bernard Bailyn observed some four decades ago, such language may help in understanding the significant role of religious texts and modes of thought in the process by which political arguments became revolutionary. Bernard Bailyn, "Religion and Revolution: Three Biographical Studies," *Perspectives in American History* 4 (1970), 85–173: 138.

5. Kalman Neuman, "Political Hebraism and the Early Modern 'Respublica Hebraeroum': On Defining the Field," *Hebraic Political Studies* 1:1 (2005), 57–70: 59, 63; Guy Stroumsa, *A New Science: The Discovery of Religion in the Age of Reason* (Cambridge: Harvard University Press, 2010), 39. The most recent work in this vein, although one that consciously distances itself from "Hebraic political studies," is Eric Nelson's *The Hebrew Republic: Jewish Sources and the Transformation of European Political Thought* (Cambridge: Harvard University Press,

2010). For the promise of this new field see the special issue of *Hebraic Political Studies*, 4:2 (2009), dedicated to Hebraic and Old Testament politics in colonial America, and Gordon Schoschet, Fania Oz-Salzberger, and Meirav Jones, eds., *Political Hebraism: Judaic Sources in Early Modern Political Thought* (Jerusalem: Shalem, 2008); see also Michael Walzer et al., *The Jewish Political Tradition*, 2 vols. (New Haven: Yale University Press, 2000). The Eurocentrism of political Hebraism is evident in the fact that it has so far ignored not only the United States, but also Czarist and Orthodox Russia that conceived itself too as a New Israel; Isaiah Gruber, *Orthodox Russia in Crisis: Church and Nation in the Time of Troubles* (DeKalb: Northern Illinois University Press, 2012).

6. The literature in the field of Atlantic History is growing exponentially. For an excellent appraisal see Jack P. Greene and Philip D. Morgan, *Atlantic History: A Critical Reappraisal* (New York: Oxford University Press, 2008).

7. Shalom L. Goldman's engrossing *God's Sacred Tongue: Hebrew and the American Imagination* (Chapel Hill: University of North Carolina Press, 2003) does not focus on political issues; see also Abraham Katch, *The Biblical Heritage of American Democracy* (New York: Ktav, 1977), and Shalom S. Goldman, ed., *Hebrew and the Bible in America: The First Two Centuries* (Hanover, NH: University Press of New England, 1993). See also Glenn A. Moot's *Politics Reformed: The Anglo-American Legacy of Covenant Theology* (Columbia: University of Missouri Press, 2010), and Nathan Perl-Rosenthal's seminal essay, "'The Divine Right of Republics': Hebraic Republicanism and the Debate over Kingless Government in Revolutionary America," *William and Mary Quarterly* 3rd series, 66:3 (2009), 535–564. Harry Stout, a dean of early American religious history, recognized a quarter-century ago that New England ministers in 1775–1776 issued sermons addressing the theme of the Jewish republic. However, since Stout's magisterial study concludes in 1776, he inevitably underscores the threats of anarchy and disunion in these sermons rather than the potent constitutional models the Hebrew republic offered only a few years later. Stout, *The New England Soul*, 293–296. Nathan Hatch, too, noticed that clergymen "found republican ideals confirmed in the experience of Israel" and that they considered that confirmation significant because it gave the defense of liberty the full force of religious argument and provided an idiom for sustaining religious identities (*The Sacred Cause of Liberty*, 158–160). Hatch has not elaborated, however, on the significance of that idiom as a political discourse. Political scientists such as the late Daniel Elazar and Donald Lutz initially produced the most innovative work in the field by analyzing the importance and the role of the Hebraic notion of covenant and compact in the American constitutional tradition. On the centrality of the concept of covenant in political thought see Elazar, *Covenant and Constitutionalism*, and Delbert R. Hillers, *Covenant: The History of a Biblical Idea* (Baltimore: Johns Hopkins University Press, 1969). See also Donald S. Lutz, *The Origins of American Constitutionalism* (Baton Rouge: Louisiana State University Press, 1988), and Donald S. Lutz, "The Relative Influence of European Writers on Late Eighteenth-Century American Political Thought," *American Political Science Review* 78 (1984), 189–197, and the several articles in A Special Issue on Covenant, Polity, and Constitutionalism, *Publius: The Journal of Federalism* 10:4 (1980).

8. Other ancient sources, such as Josephus's *Jewish Antiquities*, restated that history. Josephus's works were printed in America between 1773 and 1800 in at least nine editions, and were read in the nineteenth century throughout the North and in the South, where they were,

according to Michael O'Brien, "mined by the pious"; O'Brien, *Conjectures of Order: Intellectual Life and the American South, 1810–1860*, 2 vols. (Chapel Hill: University of North Carolina Press, 2004), 2:593. Sutcliffe, *Judaism and Enlightenment*, 26, 43.

9. Sutcliffe, *Judaism and Enlightenment*, 26–27, 43–46, 66. Stroumsa, *A New Science*, 47–48. On Dutch Hebraism see Miriam Bodian, "The Biblical 'Jewish Republic' and the Dutch 'New Israel' in Seventeenth-Century Dutch Thought," *Hebraic Political Studies* 1:2 (2006), 186–202, and Simon Schama, *The Embarrassment of Riches: An Interpretation of Dutch Culture in the Golden Age* (New York: Knopf, 1987). See also Lea Campos Boralevi, "Classical Foundational Myths of European Republicanism: The Jewish Commonwealth," in *Republicanism: A Shared European Heritage*, 2 vols., ed. Martin Van Gelderen and Quentin Skinner (Cambridge: Cambridge University Press 2002), 1:248–250. See also Christopher Hill, *The English Bible and the Seventeenth-Century Revolution* (London: Penguin, 1995).

10. Sutcliffe, *Judaism and Enlightenment*, 50. Gary Remer, "After Machiavelli and Hobbes: James Harrington's Commonwealth of Israel," *Hebraic Political Studies* 1:4 (2006), 440–461: 454; Fania Oz-Salzberger, "The Political Thought of John Locke and the Significance of Political Hebraism," *Hebraic Political Studies* 1:5 (2006), 568–592. Alan Craig Houston, *Algernon Sidney and the Republican Heritage in England and America* (Princeton: Princeton University Press, 1991). Jonathan Scott, *Algernon Sidney and the Restoration Crisis, 1677–1683* (Cambridge: Cambridge University Press, 2002).

11. Bernard Bailyn, *The Ideological Origins of the American Revolution* (Cambridge: Harvard University Press, 1967), 34; Caroline Robbins, "Algernon Sidney's Discourses Concerning Government: Textbook of Revolution," *William and Mary Quarterly* 4:3 (1947), 267–296. Algernon Sidney, *Discourses Concerning Government*, ed. Thomas G. West (Indianapolis: Liberty Fund, 1996), 127, 464. The council instituted by Moses in the Sinai desert was named Sanhedrin only during the Babylonian captivity (587–538 B.C.).

12. Lord Summers, *The Judgment of Whole Kingdoms and Nations, Concerning the Rights, Power and Prerogative of Kings, and the Rights, Priviledges, and Properties of the People* (Philadelphia, 1773). Cato, "To the People of Pennsylvania," Letter 8, *Pennsylvania Ledger*, Apr. 27, 1776. In this rebuttal of Thomas Paine's vastly influential *Common Sense*, Cato attempted to demonstrate that Sidney was not an antimonarchist per se but merely a defender of liberty against monarchical absolutism (a position that, even if true, did not save the Englishman's life in 1683). John Adams, *A Defence of the Constitutions of Government of the United States* (New York, 1787), 147.

13. For the seventeenth-century Puritan articulation of biblical theo-politics see Shira Wolosky's illuminating "Biblical Republicanism: John Cotton's 'Moses and His Judicials' and American Hebraism," *Hebraic Political Studies* 4:2 (2009), 104–127. Frank Manuel points out that "Hebraic political theory, rooted in the biblical and rabbinic tradition, was throughout the long history of the Jews rather consistently monarchical"; Frank E. Manuel, *The Broken Staff: Judaism through Christian Eyes* (Cambridge: Harvard University Press, 1992), 127–128. Eric Nelson elaborates on the early modern encounter of European thinkers with a tradition of rabbinic commentary on biblical texts that brought about a dramatic transformation in republican thought, transforming a relativist position that accepted monarchy as a legitimate (if inferior) constitutional form, into commonwealthmen's exclusive ideology that regarded kingship as a sin. Eric Nelson, *The Hebrew Republic: Jewish Sources and the Transformation of*

European Political Thought (Cambridge: Harvard University Press, 2010), 23–56: 42. Samuel Phillips, *Political Rulers Authoriz'd and Influenc'd by God our Saviour to Decree and Execute Justice A Sermon Preached at Boston* ... [etc.] (Boston, 1750), 7.

14. Nathaniel Whitaker, "An Antidote Against Toryism, or the Curse of Meroz" (1777), in Moore, *The Patriot Preachers*, 186–231: 201. "Of Monarchy and Hereditary Succession," *Connecticut Courant*, Feb. 19, 1776. For a typical discussion of the Israelite polity as a political body among many others that history offered, see "Reflections on the Origin and Forms of Government," *The Censor*, Apr. 25, 1772. For discussions of the notion of luxury see Christopher J. Berry, *The Idea of Luxury: A Conceptual and Historical Investigation* (Cambridge: Cambridge University Press, 1994), and John Sekora, *Luxury: The Concept in Western Thought from Eden to Smollett* (Baltimore: Johns Hopkins University Press, 1977). James Dana, *A sermon Preached before the General Assembly of the State of Connecticut* ... [etc.] (Hartford: Hudson and Goodwin, 1779), 17; Dan Foster, *A Short Essay on Civil Government* (Hartford: Eben, 1775), 18.

15. *A Sermon Preached at Plymouth* (Boston, 1774), 21–22. J.R., *Connecticut Courant*, May 20, 1776.

16. Harry Stout noticed the Hebraic attributes of Langdon's sermon; Stout, *The New England Soul*, 294–295. Dan Foster, too, wrote on the theme of the Hebraic constitution in the same year as Langdon, in *A Short Essay*. Nelson, *Hebrew Republic*. Samuel Langdon, *Government Corrupted by Vice* (Boston, 1775), 12.

17. The greatest statement on the corruptibility of republics is J. G. A. Pocock's magisterial *The Machiavellian Moment: Florentine Political Thought and the Atlantic Republican Tradition* (Princeton: Princeton University Press, 1975). Daniel Elazar points out that Israel has shifted from being a strong federation to a weak confederation, operationally hardly more than a league at times. Those changes have ultimately led to "a change in regime of major proportions." Elazar, "The Book of Judges: The Israelite Tribal Federation and Its Discontents," http://www.jcpa.org/dje/articles/judges.htm [viewed Jan. 24, 2012].

18. Perl-Rosenthal, "'The Divine Right of Republics.'" Thomas Paine, *Common Sense: Addressed to the Inhabitants of America* ... [etc.] (Philadelphia, 1776), 10. For useful examinations of the difference between New Englanders and ministers from southern and mid-Atlantic colonies-turned-states, see Melvin B. Endy Jr., "Just War, Holy War, and Millennialism in Revolutionary America," *William and Mary Quarterly* 41 (1985), 3–25; Mark Valeri, "The New Divinity and the American Revolution," *William and Mary Quarterly* 56 (1989), 741–769, esp. 765; and Keith L. Griffin, *Revolution and Religion: American Revolutionary War and the Reformed Clergy* (New York: Paragon, 1994). On the differences in perceptions of chosenness between New England and mid-Atlantic clergymen see Keith Griffin, *Revolution and Religion: American Revolutionary War and the Reformed Clergy* (New York: Paragon, 1994).

19. Dana, *A Sermon*, 17. Samuel Cooper, *A Sermon Preached before his Excellency John Hancock Esq* ... *October 25, 1780. Being the Day of the Commencement of the Constitution, and Inauguration of the New Government* (Boston: T. and J. Fleet, 1780), 2, 3.

20. Cooper, *A Sermon*, 1, 8. The King James Bible's translation is misleading: what should have been translated as "Greaters" was rendered as "Nobles," reflecting the political sensibilities of early-seventeenth-century England, not the original Hebrew.

21. In traditional Christian discourse the Sanhedrin was not seen as a venerable "senate" but rather was vilified as the body that was responsible for turning over Christ to his tormentors. For a contemporary representative interpretation of the Sanhedrin in such attitude see James Rogers, *Holiness the Nature and Design of the Gospel of Christ* (Hartford, CT, 1780). Elazar, "The Book of Judges."

22. Cooper, *A Sermon*, 8, 11, 14; Dan Foster concurred with this view, stating that "God did not see it fit to assume to himself the regency and supreme civil government of Israel without their consent and election of him"; Foster, *A Short Essay*, 18. For the political implications of the theo-political concept of the covenant see Glenn A. Moots, *Politics Reformed: The Anglo-American Legacy of Covenant Theology* (Columbia: University of Missouri Press, 2010).

23. Huntington, *A Discourse Adapted to the Present Day*, 8–9. Peter Onuf, *Jefferson's Empire: The Language of American Nationhood* (Charlottesville: University of Virginia Press, 2000), 65.

24. Huntington, *A Discourse Adapted to the Present Day*, 8–9.

25. Ibid., 10.

26. On the theme of federal republicanism in the Bible see Daniel J. Elazar, ed., *Kinship and Consent: The Jewish Political Tradition and Its Contemporary Manifestations* (Lanham, MD: University Press of America and Center for Jewish Community Studies, 1983), and Daniel J. Elazar, "Covenant as the Basis of the Jewish Political Tradition," http://www.jcpa.org/dje/books/kincon-ch1.htm [viewed Jan. 24, 2012]. Huntington, *A Discourse*, 9, 24, 10. John Murray, *Jerubbaal; or, Tyranny's Grove Destroyed, and the Altar of Liberty Finished. A Discourse on America's Duty and Danger* ... (Newbury Port, MA, 1783), 51.

27. Joseph Huntington, *God Ruling the Nations for the Most Glorious End. A Sermon, in Presence of his Excellency, and both Houses of Assembly* (Hartford, 1784), 24.

28. Ibid., 24–25.

29. J. G. A. Pocock, *The Ancient Constitution and the Feudal Law: A Study of English Historical Thought in the Seventeenth Century* (New York: Norton, 1967), 30–55. Elazar, "The Book of Judges." Samuel Langdon, *The Republic of the Israelites an Example to the American States* ... [etc.] (Exeter, 1788), 6–7, 15, 16.

30. Langdon, *The Republic of the Israelites*, 8, 15.

31. Ibid., 8, 9.

32. Ibid., 9–11.

33. The classic treatment of early American historical imagination is Trevor Colbourn, *The Lamp of Experience: Whig History and the Intellectual Origins of the American Revolution* (1965; Indianapolis: Liberty Fund, 1998). The first four books of the Hebrew Bible, according to Daniel J. Elazar, may be seen as "as a constitutional document," with Deuteronomy, the fifth, as the restatement of the teachings of the other four books in more systematic and properly constitutional form." Elazar, "Deuteronomy as Israel's Ancient Constitution." Langdon, *A Sermon*, 2; Huntington, *A Discourse*, 11; Huntington, *God Ruling*, 24. Harry Stout emphasizes that although we do not understand anymore the early United States as New England writ large, we should not "understate the importance of New England's religious culture to the evolving American republic." Stout, *The New England Soul*, 9.

34. Historicus, "For the Balance," *Balance and Columbian Repository*, Dec. 10, 1801. Phillips's *American Republic and Human Liberty Foreshadowed in Scripture*, published in Ohio in 1864, testifies to the national appeal of that tradition.

35. Peter Dobkin Hall convincingly describes, in *The Organization of American Culture, 1700–1900: Private Institutions, Elites, and the Origins of American Nationality* (New York: New York University Press, 1984), the processes through which New England was able to exercise more influence over the development of American culture than any other region.

36. David Tappan, *Lectures on Jewish Antiquities Delivered at Harvard University in Cambridge* (Boston: Hilliard and Lincoln, 1807); Lyman Beecher, "The Republican Elements of the Old Testament," in *Lectures on Political Atheism and Kindred Subjects* (Boston, 1852), 176–190; and Wines, *Commentaries on the Laws of the Ancient Hebrews*.

37. Tappan, *Lectures on Jewish Antiquities*, 55, 88. Beecher, "Republican Elements of the Old Testament," 176, 179, 180.

38. Wines, *Commentaries*, 520–521.

39. Ibid., 490, 521, 532. J. V. Moore took a different stance. While agreeing that "the tribes had each a separate and independent government, and possessed well-defined state rights. Over the whole was a general government, exercising distinct jurisdiction," Moore observed that unlike the United States, biblical Israel had an "oracle, to which there is nothing corresponding in the United States government, as it is not a theocracy." J. V. Moore, "Republican Tendency of the Bible," *Methodist Quarterly Review*, new series 6 (April 1846), 220.

40. The Jewish-Roman historian Josephus was the first to coin the term "theocracy": "Our legislator [Moses] had no regard to any of these forms, but he ordained our government to be what by a strained expression, may be termed a theocracy [*theokratian*], by ascribing the power and authority to God, and by persuading all the people to have a regard to him as the author of all good things" (*Against Apion*, book II, 16). Wines, *Commentaries*, 456–457 (my emphases).

41. Beecher, "Republican Elements of the Old Testament," 180, 181, 188.

42. Wines, *Commentaries*, 122, 634, 116–118.

43. Moore, "Republican Tendency of the Bible," 221; Wines, *Commentaries*, 489, 455, 487, 409.

44. Enoch Pond, "Republican Tendencies of the Bible," in the *Biblical Repository and Classical Review* 3rd series, 4 (1848), 283–298: 287. Demophilus, *Carolina Gazette*, "The Sovereignty of the People," June 1, 1804. Moore, "Republican Tendency of the Bible," 220.

45. "Of Monarchy and Hereditary Succession," *South Carolina State Gazette and Timothy's Daily Advertiser*, Nov. 4, 1794, 2; John C. Calhoun, "Speech on the Force Bill" [1833], in *John C. Calhoun: Selected Writing and Speeches*, ed. H. Lee Cheek, Jr. (Washington, DC: Regnery, 2003), 444.

46. Moses Stuart, *Conscience and the Constitution* (Boston, 1850), 32.

47. Elias Boudinot, *A Star in the West; or, A Humble Attempt to Discover the Long Lost Ten Tribes of Israel* (Trenton, NJ, 1816), 161. Boudinot further points out that Indians, "agreeably to the theocracy of Israel, think the great spirit to be the immediate head of their state, and that God chose them out of all the rest of mankind, as his peculiar and beloved people," 192.

48. Noah's speech at the cornerstone of Ararat is reprinted in the *Publications of the American Jewish Historical Society (PAJHS)* 21 (1913), 230–252. On the reasons for the failure of Ararat see Eran Shalev, "'Revive, Renew, and Reestablish': Mordecai Noah's Ararat and the Limits of Biblical Imagination in the Early American Republic," *American Jewish Archives Journal* 62:1 (2010), 1–20.

49. Although Noah certainly bought land on Grand Island, exactly how much is uncertain. Jonathan Sarna, *Jacksonian Jew: The Two Worlds of Mordecai Noah* (New York: Holmes

and Meier, 1981), 62, 65. The events of the day, including transcriptions of Noah's speech and proclamation, were reprinted in many newspapers. For example, see the *Essex Register*, Sep. 26, 1825. Richard H. Popkin, "Mordecai Noah, The Abbé Grégoire, and the Paris Sanhedrin," *Modern Judaism* 2 (1982), 131–148: 134.

50. The finest examples are Sarna, *Jacksonian Jew*, and Popkin's "Mordecai Noah, The Abbé Grégoire, and the Paris Sanhedrin."

51. The thesis that internal causes (the problem of instituting an autonomy within the United States) contributed to the failure of Ararat, and not merely external causes (the lack of enthusiasm within the ranks of European Jews), is elaborated in Shalev, "'Revive, Renew, and Reestablish.'"

52. By signing as "judge," Benjamin Seixas, Ararat's pro tem secretary, demonstrated unintentionally how different the modern judgeship was from its biblical namesake. Others agreed with Noah that the judges functioned as Israel's "executive branch." See, e.g., Wines, *Commentaries*, 537–573. Michael Schuldiner and Daniel J. Kleinfeld, eds., *The Select Writings of Mordecai Noah* (Westport, CT: Greenwood, 1999), 113.

53. "Noah's Proclamation," *Salem Gazette*, Sep. 27, 1825.

54. Schuldiner and Kleinfeld, *Select Writings of Mordecai Noah*, 110.

55. "Interesting News," *Connecticut Courant*, Sep. 27, 1825. "Revival of the Jewish Government," *Essex Register*, Sep. 26, 1825. Schuldiner and Kleinfeld, *Select Writings of Mordecai Noah*, 105, 109, 113.

56. That case was most recently and illuminatingly made by Carl J. Richard, *The Golden Age of the Classics in America: Greece, Rome, and the Antebellum United States* (Cambridge: Harvard University Press, 2009); see also Eran Shalev, *Rome Reborn on Western Shores: Historical Imagination and the Creation of the American Republic* (Charlottesville: University of Virginia Press, 2009); and Caroline Winterer, *The Mirror of Antiquity: American Women and the Classical Tradition, 1750–1900* (Ithaca, NY: Cornell University Press, 2007). Beecher, "Republican Elements of the Old Testament," 189. Tappan, *Lectures on Jewish Antiquities*, 88. Moore, "Republican Tendency of the Bible," 221. In the context of the biblical origins of civil liberty (as opposed to the classics) see Phillips, *American Republic and Human Liberty Foreshadowed in Scripture*, 23–28.

57. Jack P. Greene, *Intellectual Heritage of the Constitutional Era: The Delegates' Library* (Philadelphia: Library Company of Philadelphia, 1986).

3. "A TRULY AMERICAN SPIRIT OF WRITING"

1. "The 1st Book of the Chronicles of John," *Investigator*, Oct. 30, 1812.

2. Lester H. Cohen makes a similar argument about the role of Providence in the early histories of the American Revolution. Cohen, *The Revolutionary Histories: Contemporary Narratives of the American Revolution* (Ithaca: Cornell University Press, 1980), 15 and passim.

3. Other post-Reformation translations included the Coverdale Bible (1535), the Matthews Bible (1537), the Great Bible (1539), and the Bishops' Bible (1568). For a longer discussion of the emergence of English translations of the Bible see S. L. Greenslade, "English Versions of the Bible," in *The Cambridge History of the Bible* (Cambridge University Press, 1963), 3: 141–174, and F. F. Bruce, *The English Bible: A History of Translations* (New York: Oxford University Press, 1961), 1–113. The historian Jonathan Sheehan points out that the post-1611 inactivity

was less because the new translations were satisfying (though they were) than because existing translations were successful in stopping the radical process of religious renovation they had begun. Jonathan Sheehan, *The Enlightenment Bible: Translation, Scholarship, Culture* (Princeton: Princeton University Press, 2005), 16–25, 53. David Lawton, *Faith, Text, and History: The Bible in English* (Charlottesville: University of Virginia Press, 1990), 64. For the movement of Puritans from the Geneva to the King James translation see also Harry S. Stout, "Word and Order in Colonial New England," in *The Bible in America: Essays in Cultural History*, ed. Nathan O. Hatch and Mark A. Noll (New York: Oxford University Press, 1982), 19–38.

    4. Christopher Hill, *The English Bible and the Seventeenth-Century Revolution* (London: Penguin, 1995), 17. Barbara K. Lewalski, *Protestant Poetics and the Seventeenth Century Religious Lyric* (Princeton: Princeton University Press, 1979), ix. Sheehan, *Enlightenment Bible*, 51–52, 148–149. Murray Roston describes the rising interest in Old Testament poetry during the eighteenth century as a move from rational neoclassical poetry to biblical romanticism; Roston, *Prophet and Poet: The Bible and the Growth of Romanticism* (London: Faber and Faber, 1965).

    5. Alister McGrath, *In the Beginning: The Story of the King James Bible and How It Changed a Nation, a Language, and a Culture* (New York: Anchor, 2001), 254, 265, 269; Adam Nicolson, *God's Secretaries: The Making of the King James Bible* (New York: HarperCollins, 2003), 223; Lawton, *Faith, Text, and History*, 62, 80–81.

    6. McGrath, *In the Beginning*, 267, 273.

    7. According to Paul Gutjahr, the King James Version reigned supreme in the United States for nearly two centuries; only in the early decades of the nineteenth century did this hegemony begin to erode. Mid-nineteenth-century arguments against revising the King James Bible revealed how many Americans still saw Elizabethan English as the only appropriate language in which to enfold the holy words of Scripture. Paul Gutjahr, *An American Bible: A History of the Good Book in the United States, 1777–1880* (Palo Alto: Stanford University Press, 2002), 92, 153.

    8. For colonial cultural dependency and imitation see Jack P. Greene, *Pursuits of Happiness: The Social Development of Early Modern British Colonies and the Formation of American Culture* (Chapel Hill: University of North Carolina Press, 1988). Horace Walpole is cited in Carla Mulford's introduction to John Leacock, *The First Book of American Chronicles of the Times, 1774–1775*, ed. Mulford (Newark: University of Delaware Press, 1987), 28. "The Lessons of the Day," *New York Weekly Journal*, July 4, 1743; the piece was reprinted from the Pennsylvanian *American Weekly Mercury*. "The French Gasconade," *Boston Evening Post*, Oct. 31, 1743.

    9. Trevor Colbourn, *The Lamp of Experience: Whig History and the Intellectual Origins of the American Revolution* (1965; Indianapolis: Liberty Fund, 1998), 23. Later editions updated Robert Dodsley's original publication, *The Chronicle of the Kings of England, Written in the Manner of the Ancient Jewish Historians. By Nathan Ben Saddi, Priest of the Jews* (Newport, RI, 1744). Another pseudobiblical account, under the name of Ben-Saddi, narrated the arrest of William Smith for allowing a translation of an article from Benjamin Franklin's *Pennsylvania Gazette* to be published in a German newspaper: *A Fragment of the Chronicles of Nathan Ben Saddi . . . now published in English* (Philadelphia, 1758).

    10. See, e.g., "Israel Ben Ader (of the Tribe of Levi)," *The Chronicle of B—g, the Son of the Great B—g, that lived in the Reign of Queen Felicia; Containing an account of his might*

transactions against Gallisoniere . . . Written in the Eastern Style (Boston, 1757), originally published in London in 1756. "Chronicles," *Maryland Journal*, May 5, 1766. "The Book of America," *Boston Gazette*, May 12, 1766, rpt. in *New Hampshire Gazette*, May 22, 1766, and *Newport Mercury* May 12, 1766. Additional chapters were published in the *Boston Gazette*, May 26, 1766, and *New Hampshire Gazette*, June 6, 1766.

11. *Chronicle of the Kings of England; From the Reign of William the Conqueror (First King of England) Down to his Present Majesty George the Third . . . By Nathan Ben Saddi* (Norwich, CT, 1773), 83.

12. From its beginning, pseudobiblicism was not an exclusively New England affair. For an early southern example, published in reaction to the Stamp Act's repeal, see "A Prophecy from the East," *Virginia Gazette* (Rind), supplement, Aug. 15, 1766. Sheehan, *The Enlightenment Bible*, 116.

13. For a Republican example see "The First Book of the Kings," *Alexandria Expositor*, Feb. 21, 1803; for a Federalist example see "Book of the Democrats," *American*, Mar. 14, 1809; for the quotation see "The Political Koran," *Federal Galaxy*, Sep. 15, 1798.

14. Mulford, Introduction to Leacock, *First Book*, 11. Leacock, *First Book*, 54.

15. Leacock, *First Book*, 58, 61, 54.

16. Mulford, Introduction to Leacock, *First Book*, 28–30.

17. The story of Elijah mocking the prophets of Baal (1 Kings 18) is an example reminiscent of the derisive style of American pseudobiblical texts. For the spiteful political culture of the early republic see Joanne Freeman, *Affairs of Honor: National Politics in the New Republic* (New Haven: Yale University Press, 2001).

18. The traditional views of secularization are best illustrated in the renowned works of Paul Hazard, *The European Mind, 1680–1715: The Critical Years*, trans. J. Lewis May (1935; New York: Fordham University Press, 1990), and Peter Gay, *The Enlightenment: The Rise of Modern Paganism* (1969; New York: Norton, 1995). Sheehan, *Enlightenment Bible*, 220, 260. See also Dror Wahrman, "God and the Enlightenment," *American Historical Review* 108 (2003), 1957–1960, and Jonathan Sheehan, "Enlightenment, Religion, and the Enigma of Secularization: A Review Essay," *American Historical Review* 108 (2003), 1061–1080.

19. "Chronicles of the people of America, Chapter XCVII," *Visitor*, Nov. 13, 1802. Gilbert J. Hunt, *The Late War, Between the United States and Great Britain . . . Written in the Ancient-Historical Style* (New York, 1819), ix.

20. "Chapter 37th," *Boston Evening Post*, Apr. 20, 1782. Andrew W. Robertson, "'Look on This Picture . . . and on This!' Nationalism, Localism, and Partisan Images of Otherness in the United States, 1787–1820," *American Historical Review* 106 (2001), 1236–1280: 1267. Freeman, *Affairs of Honor*, 10.

21. For an example of serial publication of Snowden's history see *Middlesex Gazette*, Dec. 9, 1819. For Snowden's influence see Hunt's *Late War*. For similar and earlier employments of the biblical style see "First Chapter of the Book of Remembrance," *Daily Advertiser*, Mar. 5, 1787, and "The xxxvii Chapter of the Second Book of the Chronicles," *Berkshire Chronicle*, Oct. 9, 1788.

22. For an examination of the role of Providence in the revolutionary historians' work see Cohen, *Revolutionary Histories*, 23–127. Richard Snowden, *The American Revolution; Written in the Style of Ancient History* (Philadelphia, 1793), 93, 74, 225, 34, 13, 17.

23. Snowden, *American Revolution*, 64, 226.

24. Ibid., iii. Carl Kaestle, *Pillars of the Republic: Common Schools and American Society, 1780–1860* (New York: Hill and Wang, 1983), 17; Clifton Johnson, *Old Time Schools and School-Books* (New York: Dover, 1963), 19; Gutjahr, *American Bible*, 113–142. *The Holy Bible Abridged* (Boston, 1782), 5. See also Hannah Moore, *Sacred Dramas, Chiefly Intended for Young Persons: The Subjects Taken from the Bible* (1788).

25. Classical pseudonyms were a comparable convention because they too originated in Britain, migrated to America, and gained their own cultural and generic independence during the Revolution. See Eran Shalev, *Rome Reborn on Western Shores: Classical Imagination and the Creation of the American Republic* (Charlottesville: University of Virginia Press, 2009), 151–187. Jack P. Greene, "The American Revolution," *American Historical Review* 105 (2000), 93–102.

26. "Paraphrase on the First Book of Samuel, Chap. VIII," *New York Journal*, Jan. 13, 1791. For partisan battles see, e.g., the piece written by "Moses," "The last Chapter of the first Book of Samuel," *Independent Gazetteer*, Sep. 17, 1791; and *Western Star*, May 24, 1796. For a text dealing with local, as opposed to national politics, see "The First Chapter of the First Book of Chronicles," *Ostego Herald*, Apr. 20, 1797. "First Chapter of Chronicles," *Oriental Trumpet*, Oct. 18, 1798; see also "Ancient Chronicles, Chap. XX," *Windham Herald*, Oct. 9, 1800.

27. Hunt, *Late War*, 294–300. For the concept of the "Whig interpretation of history" see Herbert Butterfield, *The Whig Interpretation of History* (1931; New York: Norton, 1965).

28. For the effect of the King James Version English on American readers see Gutjahr, *American Bible*, 153, and Robert Alter, *Pen of Iron: American Prose and the King James Bible* (Princeton: Princeton University Press, 2010). For historical discourses in the American Revolution see Peter C. Messer, *Stories of Independence: Identity, Ideology, and History in Eighteenth-Century America* (DeKalb: Northern Illinois University Press, 2005), and Colbourn's classic *Lamp of Experience*.

29. By referring to settlements in biblical Israel's far north (Dan) and south (Beersheba) the biblical author described the whole of the land. Americans gladly adopted that idiom. "Paraphrase of the First Book of Samuel, Chap. VIII," *New York Journal*, Jan. 13, 1791. *Western Star*, May 24, 1796. For "space of experience" and "horizon of expectation" see Reinhart Koselleck, *Futures Past: On the Semantics of Historical Time* (Cambridge: MIT Press, 1990), 267–288. In altering conventional understandings of historical time authors went beyond the common Christian-typological understanding of time in which early biblical events signified and foretold later modern-day occurrences. For typology in the Revolution see Shalev, *Rome Reborn on Western Shores*, 87–89. "The First Book of the Kings," *Alexandria Expositor*, Feb. 21, 1803.

30. Mark A. Noll, "The Image of the United States as a Biblical Nation, 1776–1865," in Hatch and Noll, *Bible in America*, 39–58: 45.

31. Philip L. Barlow, *Mormons and the Bible: The Place of the Latter-Day Saints in American Religion* (New York: Oxford University Press, 1991), 6n9. See also Gutjahr, *American Bible*, 2; Timothy L. Smith, "The Book of Mormon in a Biblical Culture," *Journal of Mormon History* 7:1 (1980), 3–22; and Donald M. Scott, *From Office to Profession: The New England Ministry, 1750–1850* (Philadelphia: University of Pennsylvania Press, 1978). For pseudobiblical writings after 1830 see, e.g., "The First Book of Chronicles," *Rhode Island Republican*, Mar. 18,

1835; "Chronicles of the Times," *New-Bedford Mercury*, Mar. 11, 1836; "Chapter from the Whig Chronicles," *New Hampshire Patriot*, Apr. 20, 1840. The latest pseudobiblical texts I was able to locate are "First Chronicles," *Pittsfield Sun*, Feb. 2, 1854, and A. E. Frankland's Civil War–era "Kronikals of the Times—Memphis, 1862," rpt. *America Jewish Archives* 9 (October 1957), 83–125.

32. Carl J. Richard, *The Golden Age of the Classics in America: Greece, Rome, and the Antebellum United States* (Cambridge: Harvard University Press, 2009), 41–82. Kenneth Cmiel, *Democratic Eloquence: The Fight over Popular Speech in Nineteenth-Century America* (New York: Morrow, 1990), 97.

33. For language in late-eighteenth-century America see John Howe, *Language and Political Meaning in Revolutionary America* (Amherst: University of Massachusetts Press, 2004). Cmiel, *Democratic Eloquence*, 20–54. These socioeconomic forces, commonly referred to as "the market revolution," are explored in Charles Sellers, *The Market Revolution: Jacksonian America, 1815–1846* (New York: Oxford University Press, 1994), and Harry L. Watson, *Liberty and Power: The Politics of Jacksonian America*, 2nd ed. (New York: Hill and Wang, 2006). Other factors contributed to the decline in the use of the pseudobiblical style. Paul Gutjahr has noted that the undisputed dominance that the Bible enjoyed both in American print culture and as a pedagogical tool began to slip in the opening decades of the nineteenth century; Gutjahr, *American Bible*, 3, 119. Additionally, the emergent modern historicist outlook, which understood the past as fundamentally different and alienated from the altered present, began to gain credence as the nineteenth century progressed. Henceforth the appeal of pseudobiblical language considerably diminished.

34. For major studies that trace different dimension of the erosion of traditional authority in the early republic see Sean Wilentz, *The Rise of the American Democracy* (New York: Norton, 2005); Sellers, *The Market Revolution*; Gordon S. Wood, *The Radicalism of the American Revolution* (New York: Vintage, 1993).

35. Barlow, *Mormons and the Bible*, 14; see also Paul Gutjahr, *The "Book of Mormon": A Biography* (Princeton: Princeton University Press, 2012); Gutjahr, *American Bible*, 151–166; and Richard L. Bushman, *Joseph Smith: Rough Stone Rolling* (New York: Knopf, 2005), 99, 107. Walter A. McDougall, *Throes of Democracy: The American Civil War Era, 1829–1877* (New York: Harper, 2008), 182. For the Book of Mormon as accommodating Jacksonian era sensibilities see Nathan O. Hatch, *The Democratization of American Christianity* (New Haven: Yale University Press, 1989), 116, 120; Barlow, *Mormons and the Bible*, 42; and Gordon Wood, "Evangelical America and Early Mormonism" in *Religion in American History: A Reader*, ed. Jon Butler and Harry S. Stout (New York: Oxford University Press, 1998), 180–196.

36. Hence, according to Wood, their failed attempts to get scientific verification "did not matter." Wood, "Evangelical America and Early Mormonism," 192. Terryl Givens has emphasized timing as important for understanding the Book of Mormon: "A record claiming to be a literal history of ancient Israelites in America, preserved and translated by supernatural means, appeared on the scene at precisely that moment when the long Christian retreat from biblical literalism was getting under way." Hence, Givens concludes, "this was not the best climate in which to introduce another religious record even more steeped in the miraculous, and without the benefit of the veil of historical or geographical distance." Terryl L.

Givens, *The Book of Mormon: A Very Short Introduction* (New York: Oxford University Press, 2009), 112.

37. Joseph Smith was, of course, not the only one to claim Jewish Ancestry for the American Indians. For the origins of the pervasive Hebraic "Indian theory" see chapter 4.

38. Wood, "Evangelical America and Early Mormonism," 191; Jan Shipps, *Mormonism: The Story of a New Religious Tradition* (Urbana: University of Illinois Press, 1985), 32–33. For contemporary anti-Mormonism see, e.g., Alexander Campbell, *Delusions: An Analysis of the Book of Mormon with an Examination of Its Internal and External Evidences, and a Refutation of Its Pretenses to Divine Authority* (Boston, 1832). For a study which contextualizes Joseph Smith in the early-nineteenth-century culture of prophecy see Susan Juster, *Doomsayers: Anglo-American Prophecy in the Age of Revolution* (Philadelphia: University of Pennsylvania Press, 2003).

39. Texts such as "Visionary Thoughts, or Modern Prophecy" (Greenwich, MA, 1806), "A Remarkable Prophecy of Abraham Wood ... Word for Word" (Philadelphia, 1811), "The Flaming Sword, or a Sign from Heaven" (Exeter, NH, 1814), and many similar contemporary visions and prophetic texts shunned the biblical language. When a text presented itself as "A Fragment of the Prophecy of Tobias, translated from the original" and claimed biblical language, it did not pretend to consist of an authentic prophecy. The prophets and prophecies examined in Susan Juster's *Doomsayers* show no inclination to biblical language. The only possible exception to this pattern is "The Vision of Nathan Ben Ashur." However, not only was this visionary text uncharacteristically cautious in its use of biblical language, refraining from the characteristic flourish of the pseudobiblical mode of expression, it is hard to tell whether the author of that text intended to present it as a prophetic text or rather a conventional allegory; "The Vision of Nathan Ben Ashur," *Federalist and New Jersey State Gazette*, Mar. 16, 1802.

40. Barlow, *Mormons and the Bible*, 14. See also Gutjahr, *American Bible*, 151–166: 153. *Book of Mormon*, First Book of Nephi, 1:4. Bushman, *Joseph Smith*, 99n63, 107; McDougall, *Throes of Democracy*, 182. For examples of unversified pseudobiblical texts see "Chronicles," *State Gazette of South Carolina*, June 1, 1786; "A Compendium of the 4th Chap. Of the 2d Book of Kings," *New Jersey Journal*, Feb. 16, 1793; "A Fragment of the Prophecy of Tobias," *American Mercury*, Feb. 10, 1794; "A Chronicle," *Commercial Ad*, Mar. 2, 1804; "Chronicles, Chap. VII," *Weekly Inspector*, Feb. 14, 1807; "Chronicles," *Eastern Argus*, Feb. 25, 1811; "Ninth Chapter of the Third Book of Chronicles," *Alexandria Gazette*, Apr. 25, 1812.

41. Terryl L. Givens, *By the Hand of Mormon: The American Scripture That Launched a New World Religion* (New York: Oxford University Press, 2003), 64.

42. For Joseph Smith as prophet and the larger culture of prophecy in the early republic see Juster, *Doomsayers*, 200, 213, and passim. For Mormon Biblicism see Barlow, *Mormons and the Bible*; Givens, *By the Hand of Mormon*; Smith, "Book of Mormon." Bushman, *Joseph Smith*, 86. Jon Butler, *Awash in a Sea of Faith*, 242.

43. "The First Book of Chronicles, Chapter the 5th," *Investigator*, Oct. 15, 1812. Already mid-eighteenth-century texts proclaimed a Hebrew author: Israel Ben Ader (of the Tribe of Levi), *The Chronicle of B—g, the Son of the Great B—g, that lived in the Reign of Queen Felicia; Containing an account of his might transactions against Gallisoniere ... Written in the Eastern*

Style (Boston, 1757), originally published in London in 1756. "A Fragment of the Prophecy of Tobias," *American Mercury*, Feb. 10, 1794.

44. "Fragment of the Prophecy of Tobias." *Alexandria Herald*, Oct. 9, 1822. Occasionally pseudobiblical texts could present themselves merely as "Ancient Chronicles" such as in the *Litchfield Monitor*, Mar. 28, 1804. Edwin Firmage, Jr., points out that pseudoepigraphic texts commonly presented themselves as providentially recovered writings inscribed in foreign idioms. Edwin Firmage, Jr., "Historical Criticism and the Book of Mormon: A Personal Encounter," in *American Apocrypha: Essays on the Book of Mormon*, ed. Dan Vogel and Brent Lee Metcalfe (Salt Lake City: Signature, 2002), 1–16: 3.

45. Like the English Ben Saddi, Smith presented himself as "author" in the first printing of the Book of Mormon. David Persuitte, *Joseph Smith and the Origins of the Book of Mormon* (Jefferson, NC: McFarland, 1985), 11. "Chronicles," *Broom Country Patriot*, Dec. 15, 1812. For treasure digging and the supernatural in the early republic see John L. Brooke, *The Refiner's Fire: The Making of Mormon Cosmology, 1644–1844* (New York: Cambridge University Press, 1996), 30–33; Michael D. Quinn, *Early Mormonism and the Magic World View* (Salt Lake City: Signature, 1998), passim; Alan Taylor, "The Early Republic's Supernatural Economy: Treasure Seeking in the American North-East, 1780–1830," *American Quarterly*, 1986, 6–34. For another pseudobiblical text with (tongue-in-cheek) claims of antiquity see *Philadelphia Evening Post*, Apr. 28, 1804. The affinity between the two languages is evident through texts written in biblical language self-styling as prophecies. See, among others, Francis Hopkinson, "Prophecy," in *Miscellaneous Essays and Occasional Writings* (Philadelphia, 1792), 92–97.

46. Firmage, "Historical Criticism and the Book of Mormon," 3.

47. Lori Anne Ferrell, *The Bible and the People* (New Haven: Yale University Press, 2008), 148, 156. For an early example see *A Curious Hieroglyphick Bible; or, Select Passages in the Old and New Testaments, Represented with Emblematical Figures, for the Amusement of Youth: Designed Chiefly to Familiarize Tender Age, in a Pleasing and Diverting Manner, with Early Ideas of the Holy Scriptures . . . Illustrated with Nearly Five Hundred Cuts* (Worcester, MA, 1788). Many editions and similar texts were published in decades to come. Similarly, Gilbert Hunt, the author of one of the most elaborate and protracted texts in the pseudobiblical tradition, stated that he "adopted for the model of his style the phraseology of the best of books," namely the Bible, so that it will induce "the young pupil . . . to study to Holy Scriptures." Hunt, *Late War*, ix. Compare with the early commentator who described Smith as "decipher[ing] the hieroglyphics on the plates." "Mormonism," *Richmond Enquirer*, Oct. 25, 1831.

48. Bushman, *Joseph Smith*, 84, 72; Fawn M. Brodie, *No Man Knows My History: The Life of Joseph Smith*, 2nd ed. (New York: Vintage, 1971), 69. For notable examples of attempts to contextualize the Book of Mormon see Quinn, *Early Mormonism*; Brooke, *Refiner's Fire*; Persuitte, *Joseph Smith*; Givens, *By the Hand of Mormon*, 17 and passim. Hatch, *Democratization of American Christianity*, 276n169.

49. Bushman, *Joseph Smith*, xx, 72. Thus, according to Bushman, ascribing composition to Smith calls for attributing to him "precocious genius of extraordinary powers who was voraciously consuming information without anyone knowing it." McDougall, *Throes of Democracy*, 644n15.

50. Brant A. Gardner, *The Gift and Power: Translating the Book of Mormon* (Salt Lake City: Greg Kofford Books, 2011), 318. The other side of this argument is, in the words of

Brigham Young, that had anyone other than Joseph Smith translated the Book of Mormon it would "materially differ from the present translation"; *Journal of Discourses* 9:311, http://www.journalofdiscourses.org/volume-09/ [viewed June 11, 2012]. Brigham S. Roberts quoted in Gardner, *The Gift and the Power*, 320.

51. Persuitte, *Joseph Smith*, 16–17. Quinn, *Early Mormonism*, 178–193: 179. For contemporary publications in biblical style in New York, including in the *Palmyra Register*, to which we know that Smith had access, see "Chronicles," *Palmyra Register*, Mar. 8, 1820; "Dr. Franklin's Parable against Persecution," *American Journal* (Ithaca), Feb. 13, 1822; "The Origin of Tythes," *Saratoga Sentinel*, Dec. 9, 1823; "Chronicles," *Ballstone Spa Gazette*, Oct. 19, 1824, which was reprinted from *The Livingston Journal of Geneseo*. Barlow, *Mormons and the Bible*, 24, 38.

52. Joseph Smith quoted in Givens, *By the Hand of Mormon*, 80.

53. Givens, *Book of Mormon*, 106.

54. One might have expected to encounter such criticism in a work such as Campbell's *Delusions*. Yet although critical of the Mormon bible to the utmost, labeling the work a "romance," Campbell stopped short of referring to the Book of Mormon's biblical language. Campbell, *Delusions*, 7. *Vermont Gazette*, Sep. 13, 1831. *New Hampshire Patriot and State Gazette*, Sep. 19, 1831. "Mormonism," *New Hampshire Sentinel*, Nov. 8, 1832. *American Sentinel*, Jan. 30, 1833.

55. For late pseudobiblical texts see note 31.

4. TRIBES LOST AND FOUND

1. "The Rodsmen," *Salem Gazette*, July 1, 1828. Stephen A. Marini, *Radical Sects of Revolutionary New England* (Cambridge: Harvard University Press, 1982), 54. Barnes Frisbie, *History of Middletown, Vermont, in Three Discourses* (Poultney, VT, 1867), 55. For the esoteric tradition in America and its early modern genealogy see John L. Brooke, *The Refiner's Fire: The Making of Mormon Cosmology, 1644–1844* (New York: Cambridge University Press, 1996).

2. Quotation in Donald Lutz, "From Covenant to Constitution in America Political Thought," *Publius: The Journal of Federalism* 10:4 (1980), 102–103n. For a recent account of patriotism and the War of 1812 see Nicole Eustace, *1812: War and the Passions of Patriotism* (Philadelphia: University of Pennsylvania Press, 2012). John McDonald, *Isaiah's Message to the American Nation: A New Translation of Isaiah, Chapter XVIII* (Albany, NY, 1814), 12, 13. For a similar Civil War–era interpretation of the United States as prophesied in Israelite history see George S. Phillips, *The American Republic and Human Liberty Foreshadowed in Scripture* (Cincinnati, 1864).

3. Anthony Grafton, *New Worlds, Ancient Texts: The Power of Tradition and the Shock of Discovery* (Cambridge: Harvard University Press, 1995), 149; Guy Stroumsa, *A New Science: The Discovery of Religion in the Age of Reason* (Cambridge: Harvard University Press, 2010), 3 and passim. Steven Conn, *History's Shadow: Native Americans and Historical Consciousness in the Nineteenth Century* (Chicago: University of Chicago Press, 2006). 5. For the intellectual impact of the Encounter see Anthony Pagden, *European Encounters with the New World: From Renaissance to Romanticism* (New Haven: Yale University Press, 1994); Anthony Pagden, *The Fall of Natural Man: The American Indian and the Origins of Comparative Ethnology*

(Cambridge: Cambridge University Press, 1987). There is a growing literature on the different and differences in various national experiences in the New World; for a recent example on the Dutch Encounter see Benjamin Schmidt, *Innocence Abroad: The Dutch Imagination and the New World, 1570–1670* (Cambridge University Press, 2006).

4. Quotation in Robert F. Berkhofer, *The White Man's Indian: Images of the American Indian from Columbus to the Present* (New York: Vintage, 1979), 8. In the context of making sense of the presence of natives see Grafton, in *Ancient Texts, New Worlds*. A third option was to portray Indians as "a people without history"; see Eric R. Wolf, *Europe and the People without History* (Berkeley: University of California Press, 1982). For understanding natives through the classical tradition see David Lupher, *Romans in a New World: Classical Models in Sixteenth-Century Spanish America* (Ann Arbor: University of Michigan Press, 2003), especially 189–234, and Sabine McCormack, *On the Wings of Time: Rome, the Incas, Spain, and Peru* (Princeton: Princeton University Press, 2006).

5. For biblical cosmologies and the Ten Tribes see Stroumsa, *New Science*, 21, 77–79; Shalom Goldman, *God's Sacred Tongue: Hebrew and the American Imagination* (Chapel Hill: University of North Carolina Press, 2003), 15–18; Zvi Ben-Dor Benite, *The Ten Lost Tribes: A World History* (New York: Oxford University Press, 2009), 142. Contemporaries had to explain the presence of Amerindians by responding to pre-Adamite and polygenetic theories, such as the influential one by Isaac La Peyrère; see Richard H. Popkin, *Isaac La Peyrère (1596–1676): His Life, Work, and Influence* (Leiden: Brill, 1987), 115–145. There were additional apocryphal accounts of the disappearance of the Ten Tribes, such as the Book of Esdras; see Alastair Hamilton, *The Apocryphal Apocalypse: The Reception of the Second Book of Esdras (4 Ezra) from the Renaissance to the Enlightenment* (New York: Oxford University Press, 1999).

6. Richard Popkin, "The Rise and Fall of the Jewish Indian Theory," in *Menasseh ben Israel and His World*, ed. Yosef Kaplan, Henry Mechoulan, and Richard Popkin (Leiden: Brill, 1989), 64, 81; Stroumsa, *New Science*, 78–9.

7. Thomas Thorowgood, *Jewes in America; or, Probabilities that the Americans are of that Race* (London, 1660). Quotation from Popkin, "Rise and Fall," 70; see also Nicholas Guyatt, *Providence and the Invention of the United States* (New York: Cambridge University Press, 2007), 36–37.

8. Eighteenth-century French travelers, such as the Jesuit Joseph-François Lafitau, who published *Moeurs des Sauvages Amériquains, Comparées aux Moeurs des Premiers Temp*, 2 vols. (Paris, 1724), embarked on similar projects; they did not, however, share Adair's zeal to identify the Indians as the Lost Tribes. See Gordon M. Sayre, *Les Sauvages Américains: Representations of Native Americans in French and English Colonial Literature* (Chapel Hill: University of North Carolina Press, 1997). Quotation from Thomas Jefferson to John Adams, June 11, 1812, in *Notes on the State of Virginia*, ed. Frank Shuffelton (London: Penguin, 1999), 281.

9. James Adair, *The History of the American Indians; particularly those nations adjoining to the Mississippi* [sic] *East and West Florida, Georgia, South and North Carolina, and Virginia: containing an account of their origin, language, manners, religious and civil customs, laws, form of government, punishments, conduct in war and domestic life, their habits, diet, agriculture, manufactures, diseases and method of cure . . . With observations on former historians, the conduct of our colony governors, superintendents, missionaries, & c. Also an appendix, containing a description of the Floridas, and the Mississippi lands, with their productions—the benefits of colonizing Georgiana,*

and civilizing the Indians—and the way to make all the colonies more valuable to the mother country (London, 1775), 13, 19, 32, 74, 90, 38, 47.

10. Ibid., 15.

11. Quotation from "Observations on the American Indians," *Newport Mercury*, Aug. 22, 1763.

12. Ezra Stiles, *The United States Elevated to Glory and Honor* (New Haven, 1783), 9–14. On Jefferson's speculation see James P. Ronda, *Lewis and Clark among the Indians* (Lincoln: University of Nebraska Press, 1984), 3. "Benjamin Rush to Lewis, 17 May 1803," in *Letters of the Lewis and Clark Expedition: With Related Documents, 1783–1854*, ed. Donald Dean Jackson (Urbana: University of Illinois Press, 1962), 50.

13. Thomas Jefferson to John Adams, June 11, 1812, in *Notes on the State of Virginia*, 281. See also Harold Hellenbrand, "'Not 'to Destroy but to Fulfil': Jefferson, Indians, and Republican Dispensation," *Eighteenth Century Studies* 18 (1985), 523–525.

14. Goldman, *God's Sacred Tongue*, 17–18; Guyatt, *Providence and the Invention of the United States*; Conn, *History's Shadow*, 14–15; and Popkin, "Rise and Fall" are only a few works that situate the United States in that tradition.

15. Isaac McCoy quoted in Conn, *History's Shadow*, 13.

16. Guyatt, *Providence and the Invention of the United States*, 172. Elias Boudinot, *A Star in the West; or, A Humble Attempt to Discover the Long Lost Ten Tribes of Israel* (Trenton, NJ, 1816).

17. Boudinot's definite biography is George Adams Boyd, *Elias Boudinot: Patriot and Statesman* (Princeton: Princeton University Press, 1952).

18. Boudinot, *Star in the West*, iii, vi. While Boudinot derived many of his ideas, and even his phrasing, from Adair, he did shy from compulsively aggregating the ideas of many other commentators who concluded that "there was some affinity between [Indians] and the Jews"; *A Star in the West*, 214. For Boudinot and the context of the French Revolution see Popkin, "Rise and Fall," 72–74.

19. Boudinot, *Star in the West*, 79, 87, 88.

20. Ibid., 161, 165, 281.

21. Wolf, *Europe and the People without History*. Boudinot, *Star in the West*, 297–298.

22. Boudinot, *Star in the West*, 161.

23. Lucius, "A Few Observations on the Western and Southern Indians," *Independent Gazetteer*, Apr. 22, 1789.

24. X.Y., "The Lost Ten Tribes," *Boston Patriot*, Oct. 10, 1810: 2.

25. "Star in the West," *New York Courier*, Oct. 8, 1816.

26. A Son of Abraham, "North America Indians in London," *Weekly Recorder*, Oct. 9, 1818. "American Indians," *Concord Observer*, Mar. 15, 1819.

27. "Indian Jews," *New York Columbian*, Feb. 19, 1819. "On the Aborigines," *Rutland Herald*, Sep. 4, 1816. John Gambold, "Of the Aborigines," *American Beacon and Commercial Diary*, July 31, 1816.

28. Ethan Smith, *A View of the Hebrews: Exhibiting the Destruction of Jerusalem, the Certain Restoration of Judah and Israel; the Present State of Judah and Israel, and an Address of the Prophet Isaiah Relative to their Restoration* (Poultney, VT, 1823), 263.

29. Smith, *View of the Hebrews*, 84, 48–49, 78, 79.

30. Ibid., 335, 336, 346, 268.

31. N., "Smith's View of the Hebrews," *Saratoga Sentinel*, Dec. 23, 1823. "American Aborigines," *Watch-Tower*, Dec. 4, 1826.

32. "Answer to A Review of Smith on the Hebrews," *Saratoga Sentinel*, Mar. 9, 1824.

33. Dan Vogel, *Indians and the Book of Mormon: Solutions from Columbus to Joseph Smith* (Salt Lake City: Signature, 1986), 5.

34. Stephen Prothero, *America's Jesus: How the Son of God Became a National Icon* (New York: Farrar, Straus and Giroux, 2003), 173. For the classic work on the Second Great Awakening in western New York see Whitney R. Cross, *The Burned-Over District: The Social and Intellectual History of Enthusiastic Religion in Western New York, 1800–1850* (New York: Harper and Row, 1965). Smith quoted in Vogel, *Indians and the Book of Mormon*, 8.

35. Smith quoted in Vogel, *Indians and the Book of Mormon*, 8.

36. Brant A. Gardner, *The Gift and Power: Translating the Book of Mormon* (Salt Lake City: Greg Kofford Books, 2011), 132. Terryl L. Givens, *By the Hand of Mormon: The American Scripture That Launched a New World Religion* (New York: Oxford University Press, 2003), 101. "The Mormons," *Daily Picayune*, Dec. 1, 1841.

37. Givens, *By the Hand of Mormon*, 94, 101. Oliver Cowdery, "Address to the Indian Council," in *Stories from the Early Saints: Converted by the Book of Mormon*, ed. Susan Easton Black (Salt Lake City: Bookcraft, 1992), 54. Joseph Smith to N. C. Saxton, Jan. 4, 1833, in *The Personal Writings of Joseph Smith*, ed. Dean C. Jessee (Salt Lake City: Deseret, 1984), 273. For the Book of Mormon's importance not as a text closely read but rather as a "signifier" see Givens, *By the Hand of Mormon*, 64.

38. Noah's speech at the cornerstone of Ararat is reprinted in the *Publications of the American Jewish Historical Society (PAJHS)* 21 (1913), 230–252. Ararat occasionally catches the attention of modern historians. Jonathan Sarna, for example, describes in an illuminating biography of Noah the events leading to Ararat's dedication and contextualizes the scheme and its planner in Jewish, Jewish-American, and proto-Zionist history: Jonathan Sarna, *Jacksonian Jew: The Two Worlds of Mordecai Noah* (New York: Holmes and Meier, 1981). For Noah as proto-Zionist see Jacob Rader Marcus, ed., *The Jew in the American World* (Detroit: Wayne State University Press, 1996), 179. See also Richard H. Popkin, "Mordecai Noah, The Abbé Grégoire, and the Paris Sanhedrin," *Modern Judaism* 2 (1982), 131–148; and Eran Shalev, "Revive, Re-new, and Reestablish: Mordecai Noah's Ararat and the Limits of Biblical Imagination in the Early American Republic," *American Jewish Archives Journal* 62:1 (2010), 1–20, which underscores that the Jewish autonomy that Noah sought for Ararat under the protection of the young United States, subdued as it may have been, contrasted with the prevailing political and constitutional culture reigning in America. Sarna persuasively argues that Noah had misread the world Jewish situation; *Jacksonian Jew*, 74. Daniel Walker Howe also points out that "European Jewish opinion was not prepared to entertain [Noah's] plan"; *What Hath God Wrought: The Transformation of America, 1815–1848* (New York: Oxford University Press, 2009), 301. For a view of Ararat's failure due to Noah's charlatanism see James L. Erwin, *Declarations of Independence: Encyclopedia of American Autonomous and Secessionist Movements* (Westport, CT: Greenwood, 2007), 8.

39. A telling context for Noah's colonization attempt involves the repeated clashes of southern states with their Native American populations after the conclusion of the War of

1812, when western lands were opened for white settlement. In 1830, five years after Ararat's dedication, President Andrew Jackson elaborated in his annual message on "a portion . . . of the Southern [Native American] tribes, [which] have lately attempted to erect an independent government within the limits of Georgia and Alabama." The president's speech explained the intentions of the Indian Removal Act, which had been passed seven months earlier, in May 1830, for the purpose of opening Native American–held lands east of the Mississippi for white settlement. The concept of independence had, of course, a formidable significance in the United States, reverberating also in Noah's own Jewish "declaration of independence." The question confronted by the president, and the Union over which he presided, after the states claimed to be the only sovereign within their territories, was "whether the General Government had a right to sustain those people [Native Americans] in their pretensions" for tribal independence. Jackson recognized that the Constitution forbade new states from being formed within the jurisdiction of any other state, "without the consent of its legislature." Much less, Jackson added, could the federal government "allow a foreign and independent government [such as a Native American nation] to establish itself" within an existing state. Jackson asked rhetorically: "Would the people of New York permit each remnant of the Six Nations within her borders to declare itself an independent people under the protection of the United States? Could the Indians establish a separate republic on each of their reservations in Ohio?" Perpetuating Jackson's reasoning, one might have asked if the people of New York would permit *Jews* within the state's borders to declare themselves an independent people under the protection of the United States? Could *Jews* establish a separate republic, even only a semiautonomous polity, within the borders of an existing state? Jackson had no doubts as to what New Yorkers would feel about such questions and what they would do if confronted with such dilemmas; Shalev, "Revive, Renew, and Reestablish," 15.

40. Noah's speech, 248.

41. "The Ararat Proclamation and Speech," in *The Selected Writings of Mordecai Noah*, ed. Michael J. Schuldiner and Daniel J. Kleinfeld (Westport, CT: Greenwood, 1999), 110. Noah's speech, 249; that the Indians were the "rightful inheritors of the new" world may be why Noah planned to have "young Indian hunters of the Seneca tribe, dressed in their costume," with him at the celebration at New York City. *New Hampshire Sentinel*, Nov. 18, 1825: 4.

42. "Ararat Proclamation and Speech," 123.

43. "From Ararat," *Boston Commercial Gazette*, Oct. 6, 1825: 2. *Boston Semi-Weekly Advertiser*, Oct. 29, 1825: 1. "Grand Canal Celebration," *Essex Register*, Nov. 10, 1825: 1. *New Hampshire Sentinel*, Nov. 18, 1825: 4. Even after Grand Island's failure, Noah still retained the Ark on his newspaper masthead.

44. Juniper, *Salem Gazette*, Mar. 2, 1827. Mordecai Manuel Noah, *Discourse on the Evidences of the American Indians being the Descendants of the Lost Tribes of Israel* (New York, 1837).

45. "The 'Ten Lost Tribes' of Israel in America," *Sun*, Jan. 25, 1849. Europeans already identified in earlier centuries American locales as Ophir; Stroumsa, *New Science*, 78.

46. "The Ten Lost Tribes of Israel," *Wisconsin Democrat*, Nov. 23, 1850. "The Dahlias of Mexico and the Gold of Ophir," *Trenton State Gazette*, Jan. 25, 1849.

47. Paul E. Johnson and Sean Wilentz, *The Kingdom of Matthias: A Story of Sex and Salvation in 19th-Century America* (New York: Oxford University Press, 1994), 64. *Salem Gazette*, Oct. 7, 1834: 2.

48. *Connecticut Courant*, Oct. 6, 1834: 2. Margaret Matthews, *Matthias. By His Wife. With Notes on the Book of Mr. Stone, on Matthias* (New York, 1835), 9; Johnson and Wilentz, *Kingdom of Matthias*, 98, 144.

49. Matthews, *Matthias*, 9. Johnson and Wilentz, *Kingdom of Matthias*, 64.

50. Johnson and Wilentz, *Kingdom of Matthias*, 144.

51. "A Jewish Rechabite," *Weekly Gleaner* (San Francisco), Jan. 16, 1857, and "Death of a Worthy Man," *Jewish Chronicle* (London), May 11, 1860, rpt. in *American Jewish Archives* 15 (April, 1963), 3–5.

52. "Jewish Rechabite," 4. Jeremiah 35:1–19.

53. Ralph Melnick, "Billy Simons: The Black Jew of Charleston," *American Jewish Archives* 32:1 (1980), 3–8: 6.

54. "The Ten Lost Tribes and Ancient Aztecs," *Sun*, Feb. 6, 1849. The notable exception was, as we have seen, Mordecai Noah, who speculated that California was biblical Ophir.

55. James H. Moorhead, "The American Israel: Protestant Tribalism and Universal Mission," in *Many Are Chosen: Divine Election and Western Nationalism*, ed. William R. Hutchison and Hartmut Lehmann (Minneapolis: Fortress, 1994), 145–166: 149.

56. Albert J. Raboteau, "Exodus, Ethiopia, and Racial Messianism: Texts and Contexts," in Hutchison and Lehmann. *Many Are Chosen*. Quotation in Albert B. Cleage, *The Black Messiah* (New York: Sheed and Ward, 1968), 73. Prothero, *America's Jesus*, 217.

57. John Lloyd Stephens, *Incidents of Travel in Central America, Chiapas, and Yucatan* (1841; Washington: Smithsonian Institute Press, 1993), 36. This remark represents the sole agreement between debaters in a fictitious dialogue about the Book of Mormon, published in the *Times and Seasons* in 1841, quoted in Givens, *By the Hand of Mormon*, 94.

58. Even a quick glance shows that the Israelite-Indian theory still proliferates in the subculture of the internet. Nevertheless, over the past couple of decades there have been serious scholars who examined the theory and found it at least plausible. For a modern and sophisticated adherent of the theory see Cyrus Gordon, "The Ten Lost Tribes," in *Hebrew and the Bible in America: The First Two Centuries*, ed. Shalom S. Goldman (Hanover, NH: University Press of New England, 1993), 61–69. Gordon hypothesizes that ancient Jews, though by no means the first to sail from the Mediterranean to the Western Hemisphere, were among the pre-Columbian visitors and immigrants to the New World. An authority such as Richard Popkin agrees that "no other explanation could be found for the [apparently ancient] phylacteries being where they were found [in North America]"; Popkin, "The Rise and Fall of the Jewish Indian Theory," in Goldman, *Hebrew and the Bible in America*, 70–90: 81. Quotation in Conn, *History's Shadow*, 5.

59. Phillips, *American Republic and Human Liberty Foreshadowed in Scripture*, 10, 39.

5. EVANGELICALISM, SLAVERY, AND THE DECLINE OF AN OLD TESTAMENT NATION

1. Franklin proposed the image of the Egyptian army drowning in the Red Sea, while Jefferson included in his proposal the Pillar of Fire leading the Children of Israel in the desert. John F. Berens, *Providence and Patriotism in Early America, 1640–1815* (Charlottesville: University of Virginia Press, 1978), 107.

2. Historians tend to ascribe "secularization" in America to the last third of the nineteenth century; see Christian Smith, *The Secular Revolution: Power, Interests, and Conflicts in the Secularization of American Public Life* (Berkeley: University of California Press, 2003); see also Grant Wacker, "The Demise of Biblical Civilization," in *The Bible in America: Essays in Cultural History*, ed. Nathan O. Hatch and Mark A. Noll (New York: Oxford University Press, 1982), 121–138.

3. Sydney Ahlstrom, *A Religious History of the American People* (New Haven: Yale University Press, 1972), 124. More recently, William Hutchinson argued that "with respect to religious origins . . . the European component in colonial society had been well over 95 percent Protestant. At least 90 percent of the colonists, moreover, had come out of the Calvinist rather than the Lutheran side of the Protestant Reformation. . . . The colonists had been at least 85 percent English-speaking Calvinist Protestants." William R. Hutchinson, *Religious Pluralism in America: The Contentious History of a Founding Ideal* (New Haven: Yale University Press, 2004), 20–21. See also Daniel Elazar, *Covenant and Constitutionalism: The Covenant Tradition in Politics* (Piscataway, NJ: Transaction, 1997), 68. For an analysis of the cultural dominance of New England in British North America and the United States see Peter Dobkin Hall, *The Organization of American Culture, 1700–1900: Private Institutions, Elites, and the Origins of American Nationality* (New York: New York University Press, 1984). Stephen Prothero, *American Jesus: How the Son of God Became a National Icon* (New York: Farrar, Straus and Giroux, 2003), 44–45.

4. E. Brooks Holifield, *Theology in America: Christian Thought from the Age of the Puritans to the Civil War* (New Haven: Yale University Press, 2003), 36, 45. Richard W. Fox, *Jesus in America: Personal Savior, Cultural Hero, National Obsession* (New York: HarperOne, 2005), 103, 109. Kenneth P. Minkema and Harry S. Stout, "The Edwardsean Tradition and the Antislavery Debate, 1740–1865," *Journal of American History* 92:1 (2005), 47–74; David S. Lovejoy, "Samuel Hopkins: Religion, Slavery, and the Revolution," *New England Quarterly* 40:2 (1967), 227–243.

5. Michael O'Brien, *Conjectures of Order: Intellectual Life and the American South, 1810–1860*, 2 vols. (Chapel Hill: University of North Carolina Press, 2004), 2:1119. Perry Miller, *The New England Mind: The Seventeenth Century* (Boston: Beacon, 1961), 45. Prothero, *American Jesus*, 12. Fox, *Jesus in America*, 153–154. Elizabeth Fox-Genovese and Eugene Genovese, *The Mind of the Master Class: History and Faith in the Southern Slaveholder's Worldview* (New York: Cambridge University Press, 2005), 529.

6. Conor Cruise O'Brien, *God Land: Reflections on Religion and Nationalism* (Cambridge: Harvard University Press, 1999), 4. Mark Lilla, *The Stillborn God: Religion, Politics, and the Modern West* (New York: Vintage, 2008), 45. Perry Miller succinctly remarked that the Old Testament was "more dramatic" than the New; "The Garden of Eden and the Deacon's Meadow," *American Heritage Magazine* 7:1 (December 1955), http://www.americanheritage.com/content/garden-eden-and-deacon%E2%80%99s-meadow [viewed on 1/23/2012].

7. Daniel Dreisbach provides in "The Bible in the Political Rhetoric of the American Founding," *Politics and Religion* 4 (2011), 401–427, a plethora of contemporary biblical quotations, from both the Old and the New Testaments. The pervasiveness of the Old Testament in postrevolutionary America prompted Perry Miller to observe that "the Old Testament is truly so omnipresent in the American culture of 1800 or 1820 that historians have as much difficulty

taking cognizance of it as of the air the people breathed"; Miller, "The Garden of Eden and the Deacon." Henry Adams, *The Education of Henry Adams* (New York: Bnpublishing, 2008), 13. Herman Melville, *White-Jacket; Or, the World in a Man-of-War* (1850; New York: Modern Library, 2002), 151.

8. Prothero, *American Jesus*, 10.

9. Fox, *Jesus in America*, 153. Mark A. Noll, "The Image of the United States as a Biblical Nation, 1776–1865," in Hatch and Noll, *Bible in America*, 39–58: 45.

10. For pseudobiblicism see chapter 3.

11. Noll, "Image of the United States," 45, 56n56. O'Brien, *Conjectures of Order*, 2: 1119.

12. Noll, "Image of the United States," 45.

13. Philip L. Barlow, *Mormons and the Bible: The Place of the Latter-Day Saints in American Religion* (New York: Oxford University Press, 1991), 6n9. That the shift was pronounced by 1850 is indicated also in Donald M. Scott, *From Office to Profession: The New England Ministry, 1750–1850* (Philadelphia: University of Pennsylvania Press, 1978). Prothero, *American Jesus*, 172.

14. The term "market revolution" was coined by Charles Sellers in *The Market Revolution: Jacksonian America, 1815–1846* (New York: Oxford University Press, 1994). For Methodists as evangelical innovators see John Wigger, *American Saint: Francis Asbury and the Methodists* (New York: Oxford University Press, 2009), 64, 384.

15. John Wigger, "Fighting Bees: Methodist Itinerants and the Dynamics of Methodist Growth" in *Methodism and the Shaping of American Culture*, ed. Nathan O. Hatch and John Wigger (Nashville, TN: Kingswood, 2001), 126–127. Quotation in Wigger, *American Saint*, 286–287.

16. Gordon S. Wood, *Empire of Liberty: A History of the Early Republic, 1789–1815* (New York: Oxford University Press, 2009), 576. Mark A. Noll, *America's God: From Jonathan Edwards to Abraham Lincoln* (New York: Oxford University Press, 2002), 165–170.

17. Wood, *Empire of Liberty*, 581. For a useful working definition of evangelicalism see David W. Bebbington, *Evangelicalism in Modern Britain: A History from the 1730s to the 1980s* (London: Routledge, 1989), 2–17; Noll, *America's God*, 208.

18. Scott, *From Office to Profession*, 178.

19. For the most influential study of this process see: Nathan O. Hatch, *The Democratization of American Christianity* (New Haven: Yale University Press, 1989).

20. Mark A. Noll, *God and Race in American Politics* (Princeton: Princeton University Press, 2010), 24–25, 29–30. Fox, *Jesus in America*, 195, 202.

21. E. L. Magoon, *Republican Christianity; Or, True Liberty, as Exhibited in the Life, Precepts, and Early Disciples of the Great Redeemer* (Boston, 1849).

22. Enoch Pond, "Republican Tendencies of the Bible," in *The Biblical Repository and Classical Review* 4:2 (New York, 1848), 283–298: 287, my emphasis.

23. Henry Ward Beecher, "A Conversation about Christ," in *Sermons by Henry Ward Beecher, Plymouth Church, Brooklyn* (New York, 1869), 1: 473–490: 476. Prothero, *American Jesus*, 56. Campbell quoted in Paul Gutjahr, *An American Bible: A History of the Good Book in the United States, 1777–1880* (Palo Alto: Stanford University Press, 2002), 102.

24. For example, counting appearance of keywords in contemporary newspapers in such databases as Readex's *Early American Newspapers* in an attempt to demonstrate change

over time in the popularity of the Bible proves meaningless because of the exponential growth of printed material during the nineteenth century—a growth that outpaces by orders of magnitude the relative decline in the use of the Old Testament.

25. Timothy Dwight, *Conquest of Canaan: A Poem* (Hartford, CT, 1785). Hannah More, *Sacred Dramas, Chiefly Intended for Young Persons: The Subjects Taken from the Bible* (Philadelphia, 1787). John Holt Ingraham's popular novels display, too, the rise of the New Testament in the American biblical imagination: only after publishing the first novel of what would become a trilogy, *The Prince of the House of David* (1855), which consists of a fictional depiction of the life of Jesus, did Ingraham go on to compose two Old Testament novels, which focused—of course—on earlier events (*The Pillar of Fire* [1859] and *The Throne of David: From the Consecration of the Shepherd of Bethlehem to the Rebellion of Prince Absalom* [1860]). The authorial decision to compose first the New Testament novel (and reverting afterward to a chronological progress by writing first a book about the Exodus and then one about the later reign of King David) demonstrates yet again the relative importance of the testaments in the second half of nineteenth-century America. See in this context David S. Reynolds, *Faith in Fiction: The Emergence of Religious Literature in America* (Cambridge: Harvard University Press, 1981). Fox, *Jesus in America*, 219.

26. Miller, "The Garden of Eden and the Deacon's Meadow."

27. Molly Oshatz, "The Problem of Moral Progress: The Slavery Debates and the Development of Liberal Protestantism in the United States," *Modern Intellectual History* 5:2 (2008), 225–250: 225.

28. Holifield, *Theology in America*, 494–504. Historians have recently demonstrated that the debate over slavery and the Bible continued in the South, if in a much more mellow fashion, after 1865. John David Smith, *An Old Creed for the New South: Proslavery Ideology and Historiography, 1865–1918* (Carbondale: Southern Illinois University Press, 2008), 43–44.

29. O'Brien, *Conjectures of Order*, 2: 966. For proslavery not as a sectional but nationwide phenomenon see Larry E. Tise, *Proslavery: A History of the Defense of Slavery in America, 1701–1840* (Athens: University of Georgia Press, 1990).

30. Noll, *America's God*, 367–445; Fox-Genovese and Genovese, *Mind of the Master Class*, 505–527; E. Brooks Holifield considers the debate, however, as a "stalemate" or "standoff"; Holifield, *Theology in America*, 494–504.

31. Albert Barnes, *An Inquiry into the Scriptural Views of Slavery* (Philadelphia, 1846), 22. The literature on the topic is extensive; for major and recent contributions see Molly Oshatz, *Slavery and Sin: The Fight against Slavery and the Rise of Liberal Protestantism* (New York: Oxford University Press, 2011); Charles F. Irons, *The Origins of Proslavery Christianity: White and Black Evangelicals in Colonial and Antebellum Virginia* (Chapel Hill: University of North Carolina Press, 2008); Harry S. Stout, *Upon the Altar of the Nation: A Moral History of the Civil War* (New York: Penguin, 2007); Stephen R. Haynes, *Noah's Curse: The Biblical Justification of American Slavery* (New York: Oxford University Press, 2007); Mark A. Noll, *The Civil War as a Theological Crisis* (Chapel Hill: University of North Carolina Press, 2006). For proslavery examples of biblical analysis of slavery that divided into separate Old Testament and New Testament sections see Albert Taylor Bledsoe, *An Essay about Liberty and Slavery* (Philadelphia, 1856); Thornton Stringfellow, *A Brief Examination of Scripture Testimony on the Institution of Slavery* (Washington, DC, 1850), rpt. in *The Ideology of Slavery: Proslavery*

Thought in the Antebellum South, 1830–1860, ed. Drew Gilpin Faust (Baton Rouge: Louisiana State University Press, 1981); Moses Stuart, *Conscience and the Constitution* (Boston, 1850). For antislavery instances of such division see Francis Wayland, *Domestic Slavery Considered as a Scriptural Institution: In a Correspondence Between The Rev. Richard Fuller and The Rev. Francis Wayland* (New York, 1845); and Barnes, *Inquiry into the Scriptural Views*.

32. O'Brien, *Conjectures of Order*, 2: 959; Faust, *Ideology of Slavery*, 138. Stringfellow, *Brief Examination*, 149.

33. Prothero, *American Jesus*, 173.

34. Noll, *God and Race in American Politics*, 32–33. Tise, *Proslavery*, 13. See also Mitchell Snay, *Gospel of Disunion: Religion and Separatism in the Antebellum South* (Chapel Hill: University of North Carolina Press, 1997). O'Brien, *Conjectures of Order*, 2: 959. Fox-Genovese and Genovese, *Mind of the Master Class*, 490. On the proslavery discourse as one that was cumulative and legitimized evangelicalism, and in which "the South was very conscious of itself as an intellectual community," see O'Brien, *Conjectures of Order*, 2: 947, 959. Stuart, *Conscience and the Constitution*, 23. For a book-length treatment of the curse of Canaan see Haynes, *Noah's Curse*, according to which the tale of Noah and his sons came to function as a myth of origins for slaveholding culture. On the question of race and Noah's curse see Benjamin Braude, "The Sons of Noah and the Construction of Ethnic and Geographical Identities in the Medieval and Early Modern Periods," *William and Mary Quarterly* 54:1 (1997), 103–142. Theodore Dwight Weld, *The Bible against Slavery* (New York, 1837), 95.

35. Richard Fuller, in *Domestic Slavery Considered as a Scriptural Institution* (New York, 1845), 175–177. Irons, *Origins of Proslavery Christianity*, 11–12.

36. Tise, *Proslavery*, table 5.6, 117. In order "to study proslavery quantitatively," Tise writes, he chose "91 published defenses of slavery" and subjected them "to a statistical argument analysis.... The scheme adopted does test the frequency of appearance of the most common arguments in all of the periods and geographical areas under consideration"; 102–103. Mason I. Lowance, *A House Divided: The Antebellum Slavery Debates in America, 1776–1865* (Princeton: Princeton University Press, 2003), 57. This preference is evident in works that separated their treatment of the testaments to separate sections, such as Bledsoe, *Essay about Liberty and Slavery*, which dedicated to the proslavery argument eighteen pages (138–156) from the Old Testament and sixty-eight pages (157–225) from the New Testament; and Fuller, in *Domestic Slavery*, who dedicated to the argument seventeen pages (148–165) from the Old Testament and thirty-seven (165–202) from the New. Other (and shorter) works could be less decidedly New Testament biased, such as John Richter Jones, *Slavery Sanctioned by the Bible: A Tract for Northern Christians* (Philadelphia, 1861), which dedicated seven pages to the Old Testament and nine to the New Testament.

37. Stuart, *Conscience and the Constitution*, 36. A Southern Farmer [Gabriel Capers], *Bondage, a Moral Institution, Sanctioned by the Scriptures of the Old and New Testaments, and the Preaching and Practice of the Saviour and his Apostles, by a Southern Farmer* (Macon, GA, 1837), 9, 20. James Freeman Clarke, *Slavery in the United States: A Sermon Delivered in Amory Hall on Thanksgiving Day November 24, 1842* (Boston, 1843), 14.

38. An article in the *Princeton Biblical Repertory* (April 1836), quoted in Barnes, *Inquiry into the Scriptural Views*, 33. Similarly, a Virginia planter pointed out that Jesus never condemned slavery and that Paul "rather encouraged it"; quoted in Fox-Genovese and Genovese,

Mind of the Master Class, 486. Freehling, *Drift toward Dissolution: The Virginia Slavery Debate of 1831–1832* (Baton Rouge: Louisiana State University Press, 1982). *Slavery vs. the Bible: A Correspondence between the General Conference of Maine, and the Presbytery of Tombecbee, Mississippi* (Worcester, MA, 1840), 15.

39. Stuart, *Conscience and the Constitution*, 45–46.

40. Fiske quoted in Barnes, *Inquiry into the Scriptural Views*, 29, 30. Fuller, *Domestic Slavery Considered as a Scriptural Institution*, 188. Stringfellow, *Brief Examination*, 165.

41. Barnes, *Inquiry into the Scriptural Views*, 241. John Richter Jones, *Slavery Sanctioned by the Bible* (Philadelphia, 1861), 20, 27. The Synod of Virginia quoted in Barnes, *Inquiry into the Scriptural Views*, 32. G. F. Pierce, "The Word of God a Nation's Life," in *Sermons of Bishop Pierce and Rev. B. M. Palmer* (Milledgeville, GA, 1863), 5.

42. Noll, *America's God*, 400. Both sides in the debate, according to Michael O'Brien, held the "stubborn expectation that a shared truth ought to be discoverable among believers, everywhere." O'Brien, *Conjectures of Order*, 2: 948.

43. Fox, *Jesus in America*, 211.

44. Ibid., 211, 203. Tony Horwitz provides this interesting perspective in *Midnight Rising: John Brown and the Raid That Sparked the Civil War* (New York: Henry Holt, 2011), 25. John Brown, "On Being Sentenced to Death," in *The World's Greatest Speeches*, ed. Lewis Copeland, Lawrence W. Lamm, and Stephen J. McKenna (Mineola, NY: Dover, 1999), 298–299.

45. Jonathan Blanchard, *A Debate on Slavery: Held in the City of Cincinnati, of the First, Second, Third, and Sixth Days of October 1845, Upon the Question: Is Slave Holding in Itself Sinful, and the Relation Between Master and Slave, a Sinful Relation?* (Cincinnati, 1846), 44.

46. Wayland, *Domestic Slavery Considered as a Scriptural Institution*, 84.

47. Oshatz, "Problem of Moral Progress," 235. E. P. Barrows, *A View of the American Slavery Question* (New York, 1836), 50.

48. Fox, *Jesus in America*, 152. George Cheever, *The Guilt of Slavery and the Crime of Slaveholding Demonstrated from the Hebrew and Greek Scriptures* (Boston, 1860), 58. Wayland, *Domestic Slavery Considered as a Scriptural Institution*, 94. Albert Barnes, *The Church and Slavery* (Philadelphia, 1857), 42.

49. Fox, *Jesus in America*, 198. Barnes, *Inquiry into the Scriptural Views*, 346. Wayland, *Domestic Slavery Considered as a Scriptural Institution*, 94.

50. The Reverend James Pennington quoted in Fox-Genovese and Genovese, *Mind of the Master Class*, 501.

51. Henry Ward Beecher, "Our Blameworthiness, Sermon in Plymouth Church, Fast Day, Jan. 4, 1861," in *Patriotic Addresses in America and England, from 1850 to 1885, on Slavery, the Civil War, and the Development of Civil Liberty in the United States*, ed. John R. Howard (New York, 1887), 264.

52. Barnes, *Inquiry into the Scriptural Views*, 228 ff. Grimke quoted in Fox, *Jesus in America*, 207.

53. Grimke quoted in Fox, *Jesus in America*, 206. Frederick Douglass, *Narrative of the Life of Frederick Douglass: An American Slave, Written by Himself* (1845; New Haven: Yale University Press, 2001), 81. Wayland, *Domestic Slavery Considered as a Scriptural Institution*, 81.

54. Tayler Lewis, "Patriarchal and Jewish Servitude No Argument for American Slavery," in *Fast Day Sermons; or, The Pulpit on the State of the Country* (New York, 1861), 204.

55. Fox, *Jesus in America*, 210.

56. For an early colonial example of Old Testament antislavery see Samuel Sewall, *The Selling of Joseph* (1700).

57. Wayland, *Domestic Slavery Considered as a Scriptural Institution*, 55–56; Barnes, *Inquiry into the Scriptural Views*, 78–79. For a typical proslavery answer to antislavery analogies of biblical slavery to polygamy and divorce see Bledsoe, *Essay about Liberty and Slavery*, 151–152.

58. Lewis, "Patriarchal and Jewish Servitude," 180. Barnes, *Inquiry into the Scriptural Views*, 59–60.

59. Cheever, *Guilt of Slavery*, 415–420. See further Fox-Genovese and Genovese, *Mind of the Master Class*, 508.

60. Weld, *Bible Against Slavery*, 84.

61. Wayland, *Domestic Slavery Considered as a Scriptural Institution*, 59. Barnes, *Inquiry into the Scriptural Views*, 205. See also Lewis, "Patriarchal and Jewish Servitude," 181–182, and E. P. Barrows, "Saalschütz on Hebrew Servitude," *Bibliotheca Sacra* 19 (January 1862), 32–74.

62. Some southerners argued in response to such claims that biblical slavery was harsher than the slavery practiced in the South. Fox-Genovese and Genovese, *Mind of the Master Class*, 516.

63. Barnes, *Inquiry into the Scriptural Views*, 135.

64. Daniel Coker, "A Dialogue Between a Virginian and an African Minister," in *Pamphlets of Protest: An Anthology of Early African-American Protest Literature, 1790–1860*, ed. Richard Newman, Patrick Rael, and Phillip Lapsansky (New York: Routledge, 2000), 59. Wayland, *Domestic Slavery Considered as a Scriptural Institution*, 59, 49. David Barrow expounded an early argument along these lines in *Involuntary, Unmerited, Perpetual, Absolute, Hereditary Slavery, Examined* (Lexington, KY, 1808). Mark Noll points out that much of Francis Wayland's arguments, which were published in the context of a notable disputation with Fuller, built on Barrow's argument but demonstrated more erudition and detail from the Hebrew language and Old Testament history. Noll, *Civil War as a Theological Crisis*, 46.

65. Abiel Abbot, *Traits of Resemblance in the People of the United States of America to Ancient Israel* (Haverhill, MA, 1799), 6. J. M. Pendleton, *Letters to Rev. W. C. Buck, in Review of His Articles on Slavery* (Louisville, KY, 1849), 3. Wayland, *Domestic Slavery Considered as a Scriptural Institution*, 51.

66. Wayland, *Domestic Slavery Considered as a Scriptural Institution*, 51. Oshatz, "Problem of Moral Progress," 228; Holifield, *Theology in America*, 502.

67. Miller, "The Garden of Eden and the Deacon's Meadow."

68. For the use of "slavery" as a metaphor in the political discourse see Peter A. Dorsey, *Common Bondage: Slavery as a Metaphor in Revolutionary America* (Knoxville: University of Tennessee Press, 2009). Weld, *Bible against Slavery*, 87–90.

69. Barnes, *Inquiry into the Scriptural Views*, 86–87. For a proslavery response to the abolitionist reading of Exodus see Alexander McCaine, "Slavery Defended from Scripture against the Attacks of the Abolitionists" in Lowance, *House Divided*, 84.

70. Barnes, *Inquiry into the Scriptural Views*, 97, 101–102. Eddie Glaude, Jr., noticed too these inversions of America's national community, in which "the New Israel was Egypt,

and blacks were demanding that Pharaoh (white Americans) let God's people go." Eddie S. Glaude, Jr., *Exodus! Religion, Race, and Nation in Early Nineteenth Century Black America* (Chicago: University of Chicago Press, 2000), 62.

71. Prothero, *American Jesus*, 209–210. Allen Dwight Callahan, *The Talking Book: African Americans and the Bible* (New Haven: Yale University Press, 2008), 48. Callahan examines three tropes other than Exodus in the African-American biblical imagination: of Babylonian exile, of black Ethiopia, and of Emmanuel-Jesus. Glaude concurs that "No other story in the Bible has quite captured the imagination of African Americans like that of Exodus"; Glaude, *Exodus!* 29. Lawrence Levine, *Black Culture and Black Consciousness: Afro-American Folk Thought from Slavery to Freedom* (New York: Oxford University Press, 1977), 50.

72. Noll, "The United States as a Biblical Nation," 50. White soldier quoted in Albert J. Raboteau, *Slave Religion: The 'Invisible Institution' in the Antebellum South* (New York: Oxford University Press, 2004), 311–312; Polly quoted in Raboteau, *Canaan Land: A Religious History of African Americans* (New York: Oxford University Press, 2001), 44.

73. David Walker, *Walker's Appeal in Four Articles; Together with a Preamble, to the Coloured Citizens of the World* . . . (Boston, 1830), ii, 75. Glaude, *Exodus!* 56. Frederick Douglass, *Life and Times of Frederick Douglass: His Early Life as a Slave, His Escape from Bondage, and His Complete History, Written by Himself* (1845; New York: Collier, 1969), 159–160.

74. Thomas Wentworth Higginson, "Negro Spirituals," *Atlantic Monthly* 29 (1867), 691.

75. Quoted by Eugene Genovese, *Roll, Jordan, Roll: The World the Slaves Made* (New York: Vintage, 1976), 253. Protheo, *American Jesus*, 210, 213. Noll, *America's God*, 176.

CONCLUSION

1. "A New Revelation," *Macon Daily Telegraph and Confederate*, Oct. 20, 1864.

2. The literature on the religious dimensions of the Civil War is extensive; for notable and recent titles see Randall M. Miller, Harry S. Stout, and Charles Reagan Wilson, eds., *Religion and the American Civil War* (New York: Oxford University Press, 1998); George C. Rable, *God's Almost Chosen People: A Religious History of the American Civil War* (Chapel Hill: University of North Carolina Press, 2010); Mark A. Noll, *The Civil War as a Theological Crisis* (Chapel Hill: University of North Carolina Press, 2006), Harry S. Stout, *Upon the Altar of the Nation: A Moral History of the Civil War* (New York: Penguin, 2007). "God's Rule in America a Subject of Thanksgiving," *Peninsular News and Advertiser* [Delaware], Dec. 6, 1861. "Jeroboam and Jeff. Davis," *New York Herald*, Jan. 31, 1861. "Status of the Rebellion," *Weekly Wisconsin Patriot*, Mar. 15, 1862. "Be Not Discouraged," *Macon Daily Telegraph*, Feb. 13, 1862. For an impressive wartime restatement of the United States as the Second Israel see George S. Phillips, *The American Republic and Human Liberty Foreshadowed in Scripture* (Cincinnati, 1864). For a Godhead that was once more seen as "the God of battles" see "Sermon by Rev. W. W. Lord," *Macon Daily Telegraph*, Sep. 18, 1862.

3. "New Israel," *Kalamazoo Gazette*, Sep. 26, 1882.

4. John Micklethwait and Adrian Wooldridge, *God Is Back: How the Global Revival of Faith Is Changing the World* (New York: Penguin, 2010), 76. Henry Adams, *The Degradation of the Democratic Dogma* (New York: Macmillan, 1919), 30. For more similar expressions see

Sacvan Bercovitch, *The American Jeremiad* (Madison: University of Wisconsin Press, 1978), 143–144.

5. This process is evident in a collection of characteristic "religious interpretations of American destiny": while a substantive majority of references to "Israel" in an edited collection under that title appeared in America before the Civil War, only 20 percent stem from the century and a half since that war (ten postbellum references out of a total of more than fifty). Conrad Cherry, ed., *God's New Israel: Religious Interpretations of American Destiny* (Chapel Hill: University of North Carolina Press, 1998). Josiah Strong, *Our Country: Its Possible Future and Its Present Crisis* (New York, 1885); see, e.g., 30 ("We deem ourselves a chosen people"); 217 ("This country is his chosen instrument of blessing to mankind"); and 219 ("Ours is the elect nation for the age to come. We are the chosen people"). Albert J. Beveridge, "In Support of an American Empire," in *History of the United States Political System: Ideas, Interests, and Institutions*, ed. Richard A. Harris and Daniel J. Tichenor (Santa Barbara, CA: ABC-Clio, 2010), 133.

6. Lottie Davis and Moshe Davis, *Guide to Map of Biblical Names in America: Land of Our Fathers* (New York: Associated American Artists, 1954). For the concept of geopiety see Lester I. Vogel, *To See a Promised Land: Americans and the Holy Land in the Nineteenth Century* (University Park: Pennsylvania State University Press, 1993), xv–xvi. The term was coined by the geographer John Kirtland Wright. See J. K. Wright, *Human Nature in Geography* (Cambridge: Harvard University Press, 1968). Quotations in Hilton Obenzinger, *American Palestine* (Princeton: Princeton University Press, 1999), 5, and Vogel, *To See a Promised Land*, 42, 4. On Americans in the Holy Land see also Milette Shamir, "'Our Jerusalem': Americans in the Holy Land and Postbellum Narratives of National Entitlement," *American Quarterly*, March 2003, 29–60; Obenzinger, *American Palestine*; Vogel, *To See a Promised Land*; John Davis, *The Landscape of Belief* (Princeton: Princeton University Press, 1996). For a general history of American involvement in the Middle East see Michael Oren, *Power, Faith, and Fantasy: America in the Middle East, 1776 to the Present* (New York: Norton, 2007).

7. David Nirenberg, *Anti-Judaism: The Western Tradition* (New York: Norton, 2013).

8. Jewish immigrants were particularly likely to express such notions. See, e.g., Mary Antin, *The Promised Land* (Boston, 1912). For a modern treatment see Arnold M. Eisen, *The Chosen People in America: A Study in Jewish Religious Ideology* (Bloomington: Indiana University Press, 1983). Stout, *Upon the Altar of the Nation*, xviii.

9. For the latest scholarly analysis of American exceptionalism see the articles in the symposium American Exceptionalism in *American Political Thought* 1:1 (Spring 2012), 3–128. See also Joyce Chaplin, "Expansion and Exceptionalism in Early American History," *Journal of American History* 89 (March 2003), 1431–1455, and Dorothy Ross, *The Origins of American Social Science* (New York: Cambridge University Press, 1992), 22–52. Religion might be the last acceptable tenet of American exceptionalism, as the United States is still commonly seen as the exception to the secularism of the modern "post-Christian" West. However, in *God Is Back*, 25 and passim, John Micklethwait and Adrian Wooldridge argue that the American religiosity may be for the first time winning over the rest of the world in opposition to the European model of secularism.

10. Niall Ferguson, *Civilization: The West and the Rest* (New York: Penguin, 2011), 275.

11. For Christian Zionism in the United States see Shalom Goldman, *Zeal for Zion: Christians, Jews, and the Idea of the Promised Land* (Chapel Hill: University of North Carolina Press, 2009). Mark A. Noll, *God and Race in American Politics* (Princeton: Princeton University Press, 2010), 2. Gary S. Selby, *Martin Luther King and the Rhetoric of Freedom: The Exodus Narrative in America's Struggle for Civil Rights* (Waco, TX: Baylor University Press, 2008).

Index

Aaron, 20
Abbot, Abiel, 1
Abel, 185
Abolitionists, 171–79
Abraham, 154, 166, 168
Abraham ben Mordecai Farissol, 121
Achitophel, 96
The Acts and Monuments (Foxe), 54
Adair, James, 122–29, 133, 142
Adams, Henry, 155
Adams, John, 56, 57, 98, 124
Adams, John Quincy, 188
Addison, Joseph, 86
African Americans: and evangelicalism, 168, 183–84; and Exodus narrative, 181–83; as Lost Tribes of Israel, 147–48, 149. *See also* Slavery
Age of Reason (Paine), 127
The Age of Revelation (Boudinot), 127
Ahab, 7, 8
Ahasuerus (Xerxes), 27, 28, 31–33
Ahlstrom, Sydney, 152
Alexander the Great, 39
American Antiquities and Discoveries in the West (Priest), 133
American Bible Society, 4, 127
American exceptionalism, 189, 191
American Indians. *See* Native Americans
The American Revolution (Snowden), 94
The American States Acting Over the Part of the Children of Israel in the Wilderness (Street), 19
Anachronism, 92, 96
Angles and Saxons as Lost Tribes, 148–49

Anti-Federalists, 98
Antinomian controversy, 153
Antiochus Epiphanes, 42
Anti-Slavery Society, 171
Apocalypse, 127
Apocryphal texts, 39, 110
Appeal rights, 71
Appeal to the Coloured Citizens of the World (Walker), 183
Ararat, New York, 76–82, 139–44
Arminianism, 159, 161
Articles of Confederation, 65
Asbury, Francis, 158
Assyria, 121
Authority: biblical language used to convey, 85, 87; and Hebraic political studies, 7, 53; and pseudobiblical texts, 117
Avarice, 41

Babylon, 61
Bangs, Nathan, 173
Bank Wars (1830s), 102
Baptists, 158, 159–60
Barak, 34, 36, 38, 43, 44
Barlow, Philip, 157
Barnes, Albert, 174, 176, 178, 180, 181
Bayle, Pierre, 3
Beecher, Henry Ward, 161, 174
Beecher, Lyman, 70, 71, 73, 82
Ben Hur (Wallace), 163
Benjamin of Tudela, 121
Ben Saddi, Nathan, 88, 109
Bercovitch, Sacvan, 5
Bernard, Lord, 92

Beveridge, Albert J., 188
Bible: adaptations of, 86–87; language of, 4, 85; pictographic symbols published in, 110–11; popularity of, 4, 189; prophecies of restoration of Israel, 134–35; pseudobiblicism aiding study of, 93–99; translations of, 86; violence in, 179–80. *See also* New Testament; Old Testament
The Bible against Slavery (Weld), 177
Biblical republicanism: corruption's influence on, 21–27, 37; institutions of, 56; Israel as model for, 7–8, 50–83; and Maccabean Revolt, 40–41; in Revolutionary era, 13, 15–49; and theocracy, 72
Blanchard, Jonathan, 172
The Book of America (*Boston Gazette*), 89
The Book of Chronicles ("John"), 84
Book of Maccabees, 39–40
Book of Mormon: and construction of sacred American geography, 9; criticisms of, 115; language of, 107; on Native American origins, 105, 111–12, 135–38; pseudobiblicism's influence on, 104–16; as revelatory history, 138; as translation of ancient source, 108–9; verse numbering in, 107
Book of Revelation, 127
Boston Evening Post, pseudobiblical text printed in, 88
Boston Patriot: on fate of Lost Tribes, 130; on Mordecai Manuel Noah's Ark, 142
Boudinot, Elias: on Hebrew republican model, 51, 149; on Native American republican ideals, 76; on Native Americans as Lost Tribes, 126–35, 138, 140, 144; Noah influenced by, 142
Britain. *See* England
British-Israelism theory, 148–49
Brodie, Fawn, 111
Broome County Patriot, pseudobiblical text printed in, 109
Brown, John Thompson, 170, 172
Brutus, Lucius Junius, 48
Burgoyne, John, 31
Burned Over District, New York, 144
Bushman, Richard, 111, 112
Bute, Lord, 31, 92

Cain, 185, 186
Calhoun, John C., 7, 51, 75
California, Lost Tribes in, 143–44
Calvinism: and America–Israel connection, 1, 119; on corruptibility of humans, 21–22, 27; and Curse of Meroz, 35; and Geneva Bible, 4, 86; and Hebraic political studies, 54; and Old Testament, 3, 152, 153, 155; and predestination, 160
Campbell, Alexander, 162
Camp meetings, 158
Canaanites, 36
Catholics, 18, 92, 163
Cato, 56
Chapter from the Whig Chronicles (*New Hampshire Patriot*), 102
"Chapter 37th" (*Boston Evening Post*), 93–94
The Character of Haman (Reese), 32
Cheever, George, 173, 177
Chief magistrate, 62
Child, David Lee, 8
Chosenness: Americans' perceptions of, 83, 85, 118; language of, 189; Old Testament as narrative of, 53; pitfalls of, 8–9, 10–11; pseudobiblical texts portraying America as, 94, 100; and Puritans, 3
The Chronicles of the Kings of England (Dodsley), 88–89, 90, 109
Church of God and Saints of Christ, 149
Cincinnatus, Lucius Quinctius, 45, 49
Civic humanism: and corruption, 21, 23, 25–26; and Hebrew republic, 63; and Old Testament, 17–18; in Revolutionary era, 13, 16
Clark, James Freeman, 169
Classical education, 17
Classical republicanism: corruption of, 31–32, 41; in early American thought, 16–17; Gideon portrayed as model of, 46–48; and monarchy, 186; passivity and neutrality as civic sin in, 38; and religion, 18–19, 27; and sacrifice for common good, 36–37, 45; subversion from within, 31–32; and theocracy, 72. *See also* Biblical republicanism; Civic humanism
Clay, Henry, 102

Cleage, Albert B., Jr., 149
Clinton, Bill, 191
Clinton, De Witt, 141
Coke, Thomas, 158
Coker, Daniel, 178
Cole, Abner, 137
Commentaries on the Laws of the Ancient Hebrews (Wines), 50, 70
Common Sense (Paine), 29, 44, 60
The Commonwealth of Oceana (Harrington), 55
Communitarianism, 17
Congregationalists, 155, 158. *See also* Calvinism
Congress (U.S.), 64, 65, 67–68, 75, 96
The Conquest of Canaan (Dwight), 20, 162
Constantine, 3
Constitution (U.S.), 80
Continental Congress, 29, 59
Cooper, Samuel, 61–63
Corruption: of biblical republicanism, 21–27, 37, 41; Calvinism on, 21–22, 27; and civic humanism, 21, 23, 25–26; of political power, 7, 21–27; virtue affected by, 21
Covenant, 5, 63, 118
Cowdery, Oliver, 137, 138
Crowdy, William Saunders, 149
Cult of the king, 29
Cultural shifts: and biblical language, 102–3; and Native Americans as Israelites theory, 148; to New Testament, 154–63
Cunaeus, Petrus, 54
Curse of Meroz, 34–41, 43
The Curse of Meroz (Finley), 36

Dan, tribe of, 132
Dana, James, 61
Daniel, 92, 162
David, 25, 81, 92, 96, 121, 187
Davies, Samuel, 35
Davis, Jefferson, 187
Deborah, 13, 36, 38, 43
Declaration of Independence, 73, 188
Defence of the Constitutions of the United States (Adams), 56–57
Defoe, Daniel, 56

Deism, 127
Democracy, 74
Democratization: and free will, 160; and Hebraic political studies, 53, 64; language of, 103; and New Testament, 158; and Roman political model, 11
Demophilus, 74, 75
De Republica Hebraeorum (Cunaeus), 54
Determinism, 160
Discourse on the Evidences of the American Indians being the Descendants of the Lost Tribes of Israel (Noah), 142
Discourses Concerning Government (Sidney), 44, 55
Disestablishment of churches, 190
Disinterestedness, 21, 47
Divine right, 55
Dodsley, Robert, 88–89, 109
Douglass, Frederick, 175, 183
Dunton, John, 56
Dutch republicanism, 54
Dwight, Timothy, 20, 162

Education: Bible used in, 18; classical, 17; pseudobiblical texts used in, 97
Edwards, Jonathan, 35, 153
Eglon, 43
Egypt: as despotic power, 61; and Exodus narrative, 19–21; and slavery debate, 180. *See also* Exodus narrative
Ehud Ben-Gera, 43, 44, 92
Elazar, Daniel, 62
Elections, 64, 65, 79. *See also* Democratization
Elizabeth (Queen of England), 89
England: and British-Israelism theory, 148–49; Hebraic Biblicism in, 54–55; imperial policies portrayed as corrupt, 12, 28–29, 30–31, 32, 59; interregnum period, 54; legal framework in, 66; pseudobiblical texts in, 98
Enlightenment, 125, 127
Ephraim, 64
Episcopalians, 158
Equal rights. *See* Rights of man
Erie Canal, 112
Esther, 27–28, 30, 42

Eusebius, 3
Evangelicalism: and African Americans, 168, 183–84; and Native Americans, 127; New Testament focus of, 151–63; and Old Testament, 5; and slavery, 163–84
Exceptionalism, American, 179, 189, 191
Exclusive republicanism, 59, 60
Executive powers, 62
Exodus narrative, 6–7, 19–21, 180–83, 189

The Fall of Samuel the Squomicutiti (Hopkins), 89
Federalism, 13, 72, 73, 76, 79–80
Federalists, 69, 94, 100, 102
Federal republicanism, 52, 58–60, 63, 67, 83
Feminization of virtue, 48–49
"A Few Observations on the Western and Indians" (newspaper article), 129
The Fifteenth Chapter of the Chronicles (*Broome County Patriot*), 109
Filmer, Robert, 55
Finley, Samuel, 36
Firmage, Edwin, 110
"The First Book of Chronicles, Chapter the 5th" (Shaloma Ben Ezra), 108
The First Book of the American Chronicles of the Times (Leacock), 91–92
The First Chapter of the Book of Preferment (Walpole), 88
First Treatise on Government (Locke), 55
Footnotes in pseudobiblical texts, 95–96, 97
Force Bill of *1833*, 75
Foxe, John, 54
Fox-Genovese, Elizabeth, 167
Franklin, Benjamin, 20, 151, 154
Free will, 160, 177
French and Indian War (1754–1763), 4, 35
"The French Gasconade defeated, and then swept out of Germany" (*Boston Evening Post*), 88

Gage, Thomas, 92
Garrison, William Lloyd, 167, 171, 172
General assemblies, 62
Geneva Bible, 4, 86
Genovese, Eugene, 167, 183
George III (King of England): biblical tyrants equated to, 61; counselors blamed for corruption of, 28, 29, 31, 33, 34; portrayed as Rehoboam, 7; in pseudobiblical texts, 90, 92
Gibbon, Edward, 26–27
Gibeonites, 177
Gideon, 15–16, 44–47, 49, 55
Givens, Terryl, 107, 114, 137
Glaude, Eddie, 182
Gold Bible, 107. *See also* Book of Mormon
Gospel dispensation, 166, 188. *See also* New Testament
Government Corrupted by Vice (Langdon), 24
Grand Island, New York, 77. *See also* Ararat, New York
Great Awakening, 35. *See also* Second Great Awakening
Great Britain. *See* England
Great Migration (1630s), 19
Great Seal designs, 5, 20, 151
Greene, Jack, 98
Grimke, Angelina, 174

Ham (son of Noah), 167–68
Haman, 30–34, 39, 42
Hampden, John, 38
Harrington, James, 54, 55
Hasmonean dynasty, 39–40
Hebraic Biblicism, 52–60
Hebraic exceptionalism, 179
The Hebrew Republic (Nelson), 53
Herzl, Theodore, 82
Hezekiah, 162
Hieroglyphic Bibles, 110, 111
Higher Criticism, 150
Hiram of Tyre, 144
Historicus, 70
The History of the American Indians (Adair), 122–25
History of the Jews (Adams), 13
The History of the Late War (Hunt), 99
Hitchcock, Gad, 58
Hobbes, Thomas, 3, 54, 55
The Holy Bible Abridged, 97
Holy Land tourism, 188
The Hope of Israel (Ben-Israel), 122
Hopkins, Samuel, 89, 153
Horae Lyricae (Watts), 86
Humanism, 53–54. *See also* Civic humanism

Human rights. *See* Rights of man
Hunt, Gilbert J., 93, 99, 100
Huntington, Joseph, 6, 23, 26, 63–65, 68
Hutchinson, Lord, 40, 92

Imperium in imperia, 80
Indentured servitude, 176
Independence: in Israel republican model, 51; of states, 63–64, 65–66, 70–71
Independent Company of Volunteers, 35
Indians. *See* Native Americans
Individualism, 17
An Inquiry into the Scriptural Views of Slavery (Barnes), 176
Interregnum, 54
Irony, 91, 92
Isaac, 168
Isaiah, 119, 130
Isaiah's Message to the American Nation (McDonald), 119, 130
Israel: constitutional similarities with America, 50–51; corruption of republicanism in, 24–25; egalitarianism of, 74; and Exodus narrative, 19–21; judiciary in, 68–69; legal framework in, 66–67, 74; Lost Tribes of, 118–50; political institutions in, 56, 62–63; as political model, 7–8, 50–83; prophecies of restoration of, 134–35; republicanism in, 15, 23–24
Itinerary preacher circuit system, 158

Jabin, 38, 43
Jackson, Andrew, 75
Jacob, 64, 78, 121, 128, 168
James I (King of England), 86, 87
Jaredites, 136
Jedidiah, 92
Jefferson, Thomas: on Adair's scholarship, 125; education of, 123; and Enlightenment thought, 127, 154; and Exodus narrative, 20; and Great Seal design, 5, 151; on Israelites in America, 124; on rights of man, 172; and secularism, 127
Jehonadab, 147
Jephthah's daughter, 13, 48, 49
Jeremiah, 61
Jerubbaal, 44, 47

Jerubbaal (Murray), 45
Jeshurun, 25
Jesse, 92
Jews in America (Thorowgood), 122
Joash, 45
Jonadab, 147
Jones, David, 24, 25
Jones, John Richter, 171
Joseph, 64
Joshua, 43, 55–57, 62, 81, 92, 185
Jubilee year, 176
Judah, 121, 187
Judas Maccabeus, 40, 42, 77, 81. *See also* Maccabean Revolt (167–160 B.C.)
Judas Maccabeus (Handel), 77
The Judgment of Whole Kingdoms and Nations (Defoe & Dunton), 56
Judicial powers: and federal republicanism, 68–69; in Hebrew republic, 62, 71; in Noah's proposed biblical government, 79, 80; and sovereignty, 80–81
Julius Caesar, 30, 32, 46

Kahal Kodesh Beth Elohim, 147
King, Martin Luther, Jr., 191
King James Bible, 85–88, 93, 98, 102, 107, 112–13

Land ownership, 73
Langdon, Samuel, 24, 59–62, 66, 67
Leacock, John, 91, 92
Lectures on Jewish Antiquities (Tappan), 70, 130
Legal framework, 62–63, 66–67, 74
Legislative powers, 60, 62
Legitimacy: biblical language used to convey, 85, 87; and Hebraic political studies, 53, 82
The Leviathan (Hobbes), 55
Lewis, Meriwether, 124
Lewis, Tayler, 175
The Liberator newspaper, 167, 172
Lilla, Mark, 154
Lincoln, Abraham, 8, 10, 15, 151, 156–57, 187
Locke, John, 51, 54, 55
Lost Tribes of Israel, 118–50; African Americans as, 147–48, 149; Angles and

Lost Tribes of Israel (*continued*)
Saxons as, 148–49; Native Americans as, 120–35, 139–44; origins of, 121
The Loving Kindness of God Displayed in the Triumph of Republicanism in America (Smith), 161
Lowance, Mason I., 168
Loyalists, 34–41
Lust, 41
Lutz, Donald, 11
Lycurgus, 66

Maccabean Revolt (167–160 B.C.), 25, 39–41, 42–43
Machiavelli, 51
Macon Daily Telegraph and Confederate, publication of "New Revelation," 185
Madison, James, 84
Manifest Destiny, 100
Mann, Horace, 88
Mannasseh, 64
Mansfield, Lord, 92
Massachusetts, constitutional ratification debate in, 66
Matthew, 2
Matthews, Margaret, 145, 146
Matthews (Matthias), Robert, 145–47, 149
McDonald, John, 119, 130
Melville, Herman, 8
Menasseh Ben-Israel, 122, 125
Meroz, 36–39, 42, 43
Methodists, 158, 159–60
Millenarianism, 92, 119, 133, 140–41, 187
Miller, Perry: on evangelicalism, 163; on Old Testament's prevalence in early America, 1, 11, 101–2, 157; on Puritan theology, 153; on violence in Old Testament, 179
Milton, John, 54
Mixed government, 57–58
Modernism, 150
Monarchy: and biblical republicanism, 44; corruption in, 25, 59; and cult of the king, 29; and Hebraic Biblicism, 55; legitimacy of, 31; and republicanism, 186; subversion from within, 33–34
Moore, Hannah, 13
Mordecai, 32, 33, 91
More, Hannah, 162

Morgan, Edmund, 18
Mormonism, 114. *See also* Book of Mormon; Smith, Joseph
Moses: and corruption of Israelites, 25, 27; covenant of, 6; and Exodus narrative, 19, 20, 57, 182, 183, 191; and legal framework, 50, 60, 65–68, 74; nation building by, 14; and political structure, 56, 168
Murray, John, 25, 45–47, 64

Naboth, 7, 8
Nationalism, 99, 126–27, 149
Native Americans: and Ararat proposal, 139–44; Book of Mormon's account of, 105, 111–12, 135–38; language of, 123, 125, 128; as Lost Tribes of Israel, 120–35, 139–44; republican ideals of, 76; theology of, 123–24, 128, 141
Nat Turner rebellion (1831), 167
Nebuchadnezzar, 61
Neutrality, 38
New England: and biblical republicanism, 51, 119; Hebraic political studies in, 70; and Old Testament, 152
"New Revelation," 185–87
New Testament: in eulogizing sermons, 156–57; and evangelicalism, 151–63; politicization of, 166; rise in cultural importance of, 148; and slavery debate, 163–84; social stability favored in, 170
New World Israelites. *See* Lost Tribes of Israel
New York: Book of Mormon's origins in, 112–13, 135; Noah's proposed biblical community in, 76–82, 139–44; and Second Great Awakening, 144
Noah, 164–65, 166–68
Noah, Mordecai Manuel, 76–82, 139–46, 149
North, Lord, 31, 32

Old Testament: and Book of Mormon, 136; Christianity's relationship with, 2–3; and civic humanism, 17–18; cultural role of, 150; decline in cultural importance of, 148, 187; in eulogizing sermons, 156–57; and Hebraic political studies, 52–53; justified rebellions in, 42; Lost Tribes in, 121; political uses of, 1–2, 52–60, 101;

prevalence of, 1, 11, 101–2, 157; and pseudobiblical texts, 101–4, 156; and republicanism, 48; and slavery debate, 163–84; territoriality and nationhood in, 154; violence in, 179–80
On the Health and Happiness, or Misery and Ruin, of the Body Politic (Huntington), 23
Ophir, 143–44
Our Country (Strong), 188
Overton, Captain, 35

Paganism, 11
Paine, Thomas, 2, 29, 44, 60, 127
Palestine, tourism visits to, 188
Palmyra, New York, 112–13, 135
Parody, 91
Parsons, Jonathan, 35
Passivity, 38, 41
Patriarcha (Filmer), 55
Patriarchy, 57
Patriotism, 119
Paul, 2, 171
Pendleton, James M., 179
Penn, William, 122
Pequod (in *Moby-Dick*, Melville), 8
Persian kingdom, 27–28, 30
Peter, 2
Philalethes, 41
Philemon, 171
Phillips, Samuel, 57
Philo-Patria, 37
Pierce, George, 171
Pierson, Elijah, 145
Political rationalization, 82
Pond, Enoch, 74, 161
Pope, Alexander, 86
Populism, 103
Powers, Peter, 40
Predestination, 159–60
Pride, 41
Priest, Josiah, 133
Property rights, 73
Protestants: biblical supremacy in, 18, 85–86; and Book of Maccabees, 39; on corruptibility of humans, 21–22, 27; and Hebraic political studies, 54; and Israelite republicanism, 52; and Native American origins, 132; and New Testament, 153; and Old Testament, 3, 5, 152; and pseudobiblicism, 103, 117; and Second Great Awakening, 159, 184
Providence: absence in pseudobiblical texts, 85; America as agent of, 134, 149, 151; in Book of Mormon, 106; in pseudobiblical texts, 95
Psalms of David (Watts), 86
Pseudobiblicism, 84–117; biblical studies aided by, 93–99; and Book of Mormon, 104–16; historical consciousness of, 100; intellectual environment for, 90–91; and Old Testament, 156; origins of, 85–89; political use of, 99–104, 114; in Revolutionary era, 89–93; as translations of ancient sources, 110; verse numbering in, 107
Pseudoepigraphy, 110
Puritans: and Curse of Meroz, 35; and Exodus narrative, 3, 19, 118–19; and Old Testament, 3, 152–53; pseudobiblical texts on, 92

Ramsay, David, 96
Rationalization, 82
Rechabites, 147–48
Red Jacket, Chief, 140
Reese, Thomas, 32
Rehoboam, 7–8, 25, 42, 92, 121, 187
Religion and Patriotism the Constituents of a Good Soldier (Davies), 35
Renaissance, 53–54
Republican Christianity (Magoon), 161
"The Republican Elements of the Old Testament" (Beecher), 70
Republicanism. *See* Biblical republicanism; Classical republicanism
Republicans, 94, 98, 100
"Republican Tendencies of the Bible" (Pond), 161
Revelation, Book of, 127
Revolutionary era: civic humanism in, 16, 17–18, 21, 23, 25–26; corruptibility of politics in, 21–27, 37; and Exodus narrative, 19–21; and Old Testament, 189; passivity and neutrality portrayed as civic sin in, 38; pseudobiblical texts in, 89–93; Tories portrayed as corrupt in, 34–41

Rhythms of biblical language, 85, 87
Richmond Enquirer, pseudobiblical texts printed in, 84
Rights of man, 50, 58, 74, 172
Rome: corruption of republicanism in, 21, 22–23, 26, 27; legal framework in, 66; as political model, 11
Rousseau, Jean-Jacques, 3
Rule of law, 56, 66–67. *See also* Legal framework
Runaway slaves, 76
Rush, Benjamin, 124
Rutland Herald critique of *A Star in the West,* 132

Saidi, Ben, 109
Sallust, 26
Samuel, 24, 25, 27, 59, 64
Sanhedrin, 56, 62, 64–65, 67–68, 96
Satire, 88, 92–93
Saxons as Lost Tribes, 148–49
Saxton, N. C., 138
The Second Advent (Boudinot), 127
Second Great Awakening: and Native Americans, 125, 129; New Testament focus of, 151–52, 158–63; and Old Testament, 5; and pseudobiblicism, 112; and restoration of Israel, 135; theological deviancy in, 146
Secularism, 127
Selden, John, 54
Seleucid Empire, 39–40, 41, 43
Self-government, 51
Self-sacrifice, idealization of, 21, 36–37, 45
The Selling of Joseph (Sewall), 153
Sennacherib, 42
Separatist nationalism, 149
Sewall, Samuel, 153
Shaloma Ben Ezra, 108
"The Ship of Zion" (slave spiritual), 183
Shrine of the Black Madonna Church, 149
Sidney, Algernon, 44, 55, 56
Simon, 148
Sisera, 34, 36
Slavery: corruption of republicanism leading to, 38; and evangelicalism, 163–84; and Exodus narrative, 180–83; runaway slaves returned to owners, 76
Smith, Elias, 161
Smith, Ethan, 133–35, 142, 144
Smith, Joseph, 1, 105–6, 109–17, 135–38, 144, 149
Smith, Samuel, 137
Snowden, Richard, 94–97, 99, 100
Society of the Ten Tribes, 148–49
Sola scriptura doctrine, 18, 85–86
Solomon, 25, 143, 144
Song of Deborah, 34–35
Spinoza, 3
Stamp Act, 30
A Star in the West (Boudinot), 126–33, 140; reviews and critiques of, 131–33
States: independence of, 63–64, 65–66, 70–71; sovereignty of, 71, 80–81
Stephens, John Lloyd, 149
Stiles, Ezra, 9, 10, 124
Stiles, Isaac, 36
Stowe, Harriet Beecher, 155, 163, 175
Street, Nicholas, 10, 19
Stringfellow, Thornton, 166, 170
Strong, Josiah, 188
Stuart, Moses, 76, 167, 169, 170
Supreme Court (U.S.), 71

The Taking of Naboth's Vineyard (Child), 8
Tappan, David, 70, 82, 130
Teachings of the New Testament on Slavery (Thompson), 173
Ten Lost Tribes. *See* Lost Tribes of Israel
Tennent, Gilbert, 35
Theocracy, 72, 123, 124
Theology: of Hebrew republic, 63; of Native Americans, 123–24, 128, 141; of Puritans, 153
Theonationalism, 187
Thompson, Joseph, 173
Thorowgood, Thomas, 122
Tobias, 109
Tories, 34–41
Treasure hunting culture, 110
Treaty of Paris (1763), 90
Tribal government, 58, 63–66, 70–71, 123, 128

True Israelite Church, 147
Tyndale, William, 87
Typological analysis, 19, 85, 119

Uncle Tom's Cabin (Stowe), 163, 175
The United States Elevated to Honor and Glory (Stiles), 9
"United states or tribes of Israel" concept, 23, 50–83. *See also* Federal republicanism
Universalism, 50, 175

Vermont Rodsmen, 118, 120
A View of the Hebrews (Smith), 133, 134–35
Virtue, 21, 48–49, 73
Voltaire, 3

Walker, David, 183
Wallace, Lew, 163
Walpole, Horace, 88
War of *1812*, 98–99, 102, 119
War of Independence (1775–1783), 23. *See also* Revolutionary era

Washington, George: biblical figures equated to, 6, 10, 15, 20; eulogizing sermons for, 157; in pseudobiblical texts, 100; as republican model, 45–47; on sense of duty and sacrifice, 38, 42
Watts, Isaac, 86
Wayland, Francis, 173, 175
Wedgwood, William B., 6, 10
Weld, Theodore, 168, 177
Wentworth, John, 136
Whitaker, Nathaniel, 57
Whitfield, George, 35
Williams, Roger, 35, 122
William the Conqueror, 89
Wines, Enoch, 50, 51, 70, 71, 73
Women: and classical republicanism, 48–49; and New Testament cultural shift, 159; Old Testament scholarship by, 13

Zedekiah, 107